WORK-FAMILY ARRANGEMENTS IN EUROPE

Editors

Laura den Dulk

Anneke van Doorne-Huiskes

Joop Schippers

THELA · THESIS

ISBN 90 5170 4755
NUGI 681/652

This book is the result of an international expertmeeting which was subsidized by the Netherlands Organization of Scientific Research (ISW-97013).

THELA THESIS
Prinseneiland 305, 1013 LP Amsterdam, The Netherlands
Tel.: +31 (0)20 625 54 29, Fax: +31 (0)20 620 33 95
Email: office@thelathesis.nl

TABLE OF CONTENTS

WORK-FAMILY ARRANGEMENTS IN THE CONTEXT OF WELFARE STATES

Anneke van Doorne-Huiskes, Laura den Dulk and Joop Schippers

1.   Central theme of the book

Between 1987 and 1995 the average rate of women's participation in the 25-29 age group in the European Union, showed a rise from 63% to just over 70%. The rate rose during that period in all countries, except Denmark, Finland and Sweden, where it remained high, at more than 80%. The increase was especially pronounced in countries where the level was low at the start of this period, such as Spain and Ireland, eventually rising from around 40% to almost 60%. This increase implies that paid work is no longer carried out by highly educated women only. The population of working women has become as diverse as the male labour force has been for years.

An increase in working women will have, or should have, implications for the way paid labour is organised. Many women have to combine care tasks at home with paid jobs elsewhere. To make this possible, facilities and provisions are needed, such as childcare facilities, part-time work, flexible working times or possibilities for parental leave.

The increase in the number of working women also influences the allocation of men's time. In the traditional one-earner family, men are, generally speaking, fully available for work outside the home. In a two-earner family, that availability is far more restricted. This does not mean, however, that task divisions in the household between women and men have already changed substantially. In all European countries, women spend more hours on average on household work than their husbands do, regardless of the number of hours they work outside the home (e.g., Van Doorne-Huiskes, 1996). Changes in this pattern occur only slowly.

It is not only with regard to family life that the adaptation to changes in the labour market makes slow progress. Governments and firms also react differently to developments in the working population. In some countries, high priority is given to the development of work-family facilities. In the Nordic countries, the government has given much attention over the past decades to the question how the human capital of both sexes should be mobilised optimally for paid labour. In many other European countries, this approach is taken for granted far less readily. Many European welfare states are still based on traditional family models (e.g., Sainsbury, 1996).

1

Governments, but labour organisations as well, show substantial differences in the extent of facilities they offer to allow members of the workforce to combine family and work. In some companies, many facilities are available, while others hardly offer any. Work-family arrangements can be described as facilities that support a combination of paid work and family responsibilities. Examples are leave arrangements, care provisions, flexible working patterns, supportive arrangements (e.g., Den Dulk and Remery, 1997). In the next section a more detailed description of work-family arrangements will be given.

On a national scale, differences between firms in the number and nature of work-family arrangements depend, for instance, on the sector to which a firm belongs and on the number of working women in the firm. Generally, few facilities are available in sectors in which traditional "male jobs" dominate. A higher number of female employees sometimes means that more work-family arrangements are developed. In general public organisations offer more facilities to combine family and work than private organisations do.

This book goes beyond national borders and is based on international comparative research. Its central issue is the question as to how developments in work-family arrangements in firms differ in different countries and how these differences can be explained. To explain differentiation in work-family arrangements, it is not only characteristics of workplaces that have to be taken into account. Attention also needs to be given to institutional conditions at the macro level of the social policy and the political priorities in a country. An important point of view in an international comparative analysis of work-family arrangements, is the way the welfare state is institutionalised. In the literature on welfare states, there is growing attention for aspects of gender and for the implications of welfare state models for the position of women compared to men. From a gender perspective, typologies of welfare states are based, among other things, on differences in the division of tasks between women and men, ranging from more traditional to less traditional and egalitarian relations. It could be expected that different types of welfare state would also have implications for the types and number of work-family arrangements that have been realised within firms. It is this relation between institutional conditions at the macro level of societies and the type of work-family arrangements within workplaces, that is the central theme of this book. From an international comparative perspective, it will be investigated whether countries that belong to different welfare state models also show different developments in work-family arrangements within workplaces and firms. The countries included in this comparison are the Netherlands, Germany, Spain, Italy, the United Kingdom and Sweden.

One might wonder why France, as one of the central countries in the European Union, is not represented in the book. This primarily has to do with the typology of welfare states on which the choice of countries is based. In this typology of social-democratic, conservative-corporatistic and liberal models of welfare states (see section 5 of this chapter), France cannot be easily classified. On the one hand, France is certainly part of the so-called conservative-corporatistic welfare state tradition in Europe. On the other hand, France has a long tradition of working women and of supporting facilities for working parents with young children. In her article Women, Work and Welfare in France, Hantrais (1997) reports an ambivalent attitude in the area of social policy towards the welfare of women in France, fluctuating between a reluctance to introduce gender-specific measures and recognition that women require special treatment, both in their reproductive capacity and as citizens and workers in their own right. As Hantrais puts it, the constant shifting between policies supporting motherhood as a recognized social function and measures designed to integrate women into the labour force can be seen as the hallmark of post-war social welfare in France. This ambivalence is partly an effect of pronatalist concerns, which regularly surfaced in French social policy over the years, in reaction to low birth rates and a subsequent demographic decline.

Each of the following chapters focuses on one country and on the types of work-family arrangements that have been developed in that country. The contributions show a wide variety in political debates between the nations and in the provisions that have been realised. The answer to the question as to how governmental policies and activities regarding work-family arrangements within firms relate, is not clear at this point. Is it true that an active national social policy on equal opportunities and reconciling work and family life discourages firms from realising work-family arrangements? Or is it the case that a political culture that emphasizes equal roles of men and women and points out the necessity for work-family arrangements invites employers to create substantial supplementary provisions? And what is the role of the European Union in this respect? In the last chapter of this book, an overview of recent European policies and activities on work-family facilities will be given. To specify the context of the book, some recent developments regarding women's participation in European labour markets will be presented in this introductory chapter, as well as some data on the division of paid and unpaid work between women and men. Next, typologies of welfare states will be focused on. Based on these typologies, the choice of countries will be discussed. First of all, a more precise description of what is meant by work-family arrangements is needed.

2. Work-family arrangements: a definition

In the literature, an operational definition of work-family arrangements is most commonly used. Moss (1990) makes a distinction between fringe benefits for working parents (leave arrangements) and childcare. Kingston (1990) states that the concept of work-family arrangements generally refers to two main types of personnel policy. On the one hand, he lists additions to fringe benefits, such as childcare arrangements or parental leave, and on the other hand, modifications in typical work schedules, such as flexitime, part-time work or job-sharing. There is also a distinction between direct and indirect policies. Direct policies are explicitly developed to facilitate the combination of paid and unpaid work, whereas indirect policies may or may not have been initiated with this goal in mind, but their effects support this combination nevertheless (Hayghe, 1988).

Work-family arrangements in this book will be defined as facilities that, intentionally as well as unintentionally, support the combination of paid work and family responsibilities. Four types of arrangements are distinguished: flexible working patterns, leave arrangements, care provisions and supportive arrangements. Examples of flexible working patterns are part-time work, flexible working hours and job-sharing. These types of arrangement allow workers to choose either to reduce their working hours or adjust them to caring tasks. Leaves, such as parental leave and paternity leave, enable parents to (temporarily) take care of their young children. Provisions like childcare or care for the elderly mean that care functions are performed by others during the time employees are at work. Supportive measures such as the distribution of information or management training can increase the awareness of work-family issues within the organisation. In Figure 1, the different types of work-family arrangements are summarised.

Work-family arrangements can either be formal, written policies or informal arrangements within the organisation. In the case of informal policies, the implementation is usually at the discretion of the manager (Wolcott, 1991). The manager, not the employee, decides whether an arrangement can be used. In some cases, work-family arrangements are only available to certain groups of employees, for example employees with a permanent contract or female employees. According to European Union directives, it is illegal to exclude certain groups (i.e. men) from these arrangements. However, if an employer can show that women are at an unfair disadvantage, measures are allowed to eliminate this disadvantage. In such cases employers can restrict the provision of work-family arrangements to women. Nevertheless, restrictive company arrangements can raise questions about equality of access. Work-family arrangements also differ in the level of costs involved, both organisational - a temporary loss of human capital, for example - and financial. A career break, although not without costs, generally is not too complicated to arrange, whereas a workplace nursery requires a substantial investment to be made.

Figure 1 *Work-family arrangements*

Flexible working patterns
- part-time work
- flexitime (flexible working hours)
- job-sharing
- flexplace (teleworking/working at home)
- term-time work
- banking hours

Leaves
- maternity leave
- parental leave
- paternity leave
- leave for family reasons
- career break schemes
- adoption leave

Care provisions
- workplace nursery
- after-school care
- holiday play scheme
- childcare resource and referral
- financial assistance
- vouchers
- elderly care resource and referral

Supportive arrangements
- work-family management training
- employee counselling/assistance programmes
- work-family co-ordinator
- supply of information

Fertility rates in Europe

Work-family arrangements could be considered as coping strategies, as strategies aimed at reconciling conflicting demands on time. Or, from a pragmatic perspective, to make conflicting claims more manageable in daily life. Another, quite different strategy aimed at avoiding time pressure, which is often the result of combining parenthood with paid employment, is to reduce the number of children born into households. This strategy is not uncommon in the European Union. Table 1 shows fertility rates in the European member states in the mid-1990s.

Table 1 *Fertility rates in Europe (1996)*

Austria	1.40	Italy	1.17
Belgium	1.55	Luxembourg	1.69
Denmark	1.80	Netherlands	1.53
Finland	1.81	Portugal	1.40
France	1.70	Spain	1.18
Germany	1.25	Sweden	1.73
Greece	1.32	United Kingdom	1.70
Ireland	1.86		

Source: European Observatory on National Family Policies, 1997

There is an overall decline in average household size in Europe, primarily due to declining fertility rates and an increasing number of childless families in many countries. It is interesting to note, however, that fertility rates differ. Apart from Ireland, with its longstanding catholic tradition, it is the Nordic countries that show the highest fertility rates of all the European member states. And, even more remarkably, the lowest birth rates are found in Southern Europe: Italy, Spain, Greece and Portugal. Although socially, economical and legally, the family is still one of the dominant institutions in Southern Europe, while at the same time, a silent revolution is going on, which eventually will affect families in their social and cultural significance. With reference to the different family policies in Europe, it seems clear that policies that support the combination of parenthood with paid work, also support a higher number of children per household. The time when traditional, mostly religious norms and values encouraged large families, definitely seems a thing of the past. A more decisive factor for the number of children is the amount and quality of facilities and work-family arrangements available in a given country. Bigger families no longer represent traditional welfare state regimes. On the contrary, advanced welfare states seem to offer more positive incentives for having (more) children than the more traditional welfare states do. This supposed relationship implies some ambivalence, however. More detailed research on the Swedish situation reveals that the "speed premium" in the parental leave scheme encouraged parents to have their second child soon after the first one was born. If the interval between two births does not exceed thirty months, a parent may retain the level of income compensation paid after the first birth even though the parent has a drop in wages in between births because of part-time work (see also chapter 7). This behaviour caused a rise in birth rates, which disappeared in the following years. So it is uncertain what will be the effects of these favourable parental leave conditions in Sweden in the long run. In general, it is not easy to give causal interpretations of statistical relations between policy measures and the so-called demographic behaviour of people (Beets, 1998).

3. Labour force participation of European men and women

In order to describe the economic activities of men and women, we used data from the Eurostat Labour Force Survey, presented by the European Commission on Employment in Europe in 1997. It appears that 70% of the male population and 50% of the female population in the European Union were economically active in 1996. Activity rates are calculated as the percentage of people who either have jobs or are unemployed - and are looking for a job - in a population aged 15 to 64 years.

Table 2   *Activity rates by sex; population of working age 15-64 years (1996)*

	Men	Women	Total
EUR 15	70	50	55
Belgium	67	46	57
Denmark	82	69	76
Germany	71	54	63
Greece	75	40	57
Spain	62	33	47
France	68	53	60
Ireland	69	43	56
Italy	67	37	51
Luxembourg	75	44	60
Netherlands	76	54	65
Austria	79	61	70
Portugal	76	57	66
Finland	64	60	62
Sweden	72	69	70
United Kingdom	76	63	70

Source: Employment in Europe 1997

The variation in female participation, ranging from 33% in Spain to 69% in Sweden, is higher than among men. Male activity rates vary between 62% in Spain and 79% in Austria. The activity rates of women are still lower than those of men in every single member state. This is even the case in the Nordic countries, Denmark, Sweden and Finland, countries that are highly developed welfare states. Variations in female economic activity between the European member states have much to do with differences in history and in the way welfare state regimes are institutionalised. We will come to this later.

Increase in activity rates

Despite their lower activity rates in comparison to men, women are accounting for an increasing proportion of the Union's labour force, and for a considerable share of the new jobs being created. While women represent around 41% of people in employment across the European Union, they accounted for just over 62% of the rise in the number of people employed. This means that female activity rates continued to increase relative to men's. Interestingly enough, this is not the case in all countries. Whereas in Greece women accounted for all of the net addition to jobs, and in Germany and Austria the number of working men declined, the employment of women fell while that of men increased in Denmark and Luxembourg (Employment in Europe, 1996). Partly, these differences in the growth of female workforces is caused by differences in sectoral patterns in employment. In the Union as a whole, the number of people employed in agriculture and industry where men represent a disproportional large share of the workforce, is declining. But this process varies across countries.

Part-time work in relation to activity rates

An interesting phenomenon in European labour force participation patterns is the difference in numbers of part-time workers across the Union. Table 3 shows the percentages of part-time workers, broken down by sex for all member states.

Table 3   Percentages of part-time workers in the employment population, by sex (1996)

	Men	Women	Total
EUR 15	6	32	16
Belgium	3	31	14
Denmark	11	35	22
Germany	4	34	17
Greece	3	9	5
Spain	3	17	8
France	5	30	16
Ireland	5	22	12
Italy	3	13	7
Luxembourg	2	18	8
Netherlands	17	69	38
Austria	4	29	15
Portugal	5	13	9
Finland	8	16	12
Sweden	9	42	25
United Kingdom	8	45	25

Source: Employment in Europe, 1997

Part-time work in the European Union usually means working weeks of less than 31 hours. The range in variation of part-time work patterns is rather large. The range is 2 to 17 percent among men in Luxembourg and the Netherlands, and from 9 to 68 percent among women in Greece and the Netherlands, respectively. There seems to be a relation between the number of part-time working women and part-time working men. A higher percentage of female part-timers corresponds to a higher percentage of male part-time workers. This holds true for the Netherlands, as well as for Denmark and Sweden, and to a certain degree for the United Kingdom. This could be seen as an indication of a relatively "part-time friendly" culture in a country. This is not the case in all countries, however. The Netherlands could be characterised as part-time friendly, and so could Denmark and possibly Sweden. But this is not the case for the United Kingdom. More than in other countries, long working weeks are common in the United Kingdom. Statistics show the United Kingdom as having the longest working weeks for full-time working men and women across the Union. Eurostat indicates an average working week of 44 hours in the United Kingdom, in comparison to the European average number of 40 hours (Eurostat 1996). Part-time work in United Kingdom is, generally speaking, primarily found in low-skilled, female-dominated jobs.

Based on figures of part-time work by women in 12 European Member States during the period 1983-1990, Fagan and Rubery (1996) investigated possible relationships between part-time work and overall employment growth for women. Three part-time conditions are distinguished: high part-time, relevant for the Netherlands, United Kingdom, Denmark and West Germany; moderate part-time, relevant for Belgium, France, Ireland and Luxembourg and a low part-time condition relevant for Spain, Italy, Portugal and Greece. Rapid employment expansion did not turn out to be dependent on the creation of part-time jobs. The Netherlands and Spain are both countries that have experienced a fast employment growth for women over recent years. In the Netherlands, this growth was nearly entirely based on an increase in the number of part-time jobs. This was not the case in Spain, however. The integration of women into employment in Spain was primarily realised because more women worked full-time. Fagan and Rubery conclude that, from an international, comparative point of view, there is no relationship between the mobilization of women into the labour force and the growth of part-time jobs over recent years.

Part-time work patterns, at least among women, seem to be most popular in the Netherlands. In terms of work-family arrangements, part-time work in the Netherlands is a pre-eminent coping strategy used to meet conflicting claims on time and availability. We will come to this point later. Related to the fact that part-time work is used as a coping strategy to reconcile family and work, is the question whether there are other reasons why women work part-time and whether different arguments for this fact are used in European countries.

The Labour Force Survey 1996 provides some answers. Several reasons for part-time work are distinguished: education; illness or disability; could not find full-time job; did not want full-time job. Differences in the arguments "did not want full-time job" and "could not find full-time job" among European women are striking. Table 4 gives more precise information.

Table 4   European women: working part-time by reason

	Not want full-time job	Not find full-time job
EUR 15	66%	17%
Belgium	12%	25%
Denmark	58%	15%
Germany	80%	11%
Greece	43%	32%
Spain	4%	23%
France	63%	37%
Ireland	25%	21%
Italy	30%	34%
Luxembourg	63%	6%
Netherlands	81%	5%
Austria	15%	9%
Portugal	10%	25%
Finland	22%	44%
Sweden	54%	30%
United Kingdom	80%	10%

Source: The Labour Force Survey

Most part-time working women in Belgium, Spain, Ireland, Italy, Austria, Portugal and Finland work part-time because full-time jobs are not available. The reverse seems to be true for women in the Netherlands, Denmark, Germany and the United Kingdom. Many of them declare that they work part-time because it suits them. Some caution, however, should be observed, because the concept of "preference" is a rather ambivalent one in this context. It is likely, for example, that many working women in the United Kingdom have to take part-time jobs, because affordable childcare and other facilities are not available.

This is not what Hakim suggests in relation to the British situation of working women. In her "Five feminist myths about women's employment " (1995), she argues that, although it is true that women with dependent children show the highest rates of part-time work, half of the more numerous group of women with no childcare responsibilities also choose not to work at all, or only part-time. Hakim defends the thesis of British women's polarization into two groups that are currently fairly evenly balanced in size: a group giving priority to marriage and child-rearing as their central activity and another group giving priority to work as their central activity. In doing so, Hakim stresses the significance of choices, priorities, commitments and the respective differences between men and women and among women themselves. Women, as Hakim puts it, need not primarily be seen as victims who have little or no responsibility for their situation. Women give priority to one way of living or another.

Hakim's hypothesis also seems applicable to the Dutch, German and Danish situation. Most women in these countries work part-time, because they prefer to do so. This does not mean, however, that priorities are set and decisions are made in an environment that is totally free of restrictions. Women decide to be engaged in paid or unpaid work in a context of more or less favourable structural and normative conditions (e.g., Van Doorne-Huiskes and Van Hoof, 1995). Important parts of these conditions are norms, values and internalised ideas about how to behave in relation to two important domains of life: paid labour and care. If concepts such as "preferences" and "priorities" are studied from a sociological point of view, norms or other institutional facts should not be neglected. Theoretically, it is precisely the analysis of how decisions are made in restrictive environments which is a central issue.

New forms of part-time work?
Part-time work in the Netherlands does not necessarily equate with a half-time job. Interestingly enough, discussions about how managerial and higher staff positions could fit into four-day schemes and/or into working weeks of about 30 hours are prevalent. This pattern is developing slowly, primarily in the public sector and primarily among women. This does not mean, however, that men with young children and older men at the end of their careers, are not interested in such new ways of organising labour. It can be expected that four-day jobs will be more common in the near future.

Without doubt, an important condition for the rather part-time-friendly culture in the Netherlands, is the lack of economic pressure to earn two full-time incomes in many households. The traditional one-earner family is the dominant pattern in a substantial but rapidly declining number of households. In addition, the so-called one-and-a-half earner-model is becoming popular; here, men are usually the breadwinners and women the part-time workers. In sum, economic conditions and cultural priorities, rooted in a history of rather traditional views on male and female roles, have created a climate that permits the development of new patterns of work in the Netherlands. If and how these new patterns could help cope with future developments and challenges, is an interesting question. To answer this question, a big disadvantage of part-time culture also has to be taken into account. This disadvantage is the lasting and persistent economic and social inequality that is created between women and men. Such inequality, however, is not a feature of Dutch society only.

4. Inequality between the sexes: a persistent phenomenon

Although progress has been made in integrating women into the European labour market, this does not mean that inequalities between male and female workers have disappeared. Women in the labour market still tend to be more concentrated than men in a limited number of sectors of activity. In 1995, about 22% of women in employment in the European Union worked as secretaries, typists or clerks, while another 20% were employed as shop assistants or waitresses or as other sales or service workers. A further 16% was employed as technician or associate professional, a high proportion of them as nurses, care workers or teachers. These three broad occupational categories accounted for around 60% of the jobs performed by women. In the case of men, less than half worked in the three occupational groups that were most important as far as male employment is concerned in craft trade, including jobs such as builders, metal workers and mechanics. A further 12% were employed as plant and machine operators and a slightly lower proportion as technicians (Employment in Europe, 1996). Not only is women's employment more concentrated than that of men, but there also remains a sharp distinction in the type of job done. This occupational segregation between the sexes seems to have remained largely untouched by the rising activity rates of European women. This is partly caused by the fact that the important sectors for women -public administration, retailing and business activities- are among the most rapidly expanding, in terms of jobs. There is some tendency, for men's employment as well, to become concentrated in the same sectors as women (Employment in Europe, 1996). This reflects the fact that the number of jobs in industry tends to decline and the number of jobs in the service sector tends to expand. This does not mean, however, that men and women have the same access to senior positions. Whereas 10% of men were employed as managers or senior officials, only 6% of women were similarly employed (Employment in Europe, 1996).

Occupational segregation between male and female workers partly explains the differences in wages between men and women that still exists. In European countries, women earn less than men. Statistics on hourly wage differences between men and women show that pay inequality is the lowest in Sweden and Denmark, followed by France and Italy. The United Kingdom, Ireland and Luxembourg have the highest wage differences. Table 5 is based on data from the Human Development Report 1995 of the United Nations, especially written for the Fourth World Conference on Women, held in Beijing in September 1995.

Table 5   *Women's average wage as a percentage of men's*

Sweden	74.5	Portugal	76.6
Denmark	82.6	Germany	75.8
France	81.0	Belgium	74.5
Italy	80.0	Spain	70.0
Greece	78.0	United Kingdom	69.7
Austria	78.0	Ireland	69.0
Finland	77.0	Luxembourg	65.2
Netherlands	76.7		

Source: UNDP. Human Development Report, 1995

It is interesting to note that there are large differences between countries with respect to women's wages in comparison to those of men. As will be elaborated on in the next section, social-democratic welfare states offer the best conditions for reconciliation of work commitments and family obligations, but this does not seem to be related with equal wages between women and men. It is very likely that both phenomena are interrelated (e.g., Den Dulk *et al.*, 1996).

So, while some progress in social equality between men and women has been achieved, it remains slow. This can be mainly explained by the burden of care work in the home. Care work is still predominantly a woman's affair in most European countries. Caring for relatives still impacts almost exclusively on female employment, while male careers remain unaffected by the presence of relatives in need of care. Countries do differ, however, in the way they have created conditions to facilitate the reconciliation of work and family responsibilities. In the next section, these differences between countries will be focussed on.

5.   Types of welfare states

As was said in section 1, where the central theme of the book was presented, differences in work-family arrangements between nations cannot be explained without giving attention to the way welfare states are institutionalised in Europe. It is an important point of view in this book, that all welfare states are, at least implicitly, based on assumptions about the social roles of men and women, on ideas about families, and on what has to be seen as appropriate behaviour for women and for men. Another leading hypothesis featured in this book is that types and availability of work-family arrangements in countries reflect these cultural visions and assumptions.

If we look at it from a historical point of view, the origin of current European welfare states can be traced back to the years after World War ll. A significant contribution to the development of welfare states was made by William Beveridge in his 1942 publication on Social Insurance and Allied Services and in his 1944 publication on Full Employment in a Free Society. Central issues in these publications were the renewal and extension of social provisions, as directed against the great evils of modern times: want, disease, idleness, ignorance and squalor. A policy of state intervention was theoretically legitimated by Keynes' plea for state-supported employment stimulation programmes. In Keynes' view, a situation of full employment was realised, if all male potential workers had full-time jobs. Keynes as well as Beveridge based their theories on the implicit assumption of a traditional division of tasks between women and men. The unpaid care work of the wife was paid for indirectly by the paid labour of the husband. Theories on welfare states were initially based on the thesis of convergence. Because of similar technological and economic developments in Europe, welfare states were expected to develop more or less identical characteristics in terms of political and socio-economic organisations. Institutional differences were supposed to disappear gradually. Similarity between welfare states would become a dominant feature. Later on, influenced by economic crises in Europe during the seventies and beyond and by the differences in responses to these crises, the theory of convergence lost ground. Welfare states clearly reacted differently to economic recessions. It was not uniformity in institutions that was striking, but multiformity instead.

By stipulating these historically-based differences between countries, Titmuss (1974) and later Esping-Andersen (1990) constructed typologies of welfare states. The central issue in the analyses of Esping-Andersen is the principle of social rights. Social rights permit people to make their living standard independent of pure market forces. This important element of public protection against social risks in the free market is referred to as decommodification by Esping-Andersen. Based on this notion of decommodification, he distinguishes three main types of welfare state: liberal, conservative/corporatistic, and social-democratic welfare state regimes.

From a feminist point of view, much has been said already about Esping-Andersen's typology (e.g., Langan and Ostner, 1990; Siim, 1991; Plantenga and Van Doorne-Huiskes, 1992; Lewis,

1993; Sainsbury, 1996). A crucial objection brought forward in this literature is that mainstream analyses do not take into account the specific position of women in welfare states and that their analyses are mainly based on (male) paid workers. As feminist scholars argue, it is not just the degree in which people live independently of market forces that is relevant, but also the degree in which it is possible for people (women) to live independently from their families. Based on the work of Esping-Andersen, but with more emphasis on the interrelations between the market, the state and the family, the social-democratic welfare state regime can be described as one that promotes equality among its citizens and that is committed to a full-employment guarantee for men as well as women. The costs of having a family, therefore, are largely socialised to maximise the capacities for individual independence. An elaborate system of public services, including childcare, health care and care of the elderly, ensures that everyone who is able to participate in the labour market does, in fact, participate. In this welfare state regime, the state also plays an important role as an employer, especially within the service sector. When it comes to gender, men and women are regarded as equivalent in social-democratic welfare state regimes. The tax system is individualised and the government takes up a neutral position vis à vis the choice for a particular lifestyle and/or division of roles. This emphasis on equal opportunities does not necessarily mean, however, that the outcomes are also equal. The labour market is highly segregated along gender lines, because women, to a large extent, work in public services. In addition, the fact that women do most of the (remaining) unpaid work is not really challenged. What this regime does try, however, is to make the combination of paid and unpaid work less difficult to manage for women (Siim, 1991). Within the European Union, Sweden, Denmark and Finland come nearest to this particular welfare state regime. In this book, Sweden represents the social-democratic welfare state.

Within the conservative/corporatistic welfare state regime the family plays an important role as a source of social stability and individual happiness. In contrast to the social-democratic welfare state, this welfare state regime is a (financial) compensator rather than an employer. This welfare state arrangement takes care of financial compensation when the outcomes of the market are deemed unacceptable or when labour force participation is considered undesirable. The role of compensator reveals itself in an elaborate system of breadwinner facilities within the social security and tax systems. Also, in contrast to the social-democratic welfare state regime, the conservative/corporatistic welfare state regime does not treat men and women as equal. Whereas men are seen as workers, women are seen primarily as wives and mothers. This results in two different kinds of citizens: men as breadwinners and women as caretakers. Because the emphasis is on the preservation of the traditional family and not on participation in the labour force by all citizens, childcare and/or parental leave facilities are underdeveloped. Within the European

Union, Germany and Italy come nearest to this kind of welfare state regime. These two countries are represented in this book. Spain, also discussed in this book, can be considered as another representation of this welfare state regime.

In the liberal welfare state regime, means-tested assistance and modest social security plans predominate. There is a great belief in the forces of the market and in its self-regulating capacity. The state functions only as a saviour or last resort. Entitlement rules are strict and often associated with a stigma. Whereas one can say that the social-democratic welfare state regime treats men and women as equivalents, and the conservative/corporatistic regime treats them as different, the liberal welfare state regime treats men and women as equals and makes no attempt to adjust for women's heavier care responsibilities. If we take this to its extreme, it could be said that a working mother does not really exist in this regime. Childcare and parental leave facilities are seen as individual responsibilities and not as responsibilities of the government. Of course, this greatly influences the labour market position of women. Because liberal welfare state regimes only have a limited system of breadwinner facilities, however, the labour force participation of women is still rather high. This liberal welfare state regime applies, in particular, to the United States (e.g., Sainsbury, 1996). Within the European Union, the United Kingdom comes nearest to this model. This is the reason why the United Kingdom is also featured in this book.

6.   Plan of the Book

Chapters 2 to 7 discuss developments in different European countries. Chapter 2 focuses on the development of work-family arrangements by employers in the Dutch welfare state. In the Netherlands, the development of work-family arrangements is seen as a shared responsibility between government, employers, and employees. The number of work-family arrangements developed by employers or incorporated in collective agreements is increasing but there are still great differences between sectors and types of organisations. Laura den Dulk presents a theoretical model which tries to explain employer's decision-making concerning work-family arrangements.

In Britain, there are also great differences between employers' provisions. In Chapter 3, Suzan Lewis argues that the British government has constructed work-family issues as individual rather than a collective responsibility and relies on market forces as a basis for the provision of benefits and initiatives to enable employees to balance work and family obligations. In this context, a business case for work-family arrangements has been the most persuasive, despite early grounding of the work-family debate in an equal opportunities framework. The business case approach focuses on benefits to employers, especially cost benefits. Suzan Lewis argues for a wider approach, that also recognises social responsibilities of employers and state interventions. In addition, shifts in workplace values and beliefs are needed for more fundamental change.

In Chapter 4, Wolfgang Erler describes the different stages of the work-family debate in Germany and the differences between West and East Germany. In West Germany, public policy took the initiative in the 1980s by introducing parental leave legislation. At present, in the context of economic difficulties, there is less scope for new policy initiatives. Innovative programmes that are introduced, such as additional childcare facilities, are mainly developed in public-private partnership. In Eastern Germany, the work-family debate takes place in a different context. The former GDR is characterised by a high number of childcare provisions and full-time labour market participation of women. There, it is the economic recession and high (female) unemployment rates that challenge the reconciliation of work and family life.

In Chapter 5, Rossana Trifiletti focuses on the Italian welfare state and its consequences for the reconciliation of employment and family life. Although more women continue to participate on the labour market, the idea of family-friendly organisations is not widely discussed in Italy. The totalitarian past has created unwillingness to make the family the subject of political debate. Another important feature of the Italian case is the division of the labour market between well-protected workers and those in the deregulated grey economy. For instance, part-time work is often associated with the informal economy and therefore opposed by unions and employees. Still, more and more women combine paid work and family responsibilities. They rely, among other things, on help from grandparents, i.e. solidarity in the family. However, for the next generation, grandparents (-mothers) will be less available and the need for work-family arrangements will most likely increase.

In Chapter 6, Anna Escobedo identifies trends and issues related to the work-family debate in Spain. Like Italy, reconciliation between work and family life is a subject that has only recently received public attention. Low fertility rates (1.18) are connected to a strong orientation towards the employment of young adult women. Social concern, however, has been focused on unemployment, labour market flexibilisation and the reduction of labour costs. The effective use of existing legal entitlements, such as maternity leave, makes sense only in the framework of stable jobs. Work-family arrangements are seen as private matters, and employees, especially in the private sector, do not have a sense of entitlement to request facilities or make use of the possibilities that current legal provisions allow. Anna Escobedo argues that the major strategy in Spain has been family adjustment to labour market imbalances.

Sweden has a long tradition of public provisions to support people who balance work and family responsibilities. Sweden's public policies are explicitly aimed at enabling women to combine work and motherhood, to increase equality between men and women in everyday life, and to support children's development. In Chapter 7, Elisabet Näsman shows how working fathers and mothers use the available work-family arrangements in their daily life and how they do so differently. She also focuses on the role of workplace culture in the take-up rates of policies and the way organisations supplement public provisions.

Chapter 8 discusses the involvement of the European Union in the development of work-family arrangements within its member states. Over the past ten years, Directives setting minimum standards for maternity and parental leave have been adopted, as well as a Council Recommendation on Childcare. Jacqie van Stigt, Anneke van Doorne-Huiskes and Joop Schippers give an overview of the history of EU work-family policies and discuss future developments.

Finally, Chapter 9 draws conclusions about the relationship between government policies and the development of work-family arrangements in firms and organisations. We will discuss the consequences of different types of welfare state regimes and elaborate on future trends.

References

Beets, G. (1998), Kostwinnersmodel, combinatiemodel en uitstel van ouderschap: demografische effecten. In: *Naar een nieuw "sociaal contract" in de 21ste eeuw*. Ministerie van Sociale Zaken en Werkgelegenheid. Den Haag, p. 91-103.

Council of Europe (1997). *Recent demographic developments in Europe*. Strassburg.

Doorne-Huiskes, J. van and J. van Hoof. (1995), Gendered patterns in institutional constraints. In: J. van Doorne-Huiskes, J. van Hoof, E. Roelofs. *Women and the European labourmarkets*, p. 106-212. London: Paul Chapman.

Doorne-Huiskes, J. van (1996), The unpaid work of mothers and housewives in different types of welfare states. In: P. Koslowski and A. Føllesdal (eds). *Restructuring the Welfare State*, p. 202-221. Berlin: Springer.

Dulk, L. den, J. van Doorne-Huiskes and J.J. Schippers (1996), Work-family arrangements and gender inequality in Europe. *Women in Management Review*, Vol. 11, No. 5, MCB University Press.

Dulk, L. den and Ch. Remery (1997), Work-family arrangements in organisations. In: K. Tijdens, J. van Doorne-Huiskes , T. Willemsen (ed.). *Time allocation and gender*. Tilburg: University Press.

Esping-Andersen, G. (1990), *The three worlds of welfare capitalism*. Cambridge: Polity Press.

European Commission (1997), *Employment in Europe 1997*. Brussels.

European Commission (1996), *Employment in Europe 1996*. Brussels.

European Observatory on Family Policy (1997*), Developments in national family policies in 1996*. York: European Commission.

Eurostat (1997), Statistics in focus. Luxembourg.

Fagan, C. and J. Rubery (1996), The salience of the part-time divide in the European Union. *European Sociological Review*. 12/3, p. 227-250.

Hakim, C. (1995), Five feminist myth about women's employment. *British Journal of Sociology*. 46/3, p. 429-455.

Hantrais, L. (1993), Women, work and welfare in France. In: J. Lewis (ed). *Women and social policies in Europe,* p. 116-137. Hants England: Edward Elgar.

Hayghe, H.V. (1988), Employers and childcare: What roles do they play? In: *Monthly Labour Review*. September, p. 38-44.

Human Development Report 1995, Published for the United Nations Development Programme (UNDP). Oxford: Oxford University Press.

Kingston, P.W. (1990), Illusions and ignorance about the family-responsive workplace. In: *Journal of Family Issues*. 11/4 p. 439-453.

Lewis, J. (ed.). (1993), *Women and social policies in Europe*. Hants, England: Edward Elgar.

Moss, P. (1990), Kinderopvang en –verzorging in de Europese gemeenschap 1985-1990. Brussel: Europese Commissie Netwerk Kinderopvang.

Plantenga, J. and J. van Doorne-Huiskes (1992), *Gender, citizenships and welfare: A European perspective*. Paper presented at the first European Conference of Sociology. Vienna. August 26th to 29th.

Sainsbury, D. (1996), *Gender, equality and welfare states*. Cambridge: Cambridge University Press.

Siim, B. (1991), Welfare state, gender politics and equaltiy politics: Women's citizenship in the Scandinavian Welfare States. In: E. Meehan and S. Sevenhuijsen, *Equality Politics and Gender*. London: Sage.

Titmuss, R. (1974), *Social Policy*. London: Allen and Unwin.

Wolcott, I. (1991), *Work and family. Employers' view*. Melbourne: Australian Institute of Family Studies.

WORK-FAMILY ARRANGEMENTS IN THE NETHERLANDS: THE ROLE OF EMPLOYERS [1]

Laura den Dulk

1. Introduction

In the Netherlands, the participation of women in the labour market is increasing and, related to this, so is the number of dual-earner households in the labour force (Hooghiemstra, 1997). A growing number of workers combine work with family responsibilities. As a consequence, it can be asked how employees deal with the combination of paid work and caring tasks. Working parents need, for example, childcare arrangements during the hours they are at work.

This chapter focuses on the development of work-family arrangements by employers in the Dutch welfare state. What kind of arrangements are developed within organisations? How do existing government policies influence organisational practices? And finally, why do some employers get involved in the development of arrangements while others do not? Theoretically, organisational characteristics as well as such institutional conditions as government policy, influence the employer's involvement in work-family arrangements.

What is presented below is a theoretical model which includes both institutional and organisational constraints. The model is based on the assumption that employers will implement arrangements if the benefits exceed the costs. As a result of constraints such as size of an organisation, characteristics of the workforce, and government intervention, the cost and benefits will vary across employers. By specifying relevant constraints, it is possible to explain why some organisations are more likely than others to develop work-family arrangements.

In the next section, a definition of work-family arrangements is introduced in which various types of facilities are distinguished. Section 3 presents an overview of the types of arrangements offered by Dutch employers, followed by a historical description of government policy in this field. Section 5 discusses a theoretical model that tries to explain why some organisations are more likely than others to develop work-family arrangements. Finally, future developments as regards arrangements by Dutch employers are considered.

---

[1] The author wants to thank Chantal Remery for our discussions about the theoretical framework and her valuable comments.

2.   Work-family arrangements

Work-family arrangements can be defined as facilities within organisations that support the combination of paid and unpaid work (see chapter 1). Organisations can develop facilities that ease the burden of caring tasks, for instance through the provision of childcare, or provide employees with improved scope for performing these tasks themselves besides their job.[2] Work-family arrangements can either be formal policies and official statements in the personnel policy of an organisation or exist as informal arrangements. In the case of the latter, people can discuss the use of arrangements with their manager. In the first chapter of this book four types of arrangements were distinguished: flexible working patterns, leave arrangements, care provisions, and supportive measures. Flexible working patterns provide workers with an opportunity of either reducing or adjusting their working hours to their caring tasks. Examples are the possibility of varying working hours, working from home, or working part-time. It should be noted, however, that flexibility can also cause problems for workers with caring responsibility. For instance, varying work schedules are often difficult to combine with childcare arrangements. An important aspect in relation to flexible working patterns is an employee's control over working hours and the possibility of adjusting hours to caring tasks. Leave arrangements also contribute to the reconciliation of work and family life. Leaves, such as parental and maternity leave, enable working parents to take time off to care of their young children. Employers can also provide childcare arrangements, such as a workplace nursery or a childcare resource and referral service, or elderly care arrangements. Finally, supportive measures such as the distribution of information may increase awareness concerning work-family issues within the organisation and inform employees about the presence of facilities.

Different types of work-family arrangements not only differ with respect to the extent to which employees benefit from them, but also with respect to their consequences for employers. For instance, child-care arrangements usually mean that children are cared for during the time parents are at work. As such, these arrangements help to increase the availability of working parents at the workplace. In this way, childcare arrangements increase the labour supply (Glass and Fujimoto, 1995). But the financial costs of childcare can be considerable for employers. Flexible working patterns which offer employees the opportunity to reduce their working hours or to adjust them to their family life can be cheaper. However, such patterns can potentially decrease the labour supply and influence the organisation of work. For instance, flexible

---

[2] This definition refers to practical caring tasks, such as care during hours at work. The need for economic support or emotional care is not included. See Holt and Thaulow (1996).

working schedules can lead to an increase in employee control and a decrease in the ability of managers to monitor hours and productivity directly. Some employers do not wish to lose managerial control, for which reason they decide not to implement such arrangements (Kingston, 1990). It could be the case that different types of organisations prefer different types of work-family arrangements. Below, a general overview is given of the types of arrangements provided by Dutch employers.

3.   Work-family arrangements in the Netherlands

3.1   Six cases of 'family-friendly' employers

In 1996 data was collected from six organisations which were known as 'family-friendly': a bank, an insurance company, a large and a small electro-technical manufacturing company, and two government organisations.[3] These were all organisations which had implemented work-family arrangements. The government organisations and the companies from the finance sector offered five to seven different arrangements. The manufacturing companies offered fewer facilities. The large manufacturing company had recently developed work-family arrangements and the arrangements were viewed mainly as an instrument for recruiting and retaining female employees. The small electro-technical firm was responding to requests from personnel. The most important consideration for choosing family-friendly organisations is to find out the specific types of local/national facilities that are initiated.

Part-time work, extended parental leave, and the buying or hiring of childcare places are the main work-family arrangements in the Dutch cases. Part-time work had a long tradition in most organisations and the organisations had a formal policy on part-time work. However, they did not offer the *right* to work-part-time. In most cases, it was stated that part-time work is possible unless it conflicts with business interests. Sometimes, it was the manager who had to prove that part-time work was not possible in a particular job. One of the government organisations had a policy which stated that all new jobs should be offered in a 32-hour working week.

Childcare and parental leave were generally introduced only a few years ago. One option to organise childcare is to hire or buy childcare places at a childcare centre for children under

---

[3] Within the organisations, the head of personnel or a personnel officer who was responsible for the personnel policy in the field of work-family issues was interviewed. I also interviewed employee representatives (*lid ondernemingsraad*). The organisations were chosen from different sectors (manufacturing, financial services and the public sector). This way, the range of the research was increased. Also, both public and private organisations are included and the selected organisations vary with respect to the proportion of female personnel.

four years of age and after-school care. Other childcare schemes which were mentioned were a holiday play scheme, care for 24 hours and childminding. None of the organisations had a workplace nursery.

The Dutch organisations also extended the right to unpaid, part-time parental leave. In some cases, partially paid leave was offered; others continued to pay for the pension scheme during the time on leave or offered a longer period of leave. Besides enhanced parental leave, the organisations offered three days of short-term leave for family reasons. Other types of leave were mentioned less frequently. None of the organisations provided enhanced paternity leave, i.e., longer than two days, or long-term leave for seriously ill relatives. However, the respondents said that the organisation was willing to consider a request for a period of leave if a close relative fell seriously ill. Adoption leave and career break arrangements were minimal.

One of the organisations offered flexible benefit (cafeteria) packages. In this cafeteria system employees can select their own conditions of employment within a certain framework. For instance, some employees opt for childcare facilities, while others prefer to participate in an additional pension scheme. Furthermore, employees can decide on a yearly basis whether they want either to sell or to buy leisure time in exchange for salary (a maximum of 15 days). So, employees who need more free time, for example, to care for their young children, can buy extra leisure time.

Other flexible working patterns, such as flexible working hours, have been offered as an experiment or on an informal basis. Flexible working hours or flexitime allows employees to choose, within set limits, the times they start and finish work. In general, the six organisations offered a bandwidth of 1.5 hours. However, flexible working hours did not always apply to all employees. In some cases, each department made its own arrangements depending on the kind of work that is done. In that case, the implementation was at the discretion of the manager. The 36-hour working week was recently introduced in the banking sector. The implementation of this collective agreement is not without difficulties, since there are banks who try to exclude certain groups of employees from the agreement in order to get them to work longer hours. In 1997, the government also introduced a 36-hour working week. Some governmental organisations give employees the possibility of working nine hours a day, four days a week. None of the six Dutch cases offered term-time work schedules. Term-time work is a scheme that originated in the UK and makes it possible for employees to remain on a permanent contract as either full- or part-time employees, but gives them the right to unpaid leave during school holidays (New Ways to Work, 1993). In one case, the option existed of saving up overtime hours in order to take leave during school holidays. But this arrangement was abolished because the company had difficulties finding enough temporary workers during the summer holiday. Teleworking or working at home was a new development for the organisations involved. Teleworking was not related to the reconciliation of work and family life but to shortage of office space or specially organised for partially disabled workers and handicapped people. The six cases had only a few examples of job sharing.

Finally, there were no supportive measures like special management training or employee counselling. One organisation stated that there was a helpdesk for people with questions about fringe benefits while another organisation offered special courses for female employees, but not specifically related to work-family issues.

In general, within these six cases, employees with caring responsibilities can apply for a childcare place, hired by the organisation, request to work part-time or use extended parental leave. They can negotiate with their manager the hours they start or finish work or the possibility of working at home. Furthermore, their manager can grant them short-term or long-term leave in the case of a sick child or illness of another close relative.

This type of qualitative research, which focuses on a limited number of cases, shows the kind of work-family arrangements introduced by employers, but does not tell us anything about the general provision of work-family arrangements in organisations. To illustrate how widespread work-family arrangements are among Dutch companies, I will discuss a representative study on firms with more than 100 employees in the private sector conducted by the Ministry of Social Affairs and Employment (SZW, 1992, 1997).

3.2   The number of arrangements within companies

In 1990/1991 and 1996, the Ministry of Social Affairs and Employment collected data among a representative sample of firms with more than 100 employees. Both studies investigated how widespread work-family arrangements were among companies, and for some arrangements it is possible to make a comparison between 1990/1991 and 1996.

The two studies show that leaves are quite common among Dutch organisations. A majority of the companies offer working fathers two days (paid) leave after their partner has given birth (79.2%). None of the companies offer a more substantial period of paternity leave.

In 1996, the 16-week maternity leave was supplemented in 13.8% of the companies. In most cases, this meant an extended period of (unpaid) leave. In the case of adoption, no legal entitlement exists. Hence, 40% of the companies have an adoption leave arrangement; for a foreign adoption, employees are entitled, on average, to 12 days leave; for an adoption in the Netherlands, seven days. About 55% of the companies offer paid adoption leave. Compared to 1990/1991, adoption leave has increased from 28% to 40%. Short-term leave for family reasons seems widespread among Dutch companies; in 1996 80.5% of the firms offered short-term leave for sudden caring tasks at home or other emergencies, such as a broken sewer or a flood.

In a large number of companies, however, the paid or unpaid character of the leave is at the discretion of the manager. Within 88.3% of the companies, moreover, the length of the leave is not specified and in only 26.7% of the companies this leave is specifically intended for caring tasks at home. In 1990/1991, short-term leave was provided in 35% of the companies. The sharp increase is partially due to the definition used in 1990/1991, which only applied to sudden caring tasks for children. In 1996, a broader definition was adopted, which also included other emergencies. Long-term leave was not investigated before 1996; in 1996, 68% of the companies offered long-term leave for the care of seriously ill relatives. In 79% of these companies, however, the length is unknown, while 44% of these companies left payment to the discretion of the manager. The number of companies with a child-care arrangement had increased from 15 to 54% in 1996. Part-time work was also investigated in 1996. The right to work part-time, provided it did not conflict with business needs, existed in 51.6% of the companies. On the other hand, the possibility of working part-time temporarily was limited to 1.8% of the companies.

Both studies indicate that work-family arrangements are more common in larger firms, with more than 500 employees, than in smaller ones (100-500 employees). Furthermore, arrangements were introduced more frequently in the service industry than in other industries. The likelihood that an organisation will offer work-family arrangements also increases when these benefits are part of the collective agreement that applies to the firm (SZW, 1992; SZW, 1997).

The available evidence suggests that the number of work-family arrangements within organisations is increasing. However, the inclusion of informal, ad hoc arrangements in the two studies can result in an overestimation of the number of opportunities. In the case of ad hoc arrangements, it is the manager who decides whether the employee can make use of a specific arrangement. On the other hand, within some companies employees may have substantial discretion to use existing facilities (Kingston, 1990). The results also show differences between organisations in terms of branch and size. National policies seem to interact with practices of employers. In countries with advanced statutory social policies in the field of work-family arrangements, for instance, employers are not required to offer duplicate services. The next section gives an overview of public provisions in the Netherlands.

4. Governmental policies

The Netherlands is sometimes characterized as a social-democratic welfare state (Esping-Andersen, 1990). However, several authors point out that the Dutch welfare state also has characteristics of the conservative/corporatistic welfare regime (Plantenga & Van Doorne-

Huiskes, 1993; Sainsbury, 1996; Van der Veen, 1990). A social democratic feature of the Dutch welfare state is the relatively high level of benefits. However, in the Netherlands more importance is attached to the family than is done in a social-democratic welfare state regime. The breadwinner model has strongly influenced social policy in the Netherlands. For a long time, policy was based on the traditional division of paid and unpaid labour between men and women, resulting in the provision of breadwinner facilities and low labour participation of women.

In the 1970s and 1980s, Dutch women increasingly started to participate in the labour market. The growing labour market participation of women is primarily explained by social-cultural changes, such as individualisation (SCP, 1996). In this period, emancipation became an important societal issue, which also rose to prominence on the political agenda. This resulted in an emancipation policy aimed at promoting "the development from present-day society, in which inequality between the sexes is still institutionalised to a great extent, to a multiform society, in which everybody, regardless of sex or marital status, has the opportunity to earn an independent living and in which women and men have equal rights, opportunities, freedoms and responsibilities" (SZW, 1995, p. 3). One of the main issues within this policy was the realisation of a more equal division of paid and unpaid work between men and women. This emphasis on equality corresponds with the notion of socio-economic equality for all citizens, which is characteristic of social-democratic welfare states. Given this, one would expect the Dutch government to have taken the main responsibility for developing work-family arrangements. An evaluation of the concrete measures, however, points to an approach more characteristic of the conservative/corporatistic welfare state: a strong emphasis on the initiative of employers' organisations, trade unions (the social partners), and individual organisations.

Sainsbury (1996) evaluated the Dutch gender equality reforms of the 1980s. She concluded that individualization, accompanied by demands for a more equal division of paid and unpaid work between men and women, dominated the reforms. Individualization was introduced in several areas. Among other things, separate taxation was introduced. The Dual Wage Earners Act (1984) granted both spouses the same basic tax allowance. However, there still remained a generous spouse deduction for the non-working partner. During the 1980s, married women gained access to three major benefit programs: disability (1980), national retirement pensions (1985), and extended employment benefits (1987). In national insurance plans, the unit of contribution was changed from the household to individuals. This individualization has increased women's financial independence. However, total individualization has not as yet been achieved. And despite the demands for a more equal division of paid work and caring tasks, this policy issue has received less attention. It was only in the 1990s that the government started to develop concrete measures in this area.

In 1995, the minister of Social Affairs and Employment instructed a committee to consider possible future developments of the division of paid and unpaid work within society (Commissie Toekomstscenario's Herverdeling Onbetaalde Arbeid, 1995). Also, the Netherlands National Council on Equal Opportunities (*Emancipatieraad*) published a report on how to achieve a more equal income- and social security policy. Both the committee and the council advised the government to introduce a 32-hour work week as a new standard for income and employment policy (instead of 38 hours). If people spent 32 hours on paid labour, they would have enough time for caring tasks and still have a certain amount of free time to spend. For those who need more time for caring responsibilities, such as parents with young children or employees with terminally ill relatives, the government has to provide additional options, such as parental leave, and short- and long-term leave for family reasons. The remaining breadwinner facilities should be abolished and social security benefits further individualized (Emancipatieraad, 1996). Although there seems to be a development towards a shorter working week, as is evidenced by the introduction of a 36-hour working week in several industries, the introduction of a 32-hour working week as a new standard does not seem likely in the near future.

Hence, until the end of the 1980s equal opportunity policy was mainly focussed on the stimulation of the labour market participation of women. In the beginning of the 1990s, facilities which could ease the combination of paid work and caring tasks became a central issue on the political agenda. The shift to the reconciliation of work and family responsibilities is mainly due to changes in society: the increasing labour market participation of women with children since 1970, the increasing demand for childcare, the changing workforce, which was no longer dominated by the male single earner but more and more characterised by diversity of employees (male, female, dual-earners with and without care responsibilities, etc.), and changing attitudes and opinions towards the combination of work and caring tasks (Niphuis-Nell, 1997).

Part-time work is a widely adopted strategy for Dutch women to combine paid work and caring tasks. Almost 60% of working women have a part-time job. Compared to other European countries, the Netherlands has the largest share of (male and female) part-time workers in the labour force (Plantenga, 1995). This development was supported by government policy, which tried to improve the position of part-timers. Since the end of 1996, for example, employers have to treat part-timers and full-timers equally with regard to the conditions of employment (TK, 1996-1997). Recently, however, a bill entitling employees to work part-time was not accepted by the Dutch parliament (TK, 1993-1994). However, the right to work part-time is still on the political agenda. A new proposal submitted to the parliament suggests to entitle people to part-time work providing it does not conflict strongly with business needs. With the Working Time Act (1995), the government tried to stimulate the development of more flexible working patterns, including part-time work. It gives employers and employees the possibility of varying labour patterns. In addition to safety, health, and welfare of employees, the objective of this act also addresses the combination of paid work with care and other responsibilities. Employers have to consider preferences of their employees with regard to working hours (TK, 1994-1995). However, employees are not provided with the means to object to changing working hours when these make the combination between paid work and other responsibilities more difficult.

With respect to leave arrangements, the Dutch government has developed two different legal entitlements for workers with care responsibilities. In the Netherlands women are entitled to 16 weeks of fully paid maternity leave. The Parental Leave Act (1991) gives both parents the right to a period of six months unpaid, part-time leave, which can be taken until their children reach the age of eight. The Parental Leave Act is considered a minimum, which can be supplemented by collective agreements or policies of individual firms. A study which analysed collective agreements agreed upon in 1994, found that about 36% of the agreements supplement the right to parental leave. In most cases, this means that social security rights continue during this leave. Only one collective agreement provided for a (partially) paid leave (Sloep, 1996). For many employees, the unpaid character of the leave is a barrier to its use (Spaans & Van der Werf, 1994). It is less usual for collective agreements to supplement the Maternity Leave Act; in 1996 only 7% of the collective agreements extended maternity leave (Niphuis-Nell, 1997).

There are no legal entitlements to leave for family reasons or paternity leave. The government considers the development of these forms of leave to be the responsibility of the social partners (TK 1994-1995). Legally fathers can take leave to be present at the birth of their child and to register their new born child. Hence, most collective agreements provide for two days of paternity leave (94%). In 1996, 41% of the agreements offered short-term leave for sudden care problems at home and 28% provided some kind of arrangement for long-term leave (SZW, 1997).

Last year, the minister of Social Affairs and Employment introduced a legal arrangement for a career break system. The new act is mainly a financial arrangement, providing financial compensation for employees who take a career break under the condition that they are replaced by unemployed workers. It does not entitle employees to take such a break. This will be a matter of collective agreement.

Public childcare is limited in the Netherlands. Childcare is seen as the shared responsibility of parents, the government, and employers, and the organisational structure is characterised by a public-private partnership. During the period 1990-1995, the (central) government stimulated the increase in the number of child-care facilities by providing subsidies. The local government was responsible for creating child-care facilities, and organisations could buy or hire places in subsidized child-care centres. In 1989, 13% of the places were hired by employers, in 1995 39% (Niphuis-Nell, 1997). Parents also contribute to the costs, the amount paid being linked to their income. The stimulation measure on childcare has increased the number of childcare places considerably. However, supply still does not meet demand. In 1995 only 7.5% of children under four had a place in public childcare. After-school care for children between 4 and 13 is even more limited; 0.84% of school-age children had a childcare place (SGBO, 1996). At present, the local government still receives subsidy for childcare. However, the budget has been cut and there is no obligation to spend the subsidy on childcare facilities. To stimulate a further increase in childcare places, the government is offering employers and parents tax relief for (part of) the costs. Moreover, in 1958 a new package of stimulative measures was introduced with special attention for school-age children.

To summarise, although the combination of paid work and caring tasks is being widely discussed, the further development of work-family arrangements is mainly left to the initiative of the social partners and individual organisations. The development of work-family arrangements is seen as the shared responsibility between the government, employers, and employees. The government has developed a few statutory rights such as maternity and parental leave, but its policy mainly consists of recommendations and subsidies. As such, it can be characterised as stimulating, leaving social partners and organisations relatively free in their decision to implement work-family arrangements. In the view of the government, they are the right actors for developing facilities that meet the needs of both employers and employees. The role of the government is to remove existing barriers and to stimulate the development of work-family arrangements in collective agreements and organisations (TK 1994-1995).

Concerning collective agreements, the trade unions take the initiative to include work-family issues in the negotiations. But even though equal opportunities are part of the trade union policies, work-family arrangements are not a high priority. When agreement is reached on the main issues of the negotiations, work-family arrangements often become a secondary issue (Sloep, 1996). Moreover, there are still large numbers of organisations without a collective agreement or with an agreement that does not include work-family facilities.[4]

Employers can also develop work-family arrangements as part of their personnel policy. The question remains why some organisations develop these kinds of facilities and other do not. Both government policy and collective agreements influence the development of work-family arrangements within organisations. However, other conditions, such as the situation on the labour market, the cultural climate, or organisational features are also of importance.

---

[4] In the Netherlands, about 20% of the wage earners are employed in organisations with no collective agreement (Niphuis-Nell, 1997).

5. **Theoretical model explaining why some organisations introduce work-family arrangements and others do not**

Most empirical research on organisational involvement in work-family issues lacks a fully developed theoretical framework which explains why some employers adopt work-family arrangements and others do not. If a theoretical framework is used, it is usually based on institutional theories (Goodstein, 1994; Ingram and Simons, 1995). These emphasize the influence of the legal and normative environment on organisational structures and practices (DiMaggio and Powell, 1983; Scott, 1995). Organisations must not only meet technical or economic requirements, but also need to respond to regulations, norms, laws, and social expectations (Goodstein, 1994). For instance, in the Netherlands there has grown an increasing awareness that family life and work have changed and that more and more people are trying to balance work and caring tasks. Changes in the workforce have increased the demand for work-family arrangements. Moreover, the public attention to these issues, accompanied by government policies, has intensified institutional pressure on employers to respond by implementing work-family arrangements. Goodstein (1994) found some evidence for the institutional explanation of the development of arrangements by employers. His study shows that the likelihood of work-family arrangements adopted by employers was positively related to the distribution of work-family benefits among other employers in the same industry. However, institutional theorist have been critized for considering organisations as passive actors who confirm to institutional pressures (Oliver, 1991). Goodstein's study also highlights the fact that organisations do not respond uniformly to institutional pressures, but in a variety of ways. This is confirmed by other empirical data, which shows differences between organisations regarding the development of arrangements (SZW, 1997; Morgan and Milliken, 1992, Osterman, 1995). Hence, a theoretical framework in which employers are assumed to be capable of making different decisions seems more valuable (Oliver, 1991). In addition, it could be the case that when innovative programs are relatively new, interest-based considerations are more important, while, over time, institutional pressures become more salient (Tolbert and Zucker, 1983; Osterman, 1995).

Rational choice theory provides an interesting framework to elaborate the perspective that organisations make various decisions about the adoption of work-family arrangements. Rational choice theory assumes that actors generally strive for the maximum realisation of their goals given the constraints they face (Coleman, 1990). Among the constraints are the availability of resources, such as time and money, and the behaviour of other relevant actors. Constraints also refer to structural and institutional conditions, such as social norms and laws. As a result of these constraints, actors have to make choices. According to rational choice theory, actors will choose the alternative with the highest net benefit.

This general model can be applied to the behaviour of employers with regard to the introduction of work-family arrangements. Because employers are confronted with different constraints, the costs and benefits of these arrangements will vary across employers. By specifying relevant constraints, it is possible to explain why some employers are more likely to introduce work-family arrangements than others.

According to rational choice theory, actors behave purposively and intentionally; that is, their actions are aimed at the realisation of certain goals. Traditionally, neo-classical economic theory considers the maximum realisation of profit as the ultimate goal for employers. However, this was only applicable in the analysis of certain questions. Therefore, in many cases, the maximum realisation of profit was interpreted as a long-term goal, and the continuity of the company was adopted as a secondary objective. Van der Burg *et al.* (1989, p. 314) assume that actors within organisations strive for maximum realisation of their goals and that four arguments contribute to this: income, status, harmonious relations, and secure position. In the rational choice model, the unit of analysis is the individual, and goals are related to individual decision makers (Zey, 1998). However, I will apply the assumption of multiple goals to the employer as general actor.[5] The more income, the more status, the less conflicts, and the more secure the position of the organisation, the more an employer realises his goal.

Work-family arrangements can be beneficial to each of the four goals. First, the maximum realisation of income. For employers in the private sector, this argument refers to profit. For public sector organisations the income argument is not only defined in terms of profit, but also in terms of budgets (Den Dulk and Remery, 1997). If work-family arrangements contribute to the profit or budget of an organisation, the employer may decide to implement them. For example, work-family arrangements make it easier for women to combine paid work with caring tasks. Therefore, the provision of, for instance, a childcare arrangement can reduce absenteeism and turnover among female employees (Glass & Fujimoto, 1995). The benefits of reducing absenteeism and turnover can exceed the cost of implementing a childcare arrangement and contribute to the income of an organisation. As a result, an employer with a large proportion of valuable female personnel may decide to develop childcare.

Secondly, in an environment where support for working parents is considered important, the provision of work-family arrangements can contribute to the social image or status of an organisation. This image or status is important to employers for several reasons. A good image not only attracts customers but also the sufficient supply of labour. If an employer is known for

---

[5] Rational choice theory explains collective behaviour on the basis of individual actions. Whether an organisation introduces work-family arrangements is the result of decisions made by individual actors, such as shareholders, managers and employee representatives. Instead of focussing on the role of different decision makers I will focus on the role of various constrains which influence the cost and benefits of work-family arrangements. Hence, I will use the term employer as a general actor representing organisations.

his excellent working conditions, this will contribute to the recruitment of qualified personnel. Status can be of special importance to an organisation that provides services.

Thirdly, employers want to avoid conflict within the organisation. If (female) employees or labour unions make a strong request for certain work-family arrangements, the employer may conform in order to reduce the risk of a conflict and to maintain harmonious relations.

Finally, employers strive towards a secure position. The position of a company is related to its market-share. The larger the market-share and/or the more stable this share, the more secure the position of the organisation. Especially for companies that operate in a highly competitive market, a secure position is very important. For public organisations, a secure position is related to its (political) legitimacy. Loss of legitimacy endangers the survival of public organisations. If work-family arrangements increase the productivity and legitimacy of the organisation, the provision of these arrangements contributes to a secure position. However, if an organisation is in an insecure position, the employer is less likely to introduce work-family arrangements because of the costs involved.

In addition to benefits, the introduction of work-family arrangements also involves financial and organisational costs for the employer. The provision of childcare arrangements, for example, has financial consequences. Employers who offer parental leave have to be prepared to replace employees who take this leave. This leads to organisational costs. The cost and benefits of work-family arrangements are influenced by the constraints employers face. Relevant constraints are the institutional environment and organisational characteristics. By describing relevant institutional and organisational constraints, it is possible to explain why some organisations develop work-family arrangements and others do not.

Institutional constraints

Governmental policy, the influence of trade unions and collective agreements, the cultural context, and the situation on the labour market are four important institutional constraints.

As stated earlier, the Dutch government tries to influence the behaviour of employers. Its policy mainly consists of making recommendations and providing subsidies. Only maternity and parental leave are compulsory. Organisations can respond differently to existing governmental pressure to further develop work-family arrangements. Some employers will be more responsive than others. Two relevant factors are the private/public status of an organisation and the size of the organisation. Firstly, we assume that public organisations are more likely to respond to governmental pressure than private sector companies (Goodstein, 1994). The main task of public organisations is to execute governmental policy. If government policy stimulates employers to implement work-family arrangements, this creates a normative pressure on public organisations to conform. Public organisations are more often the subject of public attention and are more likely to be evaluated according to governmental standards and norms. The costs of not responding to this pressure are therefore higher for public organisations than private ones. A second factor that makes organisations more sensitive to governmental pressure is size. Larger organisations are more often subject to public discussion, for example, in the media, than smaller ones. When the government stimulates the development of work-family arrangements, the introduction of such facilities could benefit the image and social status of the employer, whereas resistance could result in public disapproval.

Another constraint refers to trade unions and the role of collective agreements. As was shown, work-family arrangements can be part of collective agreements. When this is the case, employers will be more inclined to provide these arrangements. If employers do not implement the agreed arrangements, they risk a confrontation with the trade unions. The costs and benefits of such a decision depends, among other things, on the strength of the trade unions and the importance attached to work-family arrangements.

The cultural context is a third constraint which influences the cost and benefits of work-family arrangements. Norms and values with respect to the division of paid and unpaid labour between men and women and the labour market participation of mothers with young children are changing in the Netherlands. In 1965, almost all Dutch women and men objected to the labour market participation of mothers with young children who, as a consequence, used a childcare centre; in 1995 this number had decreased to half of the population. And nowadays, a majority of the Dutch people are in favour of a equal division of paid and unpaid labour between men and women (Van Praag and Niphuis-Nell, 1997). However, in practice there is still a lot of inequality: men are responsible for about 70% of the paid work and 30% of the unpaid work. On the other hand, women do 30% of the paid work and 70% of the unpaid work (Emancipatieraad, 1996). 'One-and-a-half earner families', in which the men have a full-time job and the women a (small) part-time job, are characteristic of Dutch society. Increasing social acceptance of the idea of both parents having a job and caring responsibilities can increase societal pressure on employers to support the combination of paid and unpaid work by offering work-family arrangements to their employees. However, the cultural context in the Netherlands is still ambivalent. As a result, the pressure on organisations is not very strong.

Finally, the situation in the labour market is of importance. The unemployment rate influences the pressure on employers to develop work-family arrangements. In the case of high unemployment, there is less pressure because it is easier to replace and to recruit employees. When the labour market is tight, there is more competition among employers to retain and recruit personnel. Work-family arrangements can attract qualified employees or help to retain personnel, which saves replacement costs. Thus, in the case of a tight labour market the net benefits of keeping a qualified work force are probably higher than the costs of arrangements. Not only the institutional environment, but also organisational features influence the decision of employers to adopt work-family arrangements.

Organisational constraints

Research suggests that the size of an organisation is positively related to the presence of work-family arrangements (Kamerman and Kahn, 1987; Morgan and Milliken, 1992; Goodstein, 1994; Ingram and Simons, 1995). In addition to visibility, there are economies of scale for large organisations in benefit provision (Osterman, 1995). Consequently, adoption of work-family arrangements may be more costly for smaller organisations. Moreover, large organisations often have a specialized human resource staff, which is more likely to be aware of increasing demands for work-family arrangements and have more expertise to react to these developments (Morgan and Milliken, 1992).

A second important constraint which influences the balance of costs and benefits is the number of female employees. Because women are more likely to be responsible for caring tasks than men, the effects of work-family arrangements on productivity, absenteeism, and turnover can be significant in organisations with a large proportion of women. Moreover, a large proportion of women can result in a strong request for facilities such as childcare. On the other hand, a high demand for facilities increases the costs and may be a reason to decide against the introduction of work-family arrangements. Another strategy open to employers is to employ women with caring responsibilities only in occupations and positions where productivity losses and turnover costs are low (Glass and Fujimoto, 1995), thereby avoiding the necessity of work-family arrangements.

Hence, the position of female employees within the organisation has to be taken into account. For instance, loss of women in managerial positions means loss of human capital and is costly. In general, retainment of personnel becomes more important in terms of costs and benefits the more an employer invest in personnel. The introduction of work-family arrangements can help to reduce turnover because the organisation recognizes caring responsibilities. Besides the organisational benefits of keeping valuable personnel, female managers have the power to stimulate the development of work-family arrangements within the organisation. In the case of a strong lobby, the absence of arrangements can provoke a conflict more easily. Because employers strive towards harmonious relations, a large proportion of female managers can increase the likelihood of work-family arrangements. Flexibilisation is also an important variable. In general, flexible workers are not entitled to facilities provided by the organisation. They often work in jobs with low replacement costs. Hence, the presence of a high proportion of flexible employees will decrease the likelihood of employer's involvement in work-family arrangements.

The economic position is also linked to the development of arrangements. A good or stable economic position creates room for risk-taking and investments. There are also more resources to adopt innovative practices. Thus, the economic position is an important constraint with respect to the implementation of arrangements. This position depends largely on the situation of the industry.

Finally, the organisational culture affects the perceived costs and benefits of arrangements. Since it is difficult to measure the actual effects of work-family arrangements on, for instance, productivity, absenteeism and turnover, not all organisations are convinced that changes in work and family life are relevant to the organisation (Morgan and Milliken, 1992). Research suggests that organisations with relatively 'progressive' employment policies and philosophies are more likely to get involved with work-family arrangements (Auerbach, 1990; Osterman, 1995).

Figure 2   Institutional and organisational constraints

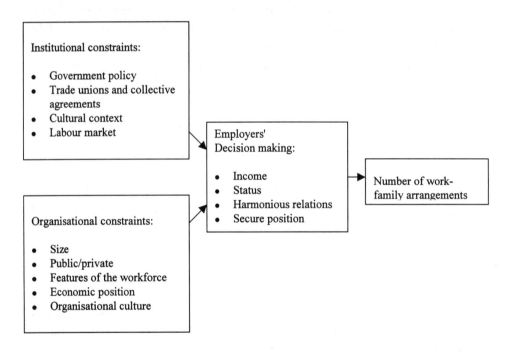

The theoretical model explains differences in the adoption of work-family arrangements between employers by specifying relevant constraints. The model is based on the assumption that employers are decision-making actors and will implement arrangements if the benefits exceed the costs. Both institutional and organisational constraints affect the costs and benefits of work-family arrangements for organisations. It is possible to formulate hypotheses, to be tested in future research, with respect to the circumstances under which organisations are more likely to introduce work-family arrangements.

The theoretical model also allows us to make comparisons between countries. The institutional constraints, such as government involvement, cultural context, and collective agreements, vary across countries. For instance, differences between types of welfare states may explain the extent to which organisations have introduced work-family arrangements. In the next section, I will discuss the implications of the model with regard to the future developments of work-family arrangements by Dutch employers.

6. Summary and extrapolations

In the Netherlands, there is not much institutional pressure on organisations to develop work-family arrangements. Firstly, government policy is restricted to encouraging organisations in their decision to implement arrangements, leaving them relatively free. Secondly, although work-family arrangements are increasingly part of collective agreements, there are still a lot of agreements without provisions. This is becoming an important issue for trade unions, but has not been a priority during negotiations (Sloep, 1996). Thirdly, social norms concerning the division of paid and unpaid labour between men and women have changed in the last few decades. However, an equal division has not yet been reached. This is reflected in the high number of women working part-time and of one-and-a-half earner households.

Finally, a growing concern about shortages of qualified employees (male and female) in the future due to demographic developments could be an incentive for employers to develop work-family arrangements. A low birth rate in combination with an ageing population can result in a shortage of young educated people. In the United Kingdom, at the end of the 1980s, this demographic forecast caused a large number of companies to implement work-family arrangements in order to attract and retain female personnel (Lewis et al., 1996). Recently the Netherlands is characterised by economic growth and declining unemployment rates. In some sectors, there is already a shortage of qualified personnel (for instance, health care or the IT-industry). But besides the growth of employment, the labour force is also increasing, mainly due to the growing labour market participation of women. As a result unemployment rates are declining slowly (SCP, 1996).

To summarize, besides some specific sectors, there is no general labour shortage expected in the near future, the cultural context is still ambiguous (i.e., in transition), and government and trade union pressure is limited. Hence, in the near future a sharp increase in work-family provisions within organisations is not to be expected. Differences between industries and organisations are expected to emerge. According to the theoretical model, work-family arrangements will mainly be developed in large organisations, in the public sector, and in those branches where employers have difficulties recruiting and retaining personnel. As a result, inequality in access to work-family arrangements between workers will arise: some workers will have access to a wide range of facilities, whereas others will have hardly any entitlements. Given the emphasis on equality in the emancipation policy of the Dutch government, this situation is not desirable. As long as the government does not implement a more compulsory policy because of economic and social-cultural developments, organisational characteristics will decide whether an organisation will develop and implement provisions.

References

Auerbach, J.D. (1990), Employer-supported childcare as a women-responsive policy. In: *Journal of Family Issues*, 11/4, pp. 384-400.

Burg, B.I. van der, J. van Doorne-Huiskes, J.J. Schippers and J.J. Siegers (1989), Loopbaan-verschillen tussen mannen en vrouwen binnen arbeidsorganisaties. Een structureel-individualistisch verklaringsschema. In: *Sociologische gids*, 5, p. 312-323.

Coleman J.S. (1990), *Foundations of Social Theory.* Cambridge: Harvard University Press.

Commissie Toekomstscenario's Herverdeling Onbetaalde Arbeid (1995), *Onbetaalde zorg gelijk verdeeld. Toekomstscenario's voor herverdeling van onbetaalde arbeid.* Den Haag: Vuga.

DiMaggio P.J. and W.W. Powell (1983), The Iron Cage Revisited: Institutional Isomorphism and Collective Rationality in Organizational Fields. In: *American Sociological Review*, 48, pp. 147-160.

Dulk, L. den and Ch. Remery (1997), Work-family arrangements in Organisations. In: *Time allocation and Gender.* J. van Doorne-Huiskes, K. Tijdens and T. Willemsen (ed.) Tilburg: University Press.

Emancipatieraad (1996), *Met zorg naar nieuwe zekerheid. Advies over een geëmancipeerd inkomens- en sociale zekerheidsbeleid.* Den Haag: Emancipatieraad, adv.nr. IV/45/96.

Esping-Andersen G. (1990), *The Three Worlds of Welfare Capitalism.* Cambridge: Polity Press.

Glass, J. and T. Fujimoto (1995), Employer characteristics and the provision of family respon-sive policies. In: *Work and Occupation*, 22/4, pp. 380-411.

Goodstein J.D. (1994), Institutional Pressures and Strategic Responsiveness: Employer Involvement in Work-Family Issues. In: *Academy of Management Journal*, 37/2, pp. 350-382.

Holt, H. and I. Thaulow (1996), Formal and Informal Flexibility in the Workplace. In: Lewis, S. & J. Lewis (eds.). *The work-family challenge. Rethinking employment.* London: Sage.

Hooghiemstra, E. (1997), *Een- en tweeverdieners.* In: Sociale atlas van de vrouw, deel 4. M.

Niphuis-Nell et al. (ed.) Sociaal en Cultureel Planbureau: Rijswijk.

Ingram, P. and T. Simons (1995), Institutional and Resource Dependence Determinants of Responsiveness to Work-family Issues. In: *Academy of Management Journal*, 38/5, pp. 1466-1482.

Kamerman, S.B. and A.J. Kahn (1987), *The Responsive Workplace, Employers and a Changing Labor Force*. New York: Colombia University Press.

Kingston, P.W. (1990), Illusions and ignorance about the family-responsive workplace. In: *Journal of Family Issues*, 11/4, pp. 439-453.

Lewis, S. et al. (1996), Developing and implementing policies: Midland Bank's Experience. In: Lewis, S. & J. Lewis (eds.). *The work-family challenge. Rethinking employment*. London: Sage.

Morgan H. and F.J. Milliken (1992), Keys to Action: Understanding Differences in Organizations' Responsiveness to Work-and-Family Issues. In: *Human Resource Management*, Fall 1992, 31/3, pp. 227-248.

New Ways to Work (1993), *Changing Times, a guide to flexible work patterns for human resource managers*. London: New Ways to Work.

Niphuis-Nell, M. (1997), *Beleid inzake herverdeling van onbetaalde arbeid.* In: Sociale atlas van de vrouw, deel 4. M. Niphuis-Nell et. al. (ed.) Sociaal en Cultureel Planbureau, Rijswijk.

Oliver, C. 1991. Strategic responses to institutional processes. In: *Academy of management review*, 16, pp. 145-179.

Osterman, P. (1995), Work-Family Programs and the Employment Relationship. *Administrative Science Quarterly*, 40, p. 681-700.

Plantenga, J. and A. van Doorne-Huiskes (1993), Verschillen in arbeidsmarktposities van vrouwen in Europa. De rol van Verzorgingsstaten. In: *Tijdschrift voor Arbeidsvraagstukken*, 9, pp. 51-65.

Plantenga J. (1995), Labour-Market Participation of Women in the European Union. In: A. van Doorne-Huiskes, J. van Hoof, E. Roelofs (eds.), *Women and the European Labour Markets*. London: Paul Chapman Publishing.

Praag, van C.S. and M. Niphuis-Nell (1997), *Het gezinsrapport*. Sociaal en Cultureel Planbureau: Rijswijk.

Sainsbury, D. (1996), *Gender, equality, and welfare states*. Cambridge: University Press.

Scott W.R. (1995), *Institutions and Organizations*. Thousand Oaks: Sage Publications.

SCP (1996), *Sociaal en Cultureel Rapport 1996*. Rijswijk: SCP.

SGBO (1996), *Kinderopvang in gemeenten: de periode 1989-1995*. Den Haag: SGBO.

Sloep, M. (1996), *Het primaat van een mannenbolwerk. Emancipatie in cao-onderhandelingen*. Den Haag: Emancipatieraad.

Spaans, J. and C. van der Werf. (1994), *Evaluatie van de Wet op ouderschapsverlof.* Den Haag: Ministerie van Sociale Zaken en Werkgelegenheid.

SZW (1992), *Emancipatie in arbeidsorganisaties.* Den Haag: Ministerie van Sociale Zaken en Werkgelegenheid, .

SZW (1995), *Emancipatie in cijfers 1995. Facts and figures.* Centraal Bureau voor de Statistiek en het Ministerie voor Sociale Zaken en Werkgelegenheid, Den Haag.

SZW (1997), *Emancipatie in arbeidsorganisaties.* Den Haag: Arbeidsinspectie, Ministerie van Sociale Zaken en Werkgelegenheid.

TK (1993-1994), *Deeltijdarbeid, initiatief wetsvoorstel Rosenmöller.* Tweede Kamer, vergaderjaar 1993-1994, 23 216.

TK (1994-1995), *Combineerbaarheid van betaalde arbeid met andere verantwoordelijkheden.* Nota om de kwaliteit van arbeid en zorg: investeren in verlof. Tweede Kamer, vergaderjaar 1994-1995, 24 332, nr. 1.

TK (1996-1997), *Gelijke behandeling deeltijd-/voltijdwerkers.* Tweede Kamer, vergaderjaar 1996-1997, 24 498.

Tolbert, P. and L. Zucker (1983), Institutional sources of change in the formal structure of organizations: the diffusion of civil service reform, 1880-1935. *Administrative Science Quarterly*, 28, p. 22-39.

Veen, R. van der (1990), De ontwikkeling van de Nederlandse verzorgingsstaat. In: K. Schuyt en R van der Veen (red.), *De verdeelde samenleving.* Leiden/Antwerpen: Stenfert Kroese.

Zey, M. (1998), *Rational Choice Theory and Organizational Theory: a Critique.* London: Sage.

WORK-FAMILY ARRANGEMENTS IN THE UK

Suzan Lewis

1. Introduction

In Britain as elsewhere in the industrialised world there has been a growth of female employment in recent decades, particularly among mothers of young children among whom employment has historically been low (Martin and Roberts, 1984). Fifty two per cent of women with children under 5, 71% of those with children aged 5-10 and 79% with children over 11 were economically active in 1995 (Labour Force Survey, 1995). The dual earner family is thus increasingly the norm. There are also a large number of single parents, but their employment levels are substantially lower than that of married mothers. Despite growing rates of female employment however, many women in the UK, especially those with young children, work part-time. Employed men continue to work mostly full-time whether they have family obligations or not. Nevertheless the increase in women's labour force participation presents challenges to the 'male model of work' (Pleck, 1977; Cook, 1992) which has developed from the assumption that employees can separate work and family (because they have the support of a homemaker), and raises issues for employers as well as governments and individual families.

This chapter discusses the ways in which employers have responded to these changes in the labour force in the context of the British welfare state. The first section discusses the impact that the particular welfare state model, institutional conditions and political debates and priorities have had in shaping workplace approaches to work-family arrangements. This is followed by an overview of the range and prevalence of workplace work-family arrangements in the UK. It is clear that within this general context, employers differ in the nature and extent of work-family arrangements developed. The next section therefore examines some of the organisational factors that influence these developments. Finally the limited impact of these arrangements on organisational culture is discussed and some necessary conditions for more fundamental change are explored.

2. Context for the development of workplace work-family arrangements

2.1 The British Welfare State Model

The welfare state in Britain can be described as liberal (Esping-Andersen, 1990) and as a strong breadwinner model (Lewis, 1992). Its liberal welfare regime is characterised by means tested welfare provisions adequate to maintain only a very modest standard of living, and a restricted role of the state. The Conservative governments in the 1980s stressed the commitment to reducing public expenditure and the size of government, and attached ever increasing importance to means testing and targeting of benefits (Lewis, 1993). The Labour government elected in 1997 is instigating some changes in policies and examining possibilities for 'modernising' the welfare benefits system, but this is in a context of a continued commitment to keeping public spending down, to avoid the need to raise taxation. At present the welfare state model remains largely unchanged.

The British welfare state has been built on a strong breadwinner model (Lewis, 1992), with only minor concessions to shifts in the structure of households. The Beveridge report on which the welfare state was based, for example, used a concept of full employment referring to the male population only. Employed women were, until the sex discrimination legislation of the 1970s permitted to choose a 'married women's option' in national insurance, which involved lower contributions in return for lower benefits, predicated on the assumption that they are dependent on their husbands' earnings rather than their own. Women's growing level of employment is increasingly recognised and even encouraged (especially for single mothers), but is treated as secondary to their family roles, while little account is taken of men's family work.

The strong breadwinner model is evident in the ambivalence towards the employment of mothers with young children, manifested in social policy and also is reflected in social attitude surveys, although this is declining to some extent (Brannen *et al.*, 1994). Successive governments have been reluctant to be seen to 'interfere' in families, by encouraging mothers to work (Brannen and Moss, 1992). The current Labour government is addressing the issue of childcare, but this has been framed largely within a welfare to work discourse, with a focus on enabling lone mothers to be able to work.

Assumptions about women's primary family role also underpin welfare policy commitment to 'care in the community', that is, encouraging elderly, disabled or otherwise vulnerable people to live independently in their own homes (Langen, 1990). In practice this relies heavily on informal family support, mainly from women, and increases pressures for those combining care and employment. Dally (1996) refers to a reserve army of nurses, that is women who can be mobilised, out of the workforce to care for family members at home when required. Welfare payments are available for carers, but this is not sufficient for income replacement.

Nevertheless it is forfeited if the carer works and earnings surpass a basic minimum. This serves to keep many carers out of the labour force or to restrict them to the most flexible, and also low paid, jobs (Lewis et al, 1996).

2.2   Gaps in social provisions

Government policy towards the family has been firmly based on the principle of individual rather than collective responsibility and the desirability of care of dependents within the family, as well as an ideal of the male breadwinner family, despite social trends towards more diverse forms of households (Pascall, 1986; van Emery, 1991/2). The ideology of individual responsibility for family members, cuts in public expenditure and an emphasis on market forces to provide services for families have resulted in gaps in social provisions to enable people to integrate work and family, which employers have been encouraged to fill in order to sustain a female workforce.

One consequence of these factors is that there is minimal provision of publicly funded childcare. What little public provision is available is targeted at children 'in need' because of health or related problems, and not directed at children of working parents. There is no tax relief for childcare expenses, but workplace nurseries are exempt from tax, to encourage employers to address childcare issues. In the early 1990s the government came under increasing pressure from voluntary organisations, employers and the EU to develop a coherent childcare strategy. Towards the end of the conservative administration a document on work and family (DfEE, 1996), acknowledged the growing number of women in the workplace, and argued the business case for encouraging the provision of affordable, accessible, quality childcare, but stopped short of taking responsibility for this provision, despite considerable pressure from leading employers for the government to play a part. The Conservative Government did encourage the growth of out of school provisions for school aged children and the current Labour government is committed to this development and talks about encouraging the development of childcare in general, but it is not yet clear how this will be achieved.

It is in this context that some employers have been motivated to fill gaps in provisions by opening their own workplace nurseries or making other provisions for carers. The extent and nature of employer's responses are discussed in a later section.

2.3   Labour market and employment policy

There is a wide range of non-standard forms of work in Britain, some of which can help in the integration of work and family. This is at least partly a consequence of government policy.

The Conservative governments of 1979-1987 pursued a Neo Liberal policy of deregulation, believing that minimal regulation of employers would best encourage economic growth. There has been for example, no national minimum wage, no statutory minimal vacation entitlement (although that is now challenged by the Working Time Directive)[1], nor limits on the growth of a variety of working time arrangements.

Part-time work is highest among mothers with young children, which, the government has argued reflects personal preference. However it is not clear to what extent this is a constrained choice made by mothers in the absence of adequate childcare provisions in Britain. Part-time work is also increasingly attractive to employers seeking a flexible labour force, defined in terms of contractual flexibility to manage changes in demands. The implications of these developments with regard to family-friendly arrangements are double edged. On the one hand it provides employers with experience of the advantages of non-standard workers, and of administering and managing diverse forms of work, which could contribute, ultimately to a questioning of the primacy of standard working hours which are incompatible with family obligations. This will, however, require a shift towards equal valuing of non-standard workers (Raabe, 1996). On the other hand, deregulation has resulted in a shift of risks from fluctuations in demand from employers to individual workers and their families, creating economic insecurity for many.

Economic policy under the current Labour government appears to be largely unchanged, albeit with more emphasis on social justice. Minimal regulation is still viewed as desirable to achieve a flexible labour market. However, there is a commitment to the implementation of a minimum wage and consultations are taking place on the rate at which it will be set. Also the opt-out from the Social Chapter of the Maastricht Treaty, has been reversed. This was negotiated by the Conservative government and enabled UK employers to be exempted from social provisions such as the Directive on Parental Leave adopted by the rest of Europe. Provisions for parental leave and leave for family reasons have been at the discretion of employers, but all employers are now preparing to implement this and also any future Directives on, for example, conditions for part-time workers. Nevertheless the growth in temporary work and short and fixed-term contracts renders maternity and parental leaves irrelevant to many employees.

---

[1] Provisions of the Working Time Directive include establishing an average limit of a 48 hour week and the provision of entitlement to 3 weeks paid annual holiday, or an equivalent pro rata entitlement for part-time workers.

2.4   Emphasis on the business case for work-family arrangements.

The emphasis on individual responsibility for family, a Neo Liberal approach to employment policy and reliance on market forces have also led to an emphasis on the business case for work-family arrangements. In the UK context, therefore, work-family arrangements have been socially constructed as a business issue, requiring minimal input or direction from the state.

The initial focus on work-family policies in the workplace grew out of discussions on equal opportunities in the 1970s, particularly in the public sector, but also in some private companies. However, by the late 1980s this was changing in the context of discussions of demographic shifts (decline in the number of young people entering the work force) and of an anticipated skills shortage (NEDO, 1988 Berry Lound, 1990; Hansard, 1990). The need to develop family-friendly policies to recruit and retain the underdeveloped workforce of women with family responsibilities was emphasized, in order to compensate for the shortfall of school leavers. This marked a shift from equal opportunities arguments to the business case for work-family arrangements.

While the recruitment and retention argument, particularly in relation to highly trained staff remains strong in areas or occupations with skills shortages, other arguments have also developed in the 1990s. In a context of downsizing and restructuring some employers recognised the need to support a reduced core workforce by ensuring that work-family problems do not create stress and interfere with work performance (Lewis, Watts and Camp, 1996). Family friendliness is seen as a way of assuaging the negative aspects of radical organisational change, especially when these changes are perceived to work against equal opportunities (Woodall *et al.*, 1997).

Another feature of the 1990s has been the promotion of the Managing Diversity approach. First developed in the USA, Managing Diversity arguments have increasingly being promoted as a replacement for, or development of Equal Opportunities arguments in Britain (Herriot and Pemberton, 1995; Institute of Personnel Management and Training, 1996). Exponents of diversity management stress the business case for optimising the contributions of a diverse workforce in order to gain competitive advantage. The aim is to develop a culture of inclusion, so that all members of the workforce can reach their full potential. This encompasses the need to take account of employees' family obligations and to dismantle barriers facing those with caring obligations. The argument is that employers should value diverse ways of working rather than regarding those who deviate from the normative full-time working pattern as having less to offer.

The business case has therefore focused on benefits to employers, and especially cost benefits. The Institute of Management Studies put the cost of every employee a company fails to retain as the equivalent of the full-time cost of the leaver (Forbes and McGill, 1988). This figure has been widely used by those making a case for work-family arrangements within organisations.

The UK context provides both incentives and disincentives for employers to become involved in developing work-family arrangements. The lack of provisions such as childcare or entitlement such as family leave propels some employers to make these provisions, if this is deemed necessary from the perspective of business needs. However, some policies which can be considered essential for work and family balance have not been widely adopted in the absence of state intervention (for example paid leave to deal with family emergencies). This is particularly the case when policies are regarded as costs. If other firms are not making these provisions there may be a fear that competitors will recruit employees in whom they have invested. Consequently the cost benefits of work-family arrangements have been emphasized by those who wish to convince employers that such provisions are a good thing (Business in the Community, 1993). A consequence of the lack of statutory intervention and the reliance on being able to demonstrate a good business case is that the provision of work-family arrangements is at best patchy and inconsistent.

3.   Range and prevalence of work-family arrangements

Work-family arrangements in British organisations tend to be largely targeted at women, who are viewed as having primary responsibility for family care. The most frequent types of initiatives which have been developed to address the work-family interface are i) assistance with caring responsibilities, primarily childcare, but also eldercare, and including benefits and leaves, and ii) flexible forms of work to enable employees to balance work and caring responsibilities.

As the number of employed mothers of young children has grown and in the context of minimal public childcare provision, much attention has focused on workplace provisions for, or contributions towards childcare. However, a recent survey of family-friendly workplace arrangements in Britain found that only 10% of the 1311 workplaces surveyed offered some form of practical assistance with childcare (Forth, Lissenbugh, Callendar and Millward, 1996). This included 2% offering a workplace nursery, 1% contributing to a nursery elsewhere, and 2% with a childcare allowance or voucher scheme. A small number of employers offer information and retrieval services, or occasionally a childcare co-ordinator is appointed. Examples of the latter include the Royal Borough of Kingston in the public sector, and Allied Dunbar in the private sector, an insurance company with a high proportion of women employees.

In the absence of statutory parental leave entitlements, career breaks and parental leave schemes represent another approach for addressing employees' childcare issues. Some employers offer enhanced maternity benefits beyond the statutory minimum and/or parental leave entitlement and paid or unpaid leave for domestic crises. The evidence suggests that these practices may be relatively common in comparison with other work-family arrangements. For example, Metcalfe (1990), suggests that enhanced maternity leave was offered by 23% of employers and leave for family reason (usually but not always unpaid) by 25%, while the Equal Opportunities Review of 1994 suggest that paternity leave, again often but not always unpaid, was offered by 69% of employers, and Forth *et al.* (1996) found that two thirds of the employers surveyed offered some form of provisions for parents to take time off in a childcare or similar emergency. In reality, however, these provisions are often at management discretion and thus not necessarily as widely available as the figures suggest. Surveys show a discrepancy between employers' and employees' reporting of the availability of such policies with employers being more likely to report their existence (McCrae and Daniel, 1991). This suggests that many employees do not know that such entitlements exist, or do not believe that they will be entitled to use them. This is borne out by qualitative research which illustrates how even in public sector organisations with long standing policies, many employees with the greatest need for flexibility of this sort are unaware that such possibilities exist, and believe that if managers do permit, for example, leave for family reasons, this is a personal favour (Lewis, Kagan and Heaton, 1996).

Career breaks are less common, reported by 10% of organisations in 1991 (McCrae and Daniel, 1991) and 17% in 1996 (Forth *et al.*, 1996), with take-up continuing to be quite rare. First developed by one of the major banks, career break schemes allow parents to take leave, usually up to 5 years, without pay but with a right to return to work at the same level. Career breaks are usually available only to highly trained staff, and although by law, required to be offered to both men and women, are predominantly taken by women. Some minimal form of professional contact is usually required during the leave. The early schemes often guaranteed a job to returners, but most organisations have now modified this to an entitlement to a job, if one is available, in view of the unpredictability of the job market. For example, Midland Bank, one of the pioneers of the schemes, no longer guarantees returners a job but states that it will make every effort to offer a suitable job to returners on receipt of 3 months notice of intention to return (Lewis, Watts and Camp, 1996). Career breakers are usually not permitted to work for any other employer during their period of leave, a condition which can create considerable financial hardship for families (Lewis, Kagan and Heaton, 1996)

Some employers are beginning to address the issue of eldercare, as this becomes evident as a pressing concern for staff. Many of the provisions for eldercare are based on and developed from those already in place for childcare, rather than developed specifically for this purpose, for example family leaves and information and retrieval services (Laszco and Noden, 1992). Recently developed provisions in some large companies include counselling and referral services, eldercare guides or booklets, financial assistance, family leaves and extended leaves. Direct provision of eldercare is very rare (Phillips, 1995).

3.1   Flexible patterns of work

There is a wide range of flexible and 'atypical' working arrangements in British organisations. Part-time work continues to be the most common non standard form of work, used, for example, by 65% of mothers returning to work after maternity leave in 1996 (Forth et al, 1996). The majority of part-time workers are still women, but some men do work part-time, sometimes for family reasons (Walton, 1995). Part-time work continues to be often associated with poor conditions and opportunities for advancement, although the law has recently changed to provide those working more than 8 hours a week with the same level of employment protection as full-time workers. Part-time or reduced hours with pro rata benefits, and job sharing are gradually becoming available in occupations and at levels previously only available to full-time workers. For example in one workplace survey 34% of respondents claims to have part-time working arrangements for senior staff (New Ways to Work, 1995). Other flexible arrangements such as term time only working arrangements are also increasing in prevalence. Reduced hours schemes, that is jobs which are just a little less than full-time, with pro rata benefits, are also offered in some organisations in occupations and at level which have not traditionally been available on a less than full-time basis (Lewis and Taylor, 1996; Brannen and Lewis, forthcoming).

Flexibility can also be available in full-time work either at a formal or informal level. In 1995, 9.5% of men and 14.7% of women working full-time reported that they had a formal flexi-time arrangement (Labour force Survey, 1995), while Forth *et al.* (1996) found formal flexitime arrangements to be available to 36% of full-time and 41% of part-time employees. The second most popular form of formal flexibility in full-time work is annualized working hours where a set number of hours are worked over the year; 6% of full-time employees in 1994 (Labour Force Survey, 1996). Formal flexi-time arrangements usually permit variations in starting and finishing times around specified core working hours. The incidence of informal flexibility is much more difficult to quantify, but qualitative studies provide examples of extremes of both flexibility and rigidity for those with pressing caring obligations (Lewis, Kagan and Heaton, 1996).

In summary, a range of formal family-friendly policies have been developed, although access to such provisions is often quite limited because of management discretion and organisational norms (Lewis and Taylor, 1996).

4.   Organisational factors influencing the development of work-family arrangements

Family-friendly policies are more likely to be available in certain workplaces than in other. What are the factors predisposing employers to develop such arrangements? Family-friendly policies are most likely to be developed in female dominated workplaces, in the public sector, or large private sector employers, in post industrial organisations which depend on flexibility, in organisations where management recognise the business advantages of such policies and in those with a recognised trade union. Many of these factors are interdependent.

The gender composition of the workplace is an important factor in the development of work-family arrangements. Women are much more likely than men to work part-time or to need other forms of working time flexibility after becoming parents, and therefore it is employers with a predominantly female workforce who are most likely to address work-family issues in order to enhance recruitment and retention. Where these policies are introduced into male dominated organisations they tend to be more marginalised, with the norm of full-time and long hours remaining very strong (Lewis, 1997). All provisions other than maternity related rights must be offered to both men and women, but in practice most policies are targeted at women.

Public sector organisations tend to be female dominated but this is only one reason why work-family arrangements are more likely to be developed than in the private sector. Meeting the demands of equal opportunities legislation is often a greater concern in the public sector, especially in local government, which has been affected more than most private sector companies by Equal Pay legislation. Equal pay claims require workers to find a comparator group of predominantly the other sex within the same organisation that is paid at a higher rate. Local Authorities are liable to Equal Pay claims because they are much more likely than other employers to provide a wide range of services including male and female dominated occupations, such as construction work and catering within the same organisations (Lewis, 1996). They are therefore motivated to pay attention to equal pay and other equal opportunities issues.

Most public sector organisations have also had to work within budgetary constraints because they are directly affected by cuts in public spending. This means that it is not possible to offer salaries and incentives to staff that are commensurate with the private sector. In these circumstances work-family arrangements, including childcare provisions, leaves and flexible forms of work have been used as a tool for recruitment and retention. The flexibility that this provides is often viewed by the predominantly female workforce as compensating for lower levels of remuneration. Most public sector organisations have some family-friendly arrangements but they differ in their implementation. Some have well thought out policies, effective implementation and practice and a culture where men as well as women can take up provisions. At the other extreme there are others where the communication and administration of policies is poor, and employees are unaware of or do not feel entitled to take up work-family arrangements (Lewis, 1997).

In the private sector, size of company is also significant although not in a straightforward way. Formal policies are more widely available in large companies, especially those with large numbers of women employees (Brannen *et al.*, 1994; Equal Opportunities Review, 1995). They are less common in small and medium enterprises, although there is some evidence of greater opportunities for informal flexibility in this sector (Erler *et al.*, 1994). The financial sector has been particularly proactive in developing formal family-friendly policies, largely because it relies on an internal market of women who are highly trained and would therefore be costly to replace if they cannot sustain work and family. Other sectors have been able to incorporate high levels of flexibility because of the nature of their work. This includes information technology, which lends itself to flexible arrangements such as working from home, and also the growth area of private health care. This sector has to provide 24-hour cover, which by definition requires shift work or other non-standard working hours. The direction of causality is not one way in these circumstances however. Not only does a particular type of work create opportunities for flexible work but it is increasingly being recognised that the availability of a flexible workforce creates new business opportunities, as for example in 24 hour opening of banks and supermarkets.

Employers are most likely to develop family-friendly arrangements if management can see the business or organisational advantages of doing so (Forth *et al.*, 1996). This contrasts with the more paternalistic companies of the past that introduced policies because of a sense of responsibility to their workers, in the days of jobs for life. Nevertheless, the legacy of this approach remains in some companies. For example, some of the best eldercare schemes exist in what used to be paternalistic companies as an extension of their policies for their retirees. Pilkington Glass, a large multinational with headquarters in the North of England, and formerly a family business has an extensive eldercare scheme funded by a charitable trust set up by the founding family. The service includes respite care, home visits, meals on wheels and other welfare services.

Family-friendly policies are also more prevalent in organisations with recognised trade unions. Although the trade unions have traditionally been male dominated the growing female membership has been associated with increased concern about work-family matters for both men and women. The TUC (Trades Union Congress) supports a number of work-family initiatives. It has published an information pack on carer's rights and has campaigned for family leave. It argues that this should be a statutory entitlement, but in its absence it published a guide on family leave, urging all unions to press for family leave rights, and including guidelines for use in negotiations. The TUC is concerned with eldercare as well as childcare issues and has published a carers' charter. While endorsing the business arguments, the trade unions have had a broader agenda of flexible working as a two way process that should benefit employees and employers. Nevertheless unions do not always play a significant role in the development of family-friendly policies in organisations (Lewis, 1997), and the possibility that other factors or combinations of factors which characterises both those organisations likely to develop work-family arrangements and also likely to recognise unions cannot be ruled out.

5. Workplace culture

A range of family-friendly policies, whether in the public or private sectors, does not guarantee a change in workplace culture to make it easier to balance work and family. In many UK organisations, including public sector organisations with long standing policies on flexible working, job sharing and other forms of reduced hours, there is a lack of awareness among employees about what they are entitled to, and often the entitlement to reduced or flexible hours depends on management discretion, inconsistently applied (Lewis, Kagan and Heaton, 1996). Take up of leaves is often blocked by line management, many of whom continue to believe that good employees should not allow family to interfere with work. Evaluation studies show that some managers can be hostile to work-family policies even in organisations with state of the art policies (Lewis and Taylor, 1996; Lewis, 1997). Furthermore, family-friendly policies often co-exist with a long hours culture, that is, a belief that long hours at the workplace are essential to demonstrate commitment and to enhance productivity (Lewis and Taylor, 1996; Lewis, 1997). Those who reduce their hours of work in this context are therefore constructed as second rate employees.

'Family-friendly' policies and practices are unlikely to become embedded in workplaces without shifts in the shared values and belief systems which comprise organisational cultures. These systems often operate unconsciously, develop over time embedded in the organization's historical experiences, are usually functional initially, but may persist inappropriately (Pemberton, 1995). Schein (1985) identifies three operational levels of culture in this sense; artefacts, values and assumptions. Family-friendly policies can be regarded as artefacts, which are surface level indicators of organizational intentions. These are underpinned by values, which in turn are underpinned by deep-seated assumptions.

Traditional workplace structures are based on assumptions of a gendered division of labour and separation of the private and public domains. This underpins the beliefs in many workplaces or among managers that family obligations are not legitimate concerns of organisations. While this assumption is being challenged to some extent other assumptions also need to be surfaced and recognised before they can be confronted. For example, a zero sum model of commitment, which assumes that if someone is committed to family they cannot be highly committed to their job, and assumptions that long hours are needed to demonstrate commitment, are often deeply entrenched and undermine efforts to change traditional patterns of work that are incompatible with family obligations (Lewis, 1997). While most work-family arrangements in Britain can be described as artefacts which continue to operate at the margins, initiatives to challenge the shared assumptions and beliefs which constitute organisational culture are beginning to emerge in a few organisations.

A small number of employers are beginning to address the issue of organisational culture, by raising issues such as the expectations of long hours of face time in, for example, management workshops and company newsletters. There are also a few examples, particularly within the public sector, where members of management and other senior staff are challenging the link between long hours and commitment by volunteering to work reduced hours, because of family demands. They serve as role models challenging the notion that only low-level work can be carried out on a part-time basis. The assumption that family concerns are not really a workplace issue has also been explicitly challenged in a few organisations, which have made family a central business concern. For example at Ikea, a process of collaboration between managers and employees, facilitated by an external researcher, led to support and counselling services being set up to specifically address employees' family issues (Burnell and Goodchild, 1996). Workplace audits carried out in organisations in each of the public, private and voluntary sectors, have also been used to raise awareness of work-family issues and the need to progress beyond family-friendly policies to consider informal practices and deeply embedded assumptions and beliefs about working time and the assumed separation between work and family life (Kagan, Lewis and Heaton, 1997).

These initiatives are small and exploratory at this stage. What is important however, is that there is an emerging recognition that policies or artefacts alone do not bring about fundamental culture change.

The relationships between family-friendly policies and shifts in cultural values needs to be addressed. There are two possible views on this. It is possible that formal family-friendly policies may be an essential first step, particularly in larger organisations, reflecting or creating shifts in cultural values. If this is the case, further progress requires sustained efforts to ensure that policies are implemented effectively at all organisational levels. An alternative possibility, however, is that formal family-friendly policies serve to marginalise work-family issues rather than to construct them as central strategic issues (Fletcher and Rapoport, 1996), which is essential for more fundamental change. In this argument the implementation of formal policies, particularly those targeted at women, allows crucial organisational systems and the assumptions on which they are based, to go unchallenged. For example, the provision of family leave arrangements, however essential, does not necessarily challenge the view that work is best performed within certain rigid hours in a specified workplace. Indeed some policies can actually perpetuate established values. For example, provisions such as job sharing schemes involve the sharing of a standard job by two people rather than challenging the standard itself.

Finally, It may also be that the necessary level of value shift within workplaces will not occur without a concomitant shift in the dominant values and structures of the wider society, in relation to family, gender and employment. Certainly the two are inter-linked, as has been argued in this chapter.

6.   Conclusions

Brewster and Hegewisch (1994) in their survey of European human resource polices suggest that high levels of statutory provisions for work and family reconciliation are not necessarily linked in a simple way with lower employer provisions. Rather, they suggest that what appears to happen is that high levels of statutory provision reflects a culture of interest in parental benefits which make employers more aware of parents' needs and more willing to enhance provisions. It has been argued in this chapter that the reverse is true of Britain; in a socio-political context where the needs of businesses are privileged over those of individuals and families, where family care is considered a private and individual responsibility, and where the regulation of employers is avoided, discussion of work and family workplace arrangements become dominated by a cost benefits, business case for action. A business argument has the advantages of appearing more rational and neutral than one based on fairness or equal opportunities (Cassels, 1997), or on an emphasis on the well being of families. However, unless this is an enlightened business argument that also recognises some social responsibility of employers, its impact will be limited, and subject to changing economic circumstances.

References

Berry Lound, D. (1990), *Work and Family. Carer Friendly Employment Policies*. London: Institute of Personnel Management.

Brannen, J., G. Meszaros, P. Moss, and Poland, G. (1994), *Employment and Family Life. A Review of Research in the UK (1980-1994)*. Sheffield: Employment Department.

Brannen, J and Lewis, S. (1998), Workplace programmes and policies in the UK, In: L.Haas, P.Hwang and G. Russell (eds), *Organizational Change and Gender Equity*. London: Sage.

Brewster, C and Hegewisch (1994), *Policy and Practice in Human Resource Management*. London: Routledge.

Burnell, A and J. Goodchild (1996), *Developing Work and Family Services*. London: Exploring Parenthood.

Business in the Community (1993), *Corporate Culture and Caring*. London: Business in the Community/Institute of Personnel management and Development.

Cassells, C. (1997), The business case for equal opportunities: implications for women in management, In: *Women in Management Review*, 12, pp. 11-16.

Cook, A. (1992), Can work requirements change to accommodate the needs of dual-earner families? In: S. Lewis, D. Izraeli and H. Hootsmans (eds), *Dual-Earner Families. International Perspectives*, pp. 204-220. London: Sage Publications.

DfEE (1996), *Work and Family: Ideas and Options for Childcare. A Consultation Document*. London: Department for Education and Employment.

Erler, G., W. Erler, M. Jaeckel, and B. Subocz (1994), *Von Europa lernen: Innovative und familienfreundliche Personalführung in kleinen und mittleren Unternehmen: Erfahrungen aus drei europäische Regionen*. Munich: Fan Consult.

Employers for Childcare (1995), *Business Blueprint for Childcare*. London: Employers for Childcare.

Employment in Europe (1996), Luxembourg: Office of Official Publications of the European Communities.

Equal Opportunities Review (1995), 60-64.

Esping-Andersen, G. (1990), *The Three Worlds of Welfare Capitalism*. London: Polity.

Every, J. van (1992), Who is 'the family'? The assumptions of British Social Policy. In: *Critical Social Policy*, Issue 33, 1991/2, pp. 62-75.

Ferri, E and K. Smith (1996), *Parenting in the 1990s*. London: Family Policy Studies Centre.

Fletcher, J. and R. Rapoport (1996), Work-family issues as a catalyst for organisational change. In S.Lewis and J. Lewis (eds), *The Work-family Challenge; Rethinking Employment*, pp. 142-158. London: Sage.

Forbes, A.. and D. McGill (1988), *Understanding Wastage.* IMS Report 105. Brighton: IMS.

Forth, J., S. Lissenburgh, C. Callendar and N. Millward (1997), *Family-friendly Working Arrangements in Britain.* Dfee Research Report 16. London: DfEE.

Hansard (1990), *The Report of the Hansard Society Commission on Women at the Top.* London: Hansard Society.

Herriot, P. and C. Pemberton (1995), *Competitive Edge Through Diversity.* London: Sage.

Institute of Personnel Training and Development (1996), *Managing Diversity.* A Position Paper. London: IPD.

Kagan, C., S. Lewis and P. Heaton (1997*), Developing workplace audits for parents of disabled children.* Paper presented at the European Work and Organisational Psychology Conference. Verona, Italy: European Work and Organisational Psychology Conference.

Laczsco, F. and S. Noden (1992), Eldercare and the Labour market. Combining Care and Work, In: F. Laczsco and C. Victor (eds), *Social Policy and Elderly People.* Aldershot: Avebury.

Langen, M. (1990), Community Care in the 1990s: the community care White Paper: Caring for People. In: *Critical Social Policy*, Issue 29, pp. 58-70.

Lewis, J. (1992), Gender and the Development of Welfare Regimes. In: *Journal of European Social Policy* 2 3, 1992, pp. 159-173.

Lewis, J. (1996), Work-family reconciliation and the law: Intrusion or empowerment? In: S. Lewis and J. Lewis (eds), *The Work-Family Challenge; Rethinking Employment*, pp. 34-47. London: Sage.

Lewis, S. (1997), Family-friendly organizational policies: a route to organizational change or playing about at the margins, In: *Gender, Work and Organization* 4, pp. 13-23.

Lewis, S. and C.L. Cooper (1987), Stress in two earner couples and stage in the life cycle. In: *Journal of Occupational Psychology* 60, pp. 289-303.

Lewis, S. and C.L. Cooper (1996), The work-family interface; A European perspective. In: *Human Resource Management Review* 5, pp. 289-305.

Lewis, S., C. Kagan and Heaton (1997), *Dual earner parents with disabled children:Pressures, needs and supports.* IOD Group Occasional paper. Manchester: MMU.

Lewis, S and K. Taylor (1996), Evaluating the impact of family-friendly employment policies: A case study. In: S. Lewis and J. Lewis (eds*), The Work-family Challenge; Rethinking Employment,* pp. 112-127. London: Sage.

Lewis, S., A. Watts and C. Camp (1996), Developing and implementing policies. The Midland Bank Experience. In: S. Lewis and J. Lewis (eds*), The Work-family Challenge; Rethinking Employment*, pp. 103-111. London: Sage.

Meadows, P. (1996), *Work Out or Work In?* Contributions to the debate on the future of work. York: Joseph Rowntree Foundation.

McCrae, S. and W. Daniel (1991), *Maternity Rights in Britain; First findings.* London: Policy

Studies Centre.

Metcalfe, H. (1990), *Retaining Women Employees: Measured to Counteract Labour Shortages.* Brighton: Institute of Manpower Studies.

NEDO (1988), *The Demographic Time Bomb.* London: National Economic development Organisation.

New Ways to Work (1995), Newsletter April 1995.

Pascall, S. (1986), *Social Policy. A Feminist Analysis.* London: Tavistock.

Pemberton, C. (1995), Organizational culture and equalities work. In: J. Shaw and D. Perrons (eds), *Making Gender Work; Managing Equal Opportunities*, pp. 108-124. Milton Keynes: Open University Press.

Phillips, J. (1995), *Working Carers.* Aldershot: Avebury.

Pleck, J. (1977), The Work-family Role System. In: *Social Problems,* 24, pp. 417-427.

Raabe, P. (1996), Constructing pluralistic work and career arrangements. In: S. Lewis and J. Lewis (eds), *The Work-family Challenge; Rethinking Employment*, pp. 128-141, op cit. London: Sage.

Schein, E. (1985*), Organizational Culture and Leadership.* San Francisco: Jossey Bass.

Walton, P. (1995), *Balanced Lives.* London: New Ways to Work.

Woodall, J., C. Edwards and R. Welchman (1997), Organisational restructuring and the achievement of an equal opportunity structure. In: *Gender, Work and Organization* 4, 1997, pp. 2-12.

WORK-FAMILY RECONCILIATION IN GERMANY: TRENDS IN PUBLIC AND CORPORATE POLICIES

Wolfgang Erler

1. Introduction

The debate on the reconciliation of work and family life in (Western) Germany since the 1980s has to be put into the context of long-term trends: the rising number of women in higher education, the growing inclination of women to look for paid labour, and the increase in female part-time work. These trends will be briefly described and related to the reconciliation of work and family life.

The concept of reconciling work and family life was born and worked out in a political context of promoting women, equal opportunities, and affirmative action. However, before 1982, while the Social Democrats together with the Liberal Democrats formed the federal government, family issues were a non-issue in the context of women's politics. Within the traditional trade-unionist and social-democratic ideologies on the equal treatment of men and women the ideal of male and female full-time employment was a vague future vision. There were no social forces in sight nor instruments worked out to realize such an 'equal treatment' vision insofar as the work-family conflict was concerned.

When the liberal-conservative government of Christian Democrats and Liberal Democrats came to power in 1982, it was not long before a path appropriate to the diversity concept of male and female roles was chosen. Parental leave and allowance were legislated, marking a remarkable breakthrough in acknowledging (female) home and child-rearing work in terms of money for work done and, additionally, tax-paid contributions to social insurance pension. The right to return to one's job was part of the parental leave act.

The origins and instruments of the work-family reconciliation policy are described in sections one and two of this chapter. Section three looks at the first steps of corporate policies in trying to define 'family-friendly' policies on the company level, especially sophisticated forms of working-time flexibility and extended parental leave.

Section four looks at the interaction between state (political) and corporate activities regarding the reconciliation of work and family life and shows that a new, interdependent pattern of action is emerging. Public-private partnership is the term used to describe this interdependent pattern where business is taking the lead. Even though the times of massive public investment in the work-family field are gone, other forms of political intervention, such as networking, and identifying and disseminating good practice, constitute an essential driving force for the change of economic, social, and cultural rules deeply rooted in the traditions of industrial society and its sexual division of paid and unpaid labour between men and women.

In section five, a detailed description of the Family and Work Audit as a management tool aimed at incorporating 'work-family balance optimization' into everyday business decisions is given. This tool is being currently developed by New Ways to Work Munich, on behalf of the Hertie Foundation.

The work-family context in the five states of Eastern Germany is examined in section six. An explanation is given as to why the reconciliation debate, seven years after the German unification, is still restricted to the West and has not really been taken up by social actors or even a social -women's- movement in the East.

The concluding section (7) sums up trends and contradictions, stating that there is no natural, self-evident trend towards an always stricter integration of work-family considerations in business decisions. Countervailing trends - the continuing decrease in birth rates, especially of women with higher education in nearly all industrialized countries being one of them - are weighed against forces that make the further development of work-family balancing strategies likely.

2.   The historical background of work-family policies in Germany

The work-family debate in Germany is still mainly a western issue. The following sketch of different stages of the work-family debate and policies therefore only refers to the old Federal Republic (FRG). The work-family conflict in the five new, eastern states of the former German Democratic Republic - GDR will be briefly discussed in section six.

The whole issue of the reconciliation of work and family life as a subject of public and political debate, of legislative decisions, and of government action, took shape in the eighties. This was partly a late response to the challenges of the traditional woman's role as mother and homemaker brought into focus by the women's movement of the seventies. However, these challenges were rooted in the education offensive of the sixties and seventies, in the increase of women's participation in higher education, and in the dramatic changes in the structure and composition of the workforce. Meanwhile - since 1992 - the number of female high school graduates has exceeded the number of male graduates. For instance, in the new eastern states, the former GDR, 57% of the high school graduates in 1993 were girls.[1] In more recent years, they are outperforming the boys more and more. Higher levels of education are, of course,

---

[1] Bundesministerium für Bildung, Wissenschaft, Forschung und Technologie1994, p. 82f.

only one determining factor within the economic context of the transformation to a post-industrial service economy increasingly based on information technologies. This is leading to a tremendous influx of women into the paid labour market. Viewed from a broader perspective, leaving aside a narrow theory of 'economistic imperialism', it is the complex pattern of cultural and social change accompanied by changing values and lifestyles acting as the driving force behind the new economic (as well as cultural and social) role of women. Even though unemployment has grown steadily from the early seventies, and women's share of unemployment has constantly been above their share of paid labour, women were the overall winners in the labour market. But what they won was mainly the segment of part-time labour where more than 90% of the sector are female. Between 1960 and 1991, female part-time employment grew by 2.9 million - up to a 30.8 % share of female employment, whereas female full-time employment at the same time only increased by 0.9 million.[2] Part-time and non-standard forms of work are not only typically female, they are, more precisely, forms of employment for working mothers. More than 50% of all mothers in paid employment work part-time. The increase in overall labour market participation by women was most significant for women aged thirty-five and older with children at least 'half grown-up'.

These are the figures of regular jobs with full social insurance benefits. In addition, the labour market sector of irregular, contingent jobs has grown considerably. In 1992, 2.1 million women held jobs of this type.[3] Related to this, 8.3% of all working women in 1992 were paid below the '610 DM'-a-month limit above which the payment of social insurance contributions is mandatory. From 1992 to 1996, the overall number of these contingent jobs increased by another 26.5%, as was reported in October 1997.[4]

The rise of contingent employment was an important issue on the political agenda in 1997. Publication of new statistical data on the fast growth of this grey labour market segment in the '90s and media comments opened a political debate on the relation between the financial crisis of the social security systems and the increase in employment free of mandatory social insurance contributions. But even far-reaching political consensus from the left (Social Democrats and Green Party) to the centre of the political spectrum (Christian Democrats) to restrict uninsured employment and to make paid employment liable to social insurance contributions from the very first hour on could not be implemented in a legislation project given the strong resistance of the Liberals, part of the government coalition. This is, however,

---

[2] Bundesministerium für Familie und Senioren 1994, p.173
[3] Cf. W. Friedrich 1993. H. Kohler, H. Rudolph, E. Spitznagel 1996 discuss extent, structure, and trends of contingent irregular forms of work and problems of data reliability.
[4] See press reports of October 30, 1997 relying on forthcoming reports of the DIW Berlin and the ISG Köln. Cf. Neue Presse Coburg 'Minijobs als willkommenes Zubrot.'

only the superficial, political business reason why contingent forms of work were not legally restricted. In fact, there are serious doubts as to whether a legislative project could really successfully transform millions of contingent jobs - cheap labour - into typical German high-wage employment, carrying a more-than-50-percent-load of taxes and insurance contributions. If the recent explosion of non standard forms of employment is taken as an indication of future trends, then we will have to deal with a growing - rather than a shrinking- variety of legal and time patterns in employment. Patterns vastly different from the traditional male model of work contracts, with no, reduced, or tax-subsidized social insurance contributions and usually covering less than 20 working hours a week will be typical for the lesser qualified working mothers who combine work and family. But at the same time, the wages earnable in these jobs will not be sufficient for many of these working mothers to sustain their children or to contribute sufficiently to their families' income. Thus, we can say that there will be a growing minority of women (with children they have to take care of) for whom the main problem is not to combine work and family, but to get any access to a form of paid employment that helps them to make a sustainable living for their family.

In the regular labour market, the influx of women has changed the workplace, moving it away from the traditional working pattern tailored to the needs and wishes of the qualified male employee: nine to five plus, often enough, overtime, five days a week. The male breadwinner/woman-homemaker model has eroded. In fact, this model has a short tradition of two decades during the economic miracle in the reconstruction period after World War II. Burkart Lutz has strikingly labelled this period and its mentality as the 'short dream of ever-lasting prosperity' (Lutz, 1989). Until well in the fifties, many married women were not just homemakers, but were also doing low paid or unpaid labour in the grey zone between households and the formal economy: doing paid housework for others, working in agriculture, trade, and other small businesses owned by family members as assistant family members. Except for the last category, these types of semi-formal jobs were notoriously underestimated by official statistics.[5] Seen against this background, the seemingly new labour market participation of women in reality only represents a change of forms rather than a fast growth of female (paid) labour in areas other than the tasks of housekeeping and rearing children.

However, the new role of women brought forth within the last decades did, and still does, seriously affect the relationship between work and family life, between the private and public roles of women. Out-of-home work is no longer looked upon by (family) women themselves as a kind of forced labour, undertaken only to meet the demands of surviving economically as a family. Women have been developing a twofold orientation: towards family values and, at

---

[5] Cf. A. Willms-Herget 1985

the same time, towards participating in paid labour, not only as a means of earning money, but also as a source of personal identity, strength, and career planning. In short, they do not want a child *or* a job, but both.[6] This has led to a situation in which, at least from the early eighties on, the supply of part-time jobs has not kept pace with women's demand for them. It was not long before both research and politics had taken up the wish of women for access to the labour market.[7]

3. Work-family reconciliation: public policy as change agent

3.1 Parental leave and allowance

Soon after the work-family debate had reached the arena of public debate, far-reaching legislative decisions were made: a parental leave law guaranteeing return to one's workplace was passed in 1986, promising to make it easier for young mothers and families to combine work and family. By law, taking a one-year leave (prolonged to two and, in 1992, to three years) should be an option for mothers and fathers. In reality, in 1993, only 1.3% of fathers were on parental leave.[8] This is related to the fairly low amount of the parental allowance (600 DM a month), originally paid for 12 months and extended to 2 years; in five states this has been prolonged by state legislation up to three years. The parental leave allowance is not seen as compensation for loss of salary but as an acknowledgement of the parents' work in bringing up children. A form of means testing is applied to payment, so that by now only 50% of parents are below income limits and receive the full allowance, compared to 56.3% in 1994 and to 83.6% in 1987.[9] Nevertheless, 97% of mothers make use of parental leave for at least a year.

3.2 Vocational training and counselling for returnees

The introduction of parental leave included a message and a promise to young parents: if they left their jobs, they would not be kept out of the labour force, but would find support in their

---

[6] Cf. the 1988 Brigitte/DJI study: G. Erler a.o. This does not mean, that the family and work orientation of women in the old FRG is evenly split between the two spheres. Only 35% of Western German women compared to 60% of women in the German East hold 'job and occupation' to be of very high importance for their lives, against 86% who think, family and children are the most important part of life. Cf. Bundesministerium für Familie und Senioren 1994, p. 172

[7] Cf. C. Born, C. Vollmer 1983; Wissenschaftlicher Beirat für Familienfragen beim Bundesministerium für Jugend, Familie und Gesundheit 1984; A. Hellmich 1986

[8] In 1992, there were 7,865 men taking parental leave, of whom 2,699, i.e. almost 35% were foreigners - this suggests that under the prevailing conditions the men who make use of parental leave and/or allowance are mainly those in a less economically secure position. Cf. R. Pettinger a.o. 1997

[9] Deutscher Bundestag, Drucksache 13/4526, May 9th, 1996

struggle to reintegrate into their job. Consequently, a number of increasingly sophisticated pilot schemes in training and counselling for female returnees was put into force. The pioneer plans were called: 'new start from 35 on'. The success of these schemes was limited. Studies showed that the majority of returnees actually had to change employers[10] because they could not get the working (time) conditions they sought, which usually meant some form of flexible part-time work.

Expansion and improvement of childcare facilities

Public policy also had to try to meet other demands that were closely connected with the work-family reconciliation promise of introducing parental leave and allowance: to support the labour market participation of young parents, childcare supply had to be improved dramatically, with respect to both the quantity and quality of the places available. During the eighties, a major focus of debate and struggle for improvement was the notorious inflexibility of kindergarten opening hours. Even today, especially in rural areas, many institutions close before 12 noon, thus making it impossible for mothers to work even a standard part-time job of four hours in the morning. The same is true with respect to school hours during the first two school years. None of the public debates on the needs of working parents have resulted in structurally reliable changes of school time patterns. There is, however, a gradual process of change going on, supported by pilot schemes like 'space for children' financed from 1991 to 1994 by the federal government.[11] Several states have started pilot schemes for a so-called 'reliable Primary School' lasting from 8 am to 1 p.m. and everywhere, not only in the big cities, but also out in rural areas, parents are taking the lead in introducing care schemes for school children after classes. As for the quantity of available childcare, not even the 1991 legislative reform of the child and youth welfare act substantially changed the situation, even though it, for the first time, acknowledged the need for childcare facilities for children under three years of age and for school children as well. It was a necessary political bargaining compromise on the new abortion law in 1993 that enforced the legal claim to kindergarten places, so that, until 1999, there will probably be a close to 100% supply for all 3 to 6 year-old children, with institutional childcare for some hours. But the road to a needs-oriented system of flexible, high-quality childcare still seems to be long and rocky.

4.   **The business community as change agent:**
      New patterns of working-time and extended parental leave

The workplaces, subject to decisions made within the business culture, could not remain

---

[10] K.A.Schneewind, L.A. Vaskovics a.o. 1994; cf. also H. Foster 1986
[11] Cf. Deutsches Jugendinstitut 1995

unaffected by the intense public debate on work-family problems. At first, very cautiously, a number of (mainly) large corporations in industry and the service sector (several banking and retailing companies acting as pioneers) began to develop specific programs of their own to support work-family reconciliation of working parents. Measures involved mainly the introduction of innovative patterns of working-time, aimed at making not just short-time (below 19 hours a week) part-time jobs compatible with family responsibilities. The second layer of new family-oriented benefits was the introduction of an extended parental leave - up to seven years from childbirth combined - in the best situations - with well worked-out training and counselling programs to keep leave-takers in contact with the company. This type of offer was developed with the strong support of company employee committees and was disseminated as a kind of standard collective agreement at company level to a good number of large well-known corporations in industry, from car-makers to large chemical corporations and the service sector. These agreements, in most cases, could not, and do not, give the entitlement to return to the company, but rather the promise to try and re-employ the leave-taker when she or he wants to return. The effects of these agreements on users (working mothers and a small minority of fathers) and on personnel management strategies of the companies working with parental leave schemes have thus far not been systematically evaluated.

Most of these family-friendly company programs are based on notions of the company's public responsibility, in a broader sense, bound to the social responsibility of large corporations. These notions apply even in Germany with its 100-year-old tradition of welfare state cash benefits and, only recently strengthened, welfare state in-kind benefits offered by social service agencies. An important factor stimulating corporate programs was the installation of equal opportunity officers throughout the business world. Flextime schemes and enforcement of collective agreements on parental leave were important fields of action for these newly established bodies to promote cultural change in favour of equality between women and men.

5. Public policy and corporate policies on family-work reconciliation
Public-private partnership as change agent: 'business is taking the lead'

Since the early 1990s, the economic context for programs aimed at balancing work and family life has changed radically. The great turnaround for Germany began with the end of the former GDR and the huge number of transfer payments that turned out to be necessary to finance the German unification and the de-industrialisation of the GDR that made the short-lived boom of 1990 and 1991 in the West possible. Social policy is back on the agenda, not to design better options for those in need of support by the community, but to - if possible - enforce cutbacks and to balance the budget. Along with this, the whole mental context of political debate has changed. Social needs are - quite similar to the fate of the ecological issues of sustainability - no longer headline number one on the political agenda. Rather, it is the question of global competitiveness, of dumping wages paid at building sites all over the country, even under the eyes of the federal government moving to new office buildings under construction in Berlin, that is taking the mental and practical lead. Furthermore, the context of a globalizing economy, pressures of international competition, etc., are the point of reference for decisions made at company level as well as at the level of public policy, on the local, state, and federal stage.

This context seems, however, to produce different results for public and corporate policies: public policy, at state and federal level more so than at local level, gives the impression of being paralyzed by the huge challenges of today and the near future; it is evident that the very foundations of the Bismarck welfare state, the social contract between the generations, and also between the sexes, has to be rebuilt and re-written. The apparently overwhelming extent of this task causes a kind of structural attentism which does not favour thinking about and aiming at far-reaching reform projects. Quite the opposite is true in regard to business culture. Driven forward by the impressive results of companies around the world that dramatically improved their performance, usually at the same time laying off staff, the new managers are trying to redefine every aspect of corporate action in the light of 'optimizing shareholder value'. As companies are inextricably bound to the abilities and inputs of their employees - human capital - they redesign their reciprocal relationship to their staff. This makes way for new perspectives. A re-evaluation of, for instance, the underused potential of the female staff. Corporate programs to ease work-family conflicts, at first designed in a spirit of social support and of promoting equal opportunities, have all of a sudden gained importance because they might be able to contribute to the all-around process of corporate re-engineering.

This can be shown with respect to all fields of action that have so far constituted the area of family-friendly corporate policies: beginning with the long-established flextime schemes and more sophisticated systems of working time organization and extending corporate support for employees with childcare - reaching from resource and referral services for childminders and au-pair-girls to buying child-care places in public childcare institutions or, finally, corporate-owned kindergartens as a comparatively expensive and, at the same time, usually selective program for only a part of staff's children.[12] Companies now dealing with the question of childcare support are moving away from an isolated evaluation of cost and effects of corporate childcare. They are trying to develop instruments that tell them how improving childcare for - usually - a minority of young children's parents is interconnected with other dimensions and preconditions of corporate performance.[13]

5.1 Public Policy 'on the retreat', but handling 'software' to communicate innovation: Public-Private Partnership

Public policy that once, in the eighties, had started the social and cultural transition to the reconciliation of work and family life with a wave of investment in 'family infrastructure', does not contain any new perspectives for further developing the legislative and financial framework for a society that will be able to guarantee not only its economic, but also its ecological and biological social reproduction. Public proposals look more like the 'race to the bottom' that is predicted to take place in the American States when it comes to implement the welfare reform bill as passed by the US Congress.

Nevertheless, there are some proposals to re-write at least the parental leave and allowance laws, making the whole project more flexible by transforming it into a three-year leave time budget that can be used within a time frame of eight, and later twelve years.[14] But these kind of proposals are only discussed in specialist circles. This is even more true of the far-reaching project for an 'education salary' (to be paid to a mother or father taking care of children up to the age of twelve), which is being proposed by a coalition of family lobby organisations.[15] There is very little political energy (manpower and finance) available to reform and transform the publicly financed sector of childcare. Research on early childhood development in Germany is a neglected issue in academic sciences. This means that the structure and future of childcare institutions are in the hands of an anti-innovative public administration and the professional lobby of a low-paid, feminized professional group that looks upon every wind of change as a threat to its own, hard won status-quo.

---

[12] For a history of corporate childcare in Germany from the end of the last century to the present see D. Höltershinken, D. Kasüschke 1996 and, for a short overview, C. Martin 1989
[13] A similar perspective based on three case studies, is convincingly outlined, by J.K.Fletcher, R. Rapoport 1996
[14] Cf., again, Deutscher Bundestag, Drucksache 13/4526, May 9th, 1996 (proposal Green faction); a similar proposal is advocated by the State of Schleswig-Holstein in the Bundesrat, the second chamber of the national legislation bodies.
[15] Ch. Leipert/M. Opielka 1997

This is perhaps too black a picture. In fact, public policy groups, largely uninfluenced by the political ideas discussed within parties, started to form innovation coalitions with very little public spending. Public agents started acting as communicators and moderators of cultural change processes.

One example of this type of public action is the public-private partnerships to create additional childcare facilities. City governments like the ones in Frankfurt/M.,[16] Munich, Stuttgart, and others have designed creative models for financing additional childcare facilities, locating them if in a new or renovated building or just in a redecorated ex-factory building or retail shop. The new frontiers that appear in these new coalitions for innovation do not just refer to the form of financial burden sharing. The public-private childcare schemes break with old habits and traditions. Open discussions on pedagogic concepts, on balancing the needs of parent, children, and the community are organized. Within the public-private childcare schemes, there are experiments with extended opening hours and mixed age groups. Parents have a voice and carry responsibility not only for organisation and finance, but also for the everyday activities involved in caring for children. Some of the schemes are avantgardistic in respect to integrating handicapped children who otherwise would have to be sent to specialised and isolated institutions. It is an impressive vision of social life where corporate childcare institutions - of course, not all of them - are similar to the initiatives organized by parents, who were and are the most engaged groups in developing new pilot schemes.

Concerning corporate involvement in childcare, it should also be noted that institutions run in partnership with private companies or public employers represent only a very small minority of the supply of childcare places. Nevertheless, the importance of the ideas and impulses emerging under the guidance of this new, non-traditional partnership goes far beyond the small number of corporate childcare institutions. They contribute to the ideas guiding the practice of tomorrow: the truth in tendencies is greater than that of sheer facts, as Oskar Negt once put it.

5.2   Federal and State governments as communicators and moderators of innovation

It is not only local governments that behave in an innovative manner by organising pilot schemes, debates, spreading ideas, and forming practice-oriented round-tables around the issue of how to make the workplaces more family-friendly. Public governments in the

---

[16] Cf. C. Busch *et al.* 1991

eighties were economically strong partners, active in promoting and investing in the process of socially reengineering the labour market reality towards more family-friendliness. Today, however, the trends and influences of the global economy and the foreshadowing of the European Currency Union, together with the number one task of consolidating the budgets, keep politics from actively intervening in the field of social reality. Instead, politics approaches business anxiously, asking business people to act and innovate, in a word: to take on the task of organising change. The Federal Government and more than 10 state governments have, for instance, organised a family-friendly employer award to encourage hundreds of - often small and medium-sized - enterprises to communicate their hidden good practice to the public.

In trying to monitor future trends in the work-family field, state and federal governments regularly contribute to a conceptual widening of our -and the business world's- understanding of work-family conflicts. The Baden-Württemberg state agency which promotes economic development, for instance, organised several large meetings of women willing to start their own businesses. In addition, a survey held on that occasion found that reconciling work and family is an important motive of the female business starters. About 42% of 130 business women surveyed think that it would be easier to balance work and family obligations in their own firm than as dependent employees.[17]

Other issues brought forth by the innovation-openness of state or federal governments include the problem of reconciling education (vocational training) with pregnancy and childcare obligations,[18] the problem of balancing obligations of caring for elderly relatives with workplace demands,[19] and last but not least, the problem of work-family reconciliation for women as wives and partners of master craftsmen[20] - a group that comprises several hundred thousand women who bear a large portion of business responsibility on their shoulders.

5.3   Other change agents: Foundations
The Hertie Foundation Family & Work Audit Project

Communication networks of change promoters and innovators in the field of work and family

---

[17] Cf. Landesgewerbeamt Baden-Württemberg und Förderkreis 'Frauen in Verantwortung' 1995, p.113. Similarly: C. Rosenberger-Balz 1993
[18] Cf. J. Zierau, M. Bartmann 1996
[19] Cfg. B. Beck, G. Naegele 1997, Die Vereinbarkeit von Erwerbstätigkeit und Pflege. Stuttgart u.a.
[20] Cf. Landesverband der Meisterfrauen im Handwerk Bayern e.V. 1995

reconciliation emerged around the European,[21] federal, and state awards for family-friendly employers. One of these agents of change and innovation is the Hertie Foundation, Frankfurt/M. In 1995 it started a large-scale research study and good practice project under the title 'family-friendly personnel management as part of strategic management'. It co-ordinated the activities of six working groups, covering practices in large industrial corporations, the service industry, and in small and medium sized companies. The main aim of the project was to systematically collect knowledge of best practice firms and to integrate that knowledge into a management tool that could demonstrate that elements of personnel management, such as family-friendly measures, can contribute to business performance as efficiently as technical, marketing or logistical strategies. Inspired by the 'Family Friendly Index' developed in 1991 by the New York-based Families and Work Institute, this management tool was constructed in analogy to well established managerial methods like benchmarking, total quality procedures, and the European Ecological Audit Certificate, which is well on its way into mainstream business practice after a long discussion and preparation process. According to this analogy, the management tool developed within the Hertie Foundation project was called Family & Work Audit. In a process of conceptualization, the rating criteria of the American family-friendly index were adapted to the context of the German labour market situation and working culture. Workshops with personnel managers from a range of companies with an open-minded, innovative approach to personnel development issues helped to make the instrument compatible with the everyday strategies of people involved in corporate decision-making. In a pilot phase that started in the autumn of 1997, the first version of the complete Audit is being tested within three to four participating companies. Their personnel management practice on all levels (of a certain establishment) will be rated according to the criteria defined in the Audit scheme. Rating points not only refer to written statements and legal entitlements, but also to real practice and implementation. Also the degree of co-determination of employees is evaluated. For example: flexible working time schemes do not automatically ease the time restrictions of working parents if they are tailored mainly to the production or service needs of the company. They will only help balance work and family duties if employees themselves can rely on - often short-time - flexibility dispositions. Similarly, it is critical that supervisors act on the grounds of work and family reconciliation instead of favouring a long hour working culture.

The aim is to enlist about 50 companies, both non-profit and public sector organisations, to participate in 1998. Beyond that time, it is hoped and expected that the Work

---

[21] The European prize awarded by the European Commission in 1995 was called 'European prize for social innovation'; its main focus were family-friendly employer practices, but there were some broader criteria of innovativeness included.

and Family Audit will gain some popularity and acceptance in the business community and can contribute to establishing standards of everyday practice in other than pioneer companies.

Within the family and work network financed by the European Commission, there has been some discussion on the transferability of the Family and Work Audit concept into a European agenda. That would require further cultural adaptation of the concept to the specific institutional framework and context in other EU member states.

6.   **The powerlessness of power: Work-family conflicts in the five new states of the former German Democratic Republic (GDR)**

During socialist times, reconciling work and family life was much easier in the GDR than in the West of Germany. Childcare institutions covered nearly 100% of all 3 to 6 year old children; opening hours of institutions were adapted to the working times of big plants and employing institutions; even women working shifts including nightshifts and weekends could also rely on a supply of institutional childcare for children under three. The same was true for school-age children.

Childcare provision rates are still considerably higher than in the former FRG. This is true for all types of institutions: crèches as well as kindergartens and latchkey centres for children between the ages of six to twelve/fifteen years. However, the greatest challenge for women in the former GDR is not the adaptation of social infrastructure standards to the rules of the West. Instead, the greatest challenge is the dramatic collapse of economic and industrial structures in all the five new states, which is in particular affecting the labour market situation of women. Seven years after German unity, the opportunities for women in the East German labour market are noticeably worse than those for men. By the end of the '80s, the female employment rate in the GDR was still over 90%. In 1992, it had gone down to 73%, and in 1995, it was as low as 63% for all women between 18 and 60 years.[22] The proportion of mothers with children under four in paid full-time employment in 1995 had decreased to nearly half of the 1991 level - from 38% to 20%.[23] Mothers on parental leave in the Eastern part of Germany more often receive the - now means-tested - parental allowance than in Western Germany, but more often than in the West, they take their leave for less than three years - which is clearly due to lower family earnings in the East. While 36% of Eastern German mothers on parental leave want to return to the workplace after one to two years -

---

[22] G. Engelbrecht/ H. Gruber/ M. Jungkunst 1997, 156.
[23] G.Engelbrecht/M.Jungkunst 1998, 12

compared to only 11% of Western German women on parental leave -, they are in fact confronted with serious difficulties when trying to reintegrate into the labour market. Only 55% of the returnees are re-employed by their former company and 25% of them find themselves unemployed after parental leave.[24] The female unemployment rate in East Germany in 1995 was twice as high as the rate for men, and this also applies to the rate for women who had been unemployed for a long time. Women in East Germany are also over-represented in job creation, further training, and retraining schemes.

The high level of publicly (co)financed childcare in the Eastern states can explain why the percentage of mothers working full-time in the Eastern German states is nevertheless much higher than in the Western regions. The following table shows percentages of mothers working fulltime and part-time in the East and West respectively.

Table 1 *Employment structure of mothers with children >3 in percentages for East and West Germany*

	youngest child: 3 to 6		youngest child 6 to 15	
	fulltime	part-time	fulltime	part-time
West	15	28	24	40
East	42	17	56	18

Source: G. Engelbrech, H. Gruber and M. Jungkunst (1997)

The stable structure of childcare services in Eastern Germany even includes projects offering flexible home-childcare in the evenings for low-wage retail workers to cover their weekly evening shifts, financed by second labour market subsidies to secure jobs in the personal service sector. Nevertheless, the childcare infrastructure is but one factor explaining the high percentage of mothers with young children working fulltime. Another explanatory factor is the cultural tradition of female fulltime employment that is reflected in the value orientations and attitudes of working women in Eastern Germany. Low salaries in the East fortify these attitudes - and one of the paradoxical trends seen in Eastern Germany is that the least qualified women with the highest need to contribute to family incomes are the ones most likely to become unemployed.[25]

The title of this section reflects the paradox that no social or political force is in sight which develops *realistic* perspectives for the future economic and social role of women, including their labour market participation. Apparently, all full-employment scenarios have

---

[24] G.Engelbrech 1997, 1, 3,4.
[25] ibid.

failed - much more dramatically in the East than in the West of unified Germany. The traditional pattern of a paternalistic, over-protective state is still shaping ideas and concepts on how society, local governments, and the local communities should deal with women, their mother-role and their labour market participation. The low proportion of mothers working part-time shows that even the first and evident instrument of harmonizing (paid) work and family and childcare obligations, part-time work and flextime, is blocked by a far-reaching consensus on full-time employment as the normal pattern. So far, there is no debate, no social force in sight that could influence the process of ongoing social change in Eastern Germany in such a way that the old 'female privileges' could be gently transformed into a new, modernized form of gender partnership and division of labour at the workplace. Thus, the whole concept of work-family balancing that is advocated by the innovators discussed in this chapter does not fit the living conditions, experiences, wishes, and needs of former GDR women precisely enough, at present. The whole concept would entail a cultural adaptation process which requires resources and funding institution that actively promotes and funds this process.

7.   Conclusion

New forms of work organisation, pushed forward by the pressures of enforced competition and industrial restructuring, reaching out well into the public and even the non-profit social service sector, have brought forward a tremendous valuation and modernization of human resource management in organisations. Part of this modernization process is the implementation of family-friendly personnel policies. Personnel management strategies of this type acknowledge that the workforce has changed dramatically within the last decades. Well-trained and highly educated employees now represent the majority of the workforce (in the post-industrial, service economies of the upcoming information-oriented, multi-media age). Organising their work according to the ideas of Ford and Taylor, with tight supervision and leadership by middle-level managers bearing an overload of decision-making authority referring to every single workplace within their range of responsibility would just cause losses in motivation, productivity, and therefore profits. This background explains why the philosophies of leading employees have changed so enormously and why organising a continuous dialogue - corporate communication process - between companies and employees about their needs and wishes, their strengths and weaknesses, has become a kind of human resource management standard. But that does not mean that this standard is being implemented without resistance and difficulties. Without continuing efforts of debate, trial and error, evaluation, and further development of state of the art standards there is always a threat of stagnation. Moreover, the globalization debate every now and then produces a revival of paradigms that one might attribute to the remote past of industrialism: organisations driven by low-wage 'work on command', organised according to the imperatives of an effective, traditional military machine. As long as these revivals of organisational traditionalism, strengthened by habits of patriarchalism deeply rooted in the industrial working culture, are able to - at least partly - shape reality, there is still a long way to go until the often predicted mega-trends towards a new culture of 'high touch' determine the everyday life of working mothers and fathers.

There is yet another threat to a lasting and stable implementation of a working culture supporting the family-work balancing tasks of working parents: the overall shrinking of the 'family sector' in all post-industrial societies of Western Europe. As long as a growing proportion of the best-trained women find it impossible or unattractive to combine a career and a family with children (as is, apparently, the case, at least, in West-Germany), the representation of family worries, family problems, family values within the corporate cultures is on the retreat. If working parents become a shrinking minority in the workplace, we will witness a decrease of family awareness, especially in the most advanced sectors of the economy employing the best trained segments of the workforce. There will be no need for innovations with respect to family needs, beginning with the time constraints of working parents, in these most advanced sectors of the economy. On the contrary, in traditional sectors with roots back in the industrial age, the imperatives of 're-inventing' the organisation of work will not be strong enough to be followed - thus forcing employees, many of them belonging to the less trained and qualified 'traditional working-class' segment of the workforce, to live with outdated rules and forms of work organisation.

Future trends in work-family and life configurations are all but secure and stable. It will depend upon creative and intelligent action and engagement.

References

Beck, B. and G. Naegele (1997), *Die Vereinbarkeit von Erwerbstätigkeit und Pflege*. Stuttgart u.a.

Born C. and C. Vollmer (1983), *Familienfreundliche Gestaltung des Arbeitslebens*. Stuttgart u.a. (Schriftenreihe des Bundesministers für Jugend, Familie und Gesundheit, Bd. 135).

Bundesministerium für Bildung, Wissenschaft, Forschung und Technologie (1994), *Grund- und Strukturdaten 1994/95*, Bonn.

Bundesministerium für Familie und Senioren (1994), *Familien und Familienpolitik im geeinten Deutschland - Zukunft des Humanvermögens. Fünfter Familienbericht.* Bonn .

Busch, C. *et al.* (1991), *Frankfurter Studie zu Modellen betriebsnaher Kinder-betreuung.* Eschborn Deutscher Bundestag, Drucksache 13/4526, May 9th, 1996.

Deutsches Jugendinstitut (1995), *Orte für Kinder.* München.

Engelbrecht, G. (1997), *Erziehungsurlaub - und was dann? Doie Situation von Frauen bei ihrer Rückkehr auf den Arbeitsmarkt.* Ein Ost/West-Vergleich (IAB Kurzbericht Nr. 8/1997. Nürnberg).

Engelbrecht, G., H. Gruber and M. Jungkunz (1997), Erwerbsorientierung und Erwerbstätigkeit ost- und westdeutscher Frauen unter veränderten gesellschaftlichen Rahmenbedingungen, In: *Mitteilungen aus der Arbeitsmarkt- und Berufsforschung,* 1/1997, 151ff.

Engelbrecht G. and M. Jungkunz (1998*), Erwerbsbeteiligung von Frauen und Kinderbetreuung in ost- und westdeutschen Familien.* (IAB Werkstattbericht, forthcoming, Nürnberg).

Erler, G. *et al.* (1988), *Kind? Beruf? Oder Beides? Eine repräsentative Studie über die Lebenssituation und Lebensplanung junger Paare zwischen 18 und 33 Jahren in der Bundesrepublik Deutschland.* Im Auftrag der Zeitschrift Brigitte. München.

Fletcher, J.K. and R. Rapoport (1996), Work-Family Issues as a Catalyst for Organizational Change. In: S. Lewis and J. Lewis (1996), *The Work-Family Challenge. Rethinking employment.* London a.o., 142-158.

Foster, H. (1986), Verlernt Frau das Pflegen in der Familie? Wiedereingliederung von Krankenschwestern nach der 'Familienphase'. In: Hedwig Rudolph *et al.* (1986), *Berufsverläufe von Frauen.* München (DJI Materialien), 217-232.

Friedrich, W. (1993), *Sozialversicherungsfreie Beschäftigungsverhältnisse 1987 und 1992.* Ergebnisse einer Untersuchung im Auftrage des Bundesministers für Arbeit und Sozialordnung. Köln.

Hellmich, A. (1984), *Frauen zwischen Familie und Beruf.* Eine Untersuchung über Voraussetzungen und Nutzungen einer Berufskontaktpflege von Frauen in der Familienphase. Stuttgart u.a. (Schriftenreihe des Bundesministers für Jugend, Familie, Frauen und Gesundheit, Band 184).

Höltershinken, D. and D. Kasüschke (1996), *Betriebliche Kinderbetreuung von 1875 bis heute.* Kindergärten und Tageseinrichtungen in Deutschland. Opladen

Kohler H., H. Rudolph and E. Spitznagel (1996), *Umfang, Struktur und Entwicklung der geringfügigen Beschäftigung. Eine Bestandsaufnahme.* Nürnberg (IAB Kurzbericht Nr. 2/1996. Institut für Arbeitsmarkt- und Berufsforschung der Bundesanstalt für Arbeit).

73

Landesgewerbeamt Baden-Württemberg und Förderkreis 'Frauen in Verantwortung' (1995), *Unternehmerinnen-Forum*. Stuttgart.

Landesverband der Meisterfrauen im Handwerk Bayern e.V. (1995), 1. *Forum der Frau. Vereinbarkeit von Familie und Erwerbstätigkeit. Nachweis von Kinderbetreuungseinrichtungen*. Augsburg.

Leipert, Ch. and M. Opielka (1997), *Erziehungsgehalt 2000*. Konzeption. Institut für Sozialökologie. Bonn.

Lutz, B. (1989), *Der kurze Traum immerwährender Prosperität: eine Neuinterpretation der industriell-kapitalistischen Entwicklung im Europa des 20. Jahrhunderts*. New edition. Frankfurt/M. - New York.

Martin, C. (1989), Ökonomische Bewertung betrieblicher Maßnahmen für die Koordination von Familie und Beruf. Am Beispiel von Unternehmen in den USA und Baden-Württemberg. In: H. Seehausen (Hrsg.) (1989), *Sozialpolitisches Forum '89. 'Arbeitswelt kontra Familienwelt'? Zur Vereinbarkeit von Familie, Beruf und Kindertagesstätte*. Dokumentation. Frankfurt/M.

Neue Presse Coburg (1997), *'Minijobs als willkommenes Zubrot' - Die 610-Mark-Jobs zahlen sich auch für viele Beschäftigte aus*. October 30th, 1997.

Pettinger, R. *et al.* (1997), *Reconciliation of Work and Family Life and Quality of Care Services*. Paper, Munich (DJI).

Rosenberger-Balz, C. (1993), *Frauen als Existenzgründerinnen unter besonderer Berücksichtigung der Wiedereinsteigerinnen im ländlichen Raum*. Freiburg (= EURES discussion paper 27).

Schneewind, K.A., L.A. Vaskovics *et al.* (1994*), Optionen der Lebensgestaltung junger Ehen und Kinderwunsch*. Verbundstudie im Auftrag des Bundesministeriums für Familie und Senioren. Projektbericht 2, Stuttgart u.a. (=Schriftenreihe des Bundesministeriums für Familie und Senioren, Band 9.1).

Willms-Herget, A. (1985), *Frauenarbeit. Zur Integration der Frauen in den Arbeitsmarkt*. Frankfurt/M.

Wissenschaftlicher Beirat für Familienfragen beim Bundesministerium für Jugend, Familie und Gesundheit (1984), *Familie und Arbeitswelt*. Gutachten, Stuttgart u.a. (Schriftenreihe des Bundesministers für Jugend, Familie und Gesundheit, Band. 143)

Zierau, J. and M. Bartmann (1996), *Recherche zur Vereinbarkeit von Berufsausbildung und früher Mutterschaft*. Hrsg. Vom Bundesministerium für Bildung, Wissenschaft, Forschung und Technologie

WOMEN'S LABOUR MARKET PARTICIPATION AND THE RECONCILIATION OF WORK AND FAMILY LIFE IN ITALY

Rossana Trifiletti

1.   Introduction

Before considering the changes taking place in the organization of work to make it more compatible with family duties for both men and women, we should examine two basic features which are essential to understanding the Italian situation. First, there exists in Italy a certain cultural inertia that creates great unwillingness to make the family the subject of political debate and policy decisions. In the post-war period, all parties, regardless of their politics, have studiously avoided becoming involved in policies regarding the family. Memories of the familist policies of the totalitarian regime were still uncomfortably close; policy proposals to ease family burdens might appear too conservative, while protecting the rights of the individual within the family or supporting new forms of parenthood might be seen as subversive. In this way there came about a sort of collective repression of the subject of the family, and it was preferable to regard it as a private affair, whose problems could be, and usually were, solved privately.

Secondly, there is a characteristic trend in Italian social policies to protect the children of reportedly 'inadequate' families, on the one hand, and a total refusal to intervene in supposedly 'normal' families, on the other. This dualism is an expression of a more general practice of the principle of subsidiarity to be found in many areas of welfare policy. Thus, the line between public responsibility and private obligations defines a certain area of legitimate public welfare intervention. In this area the state's duty to support, rather than substitute, the family in its task of maintaining, caring, rehabilitating and guaranteeing the subsistence of all its members has been totally removed. The family is expected to make up for the shortcomings of welfare policies and provide the resources to cope with the problems associated with looking after its weaker members. Civil law, in point of fact, imposes heavy responsibilities on the family in this regard.

The combination of endless obligations to other family members and their undisputed acceptance has meant that in Italy, as in other Mediterranean welfare regimes (Guillen, 1996; Tobio, 1994), the principle of subsidiarity has taken the form we mentioned above; extreme regulation combined with extreme delegation produces particular effects on social policy. The state intervenes only when the family is unable to cope with its vast burden of duties. Until the family is declared inadequate, the state does not concern itself with supporting the family or setting itself the task of facilitating the normal functioning of the family. This is not the case in other countries with a continental welfare regime where the principle of subsidiarity is less contradictory, as there is no desire to repress the theme politically.

In other countries it is generally accepted that the degree of difficulty of access to entitlements and services inevitably favours one type of family behaviour over another. In Italy, however, it often seems that policy makers regard the family as being of a single type whose every feature is known and which cannot be influenced in any way. Or rather, it is often the case that the family unit which shoulders the burden or whose income or financial resources are means-tested is in fact the extended family, whereas the unit which might possibly obtain some limited form of assistance is the nuclear family (Trifiletti 1995; cf. Eardley *et al.*, 1996).

Of course, as we shall see, not all that applies to social policy also applies to labour policy, but this questionable public image of the family is the basic reason why the state assigns so little responsibility to employers to make the duties of work compatible with those of the family.

For this reason, we should proceed step by step in examining the differences in precise detail. In particular we must show clearly how women's paid work in Italy has, for the most part, retained the traditional 'confusion' with women's unpaid work and is thus, in many respects, socially invisible. Mention must be made of the inadequacy, in the context of Italy, of the criteria for measuring women's work used in other countries, as regards our aim to gain a more realistic assessment of the effective burden of difficulties which falls to Italian women reconciling work and family obligations. We compare the picture that emerges from the statistical data with the findings of surveys conducted on the family to explain the changes that have come about in recent years and the role of social policy in bringing them about. We will then go on to examine the scope for existing and possible future interventions by employers against the background of a hypothetical Mediterranean model of a welfare regime.

2. The visibility of women's work

A premise that needs to be explored is the question of family obligations and women's work in particular. In every country, the family could be a useful observation point for investigating the work of both men and women, since it is where their paths within and outside the labour market cross, combine and take on meaning. Instead, with very few exceptions (Pleck, 1977, 1985; Balbo, 1974, 1978; Saraceno, 1986, 1993), only women's work has been investigated, especially when this work is variously blamed for the breakdown of the family, the decline of the birth rate, the loss of values and so on. It offers a limited and characteristically distorted representation of the ties which exist, but which are in fact considerably more intricate. It would be better to conceptualise them within the framework of twofold complementary roles for both genders (Saraceno, 1992). This inbalance, however, is by no means accidental; on further investigation, the lack of such a consciousness proves to be especially significant in Italy.

Unlike the types of work performed by men, those chiefly performed by women are still deeply 'embedded' in everyday interpersonal relations, so that even today women's work is confusingly divided into work inside and outside the home, and between private and public domain. This feature of women's work is changing particularly slowly in Italy since it appears to be linked to global changes in society and because women's work continues to be perceived partly as closely linked to emotional work, outside the labour market. This seems to apply, for better or worse, to very different types of work, such as a woman doctor's more human, chatty approach and greater care with diagnosis, the less technical, more supportive approach of a woman lawyer (David and Vicarelli, 1994) and the quasi right enjoyed by certain categories of civil servants to do their shopping in office hours. It is no accident that the process of 'disembedding' women's work, i.e. its gradual emergence from the gender shell, has been particularly marked by the *naming* procedure, whereby new and often provocative terms are coined to highlight the utility and economic value of what had previously been part of what was taken for granted in everyday life and therefore invisible and nameless. This procedure has given rise to a series of allusive terms, sometimes deliberately disturbing, which help those directly involved (Ronco and Peattie, 1988) to clarify and give a social representation of specific items of women's lifetime activities which were previously regarded as merely natural. In Italy, these terms, generalized from the private domain to the outside world are: *lavoro familiare (family work)* (Bianchi, 1978; Kickbutsch, 1979), a concept which explicitly expands that of house-work, and types of work which are mainly projected outside the family such as, in broader terms, *lavoro di servizio (servicing work)* (Balbo, 1983; Bianchi, 1991) or *patrimonio invisibile (invisible assets)*, the work done to support the husband's job (Barbagli, 1991; cf. Papanek, 1973). This naming process is now beginning to involve not only unpaid activities such as *emotion work* in large organizations (Piva, 1994; Cevoli, 1996 cf. Hochschild, 1983), or the expression *lavoro d'amore, labour of love,* which is not yet used in the context of help for elderly members of the family (Taccani, 1992; cf. Finch and Groves, 1983). There have been many attempts, in Italy too, to bring social reproduction work back within the terms of economic analysis (Picchio, 1992 and 1993; cf. Humphries and Rubery, 1984), showing that work and family are not two separate worlds between which individuals divide themselves, but a unified construction based on the form of their relationships.

However, in the task of theoretical re-unification, which highlights the structural similarities of the various pieces which have so far been named, it is important to bear in mind that all types of atypical work are somewhat backward in the process, and tend to agglomerate with the gender shell. Not only, as elsewhere, are these types of work often undifferentiated, having less well consolidated social recognition and a more precarious position in the labour market (European Foundation for the Improvement of Living and Working Conditions, 1988), but in Italy these are jobs which have an especially ambiguous role within and outside the family. For this reason too, we can say that women's work *in* the market is not yet entirely commodified and tends to remain embedded in non-economic relations, particularly when forms of atypical work are concerned, for example in industrial districts. This might explain why Italian women rightly prioritize the promotion of cultural emergence and social recognition of those activities which have tended to disappear within the framework of a gender division of labour perceived as aproblematic. This is especially true in operations such as the city times experiments (described later), which explicitly and publicly refer to the problem.

3.   How to assess the extent of women's presence on the labour market in Italy

The fact that women are generally underrepresented statistically on the labour market has been known for some time. At the international level, the phenomenon is more marked in countries where activities which create economic wealth are less commodified (Beneria, 1988), with the added difficulty that non standard jobs or those of limited duration, commonly characteristics of women's work, often escape the statisticians notice. At the European level, these features are typical of the Southern countries' situation and of Italy in particular. We could therefore ask ourselves on the basis of the recent data released by the National Institute of Statistics (ISTAT) and recently reformulated so as to better reflect the real situation, if Italy is really so radically different from other European countries with a similar level of economic development as regards women's presence on the labour market. The answer based on a direct comparison of women's employment rates is that Italy is not as different as it would appear to be.

The rate of women's employment in Italy is well below that of other European countries. In 1994 and 1995 it was 33.7% and 33.9% respectively, the lowest of all 15 EU members, and 11% below the EU average (Eurostat, 1996a and 1996b). Why then has this difference increased in recent years, at a time when there has been a structural increase in women's presence in paid work in Italy, and that the new generation of better educated and more highly qualified women have increasingly come to construct their identity on the basis of work (Abburrà, 1989; Gesano, 1990; Fadiga Zanatta, 1988; Carmignani and Pruna, 1991; Altieri, 1993)? In the previous two decades (but not in the 1960s) the rate of increase in women's presence was similar to the average in OECD countries, 2.3% in the 1970s and 1.9% as against 2.0% in the 1980s (OECD, 1991: 31). But the situation changed at the end of the 1980s. If a feasible comparison is made at that time with the 12 European Community countries, the figure ranges from a difference of 7% in 1989 (Eurostat, 1991b) when three other European countries had lower rates than Italy, to 10.5% only five years later in 1994 when Italy's average was the lowest. We must see whether it is possible to 'purge' women's activity in paid work of the phenomena that could, hypothetically, accentuate the differences.

In the first place, heeding the criticisms voiced in the international debate, we could question the validity of a direct comparison without distinguishing between full and part-time work. Without this distinction, an increase in part-time work only may be interpreted as an overall increase (Hakim, 1992, 1993; Jonung and Persson, 1993).

Table 1   *Women's presence in paid work accounted for by part-time work in some European countries.*

	France	Germany	Netherl.	UK	Sweden	Denmark	Italy Istat	Italy	Greece	Spain
1979*	23.3	27.6	44.0	39.0	46.0	46.3		10.6	--	--
1983*	26.1	30.0	50.1	42.4	45.9	44.7		9.4	12.1	--
1989	23.8	30.6	57.7	44.2	--	41.5		10.4	10.3	13.0
1990*	24.4	--	61.7	43.8	40.5	--		10.9	--	12.0
1993	26.4	32.0	64.5	43.9		37.3	11.0	10.8	7.6	14.8
1994	27.9	33.1	65.9	44.3		34.4	12.4	11.7	8.0	15.2
1995	28.9	33.8	67.3	44.3	40.9	— 35.4	12.6	12.3	8.3	16.6
1996							12.7			

Source: *OECD 1990 (UK, Spain, Italy data 1989), Eurostat 1991a for 1993. 1996a for 1994 1996b for 1995.

In Italy, the overall figure for part-time work is very low; at present around 12% of working women have a part-time job, and a little over 70% of part-timers are women. This figure is low but the situation is the same in other Mediterranean countries with the exception of Spain. In contrast, in countries with a large presence of women in paid work, particularly continental regimes, part-time is characteristic of women's work and the figure for feminization usually exceeds 80% (OECD, 1994: 198). If we compare other aspects, perhaps Italy regains a little numerical advantage, in that although fewer women work, most of those who do, work full-time.

The difference between Italy and certain other European countries is considerable. It remains so even if we take into account the fact that the 30/35 hours per week threshold for part-time work is very close to the 36 hours per week standard for certain posts in the public sector, which in Italy are mainly allocated to women. What we might more usefully hypothesise is a difference between old and new forms of part-time. In southern European countries, part-time was largely related to the context of self-employed agricultural labour for limited periods of time, an industry which has decreased greatly which may, to some extent, account for the drop in figures at the end of the 1980's (Meulders *et al.,* 1994: 17). We should perhaps be thinking of part-time in terms of a much more traditional phenomenon which is on its way out, rather than the creation of job opportunities that allow for reconciliation between work and the family such as can be seen in avant-garde countries. It is true that even in countries with greater equality, the creation of part-time jobs is often a move undertaken by employers to create greater flexibility and is implemented mostly when women form the labourforce; it is thus a gender management strategy. Nevertheless, in this case it is a legitimate choice that reduces unemployment (Hakim, 1995). In Italy, on the other hand, part-time work still seems to be limited to a rarely used form of underemployment or for restricting full-time work in bad times. It is therefore understandable why the trade-union movement until recently had a marked aversion to part-time work as it was concerned that it would confirm the marginal position of women and young people vis-à-vis the labour market.

Evidence of a hesitant initial promotion of 'new part-time' were contained in a Decree Law as late as 1994 and in the Budget Law for 1996 which reduced social security contributions to encourage flexibility and create job opportunities. However, protective clauses have often been introduced in collective agreements to limit the overall number of part-timers in a given firm or to give workers the right to work full-time if new posts become available. In actual fact, there has been a slight increase in new part-time work and women's presence in this sector, but we are still at the initial stages.

Nevertheless, unlike those countries where modern and feasible forms of part-time work, often in the public service sector, account for most atypical work and its recent growth - a phenomenon which involves mainly women - in Italy, atypical work still encompasses mainly the self-employed, the unskilled and full-time employees in commerce or 'various services', a sector notoriously full of jobs with little protection that often form part of the informal economy (Altieri, 1995: 54-55). It emerges from

Table 2   *The slow increase of part-time and its feminisation in Italy*

	1991	1992	1993	1994	1995	1996
Women working part-time: index numbers	100	105.6	103.5	110.3	115.9	121.2
Feminisation of part-time: % of women	65.7	67.8	69.8	70.3	70.4	70.2
Total women part-time workers (a.v.)	756,000					909,000

Source: elaboration of ISTAT's Labour Surveys, yearly averages, various years.

this that Italian women of the 'double presence' have one fewer resource for flexibility and have to cope with more radical conflicts and choices. In Italy, in point of fact, what we might call second-rate work, as opposed to jobs involving normal 'male conditions', is not covered by part-time jobs as it is elsewhere; for many women who are denied access to normal full-time work, there is the possibility to work in family firms, for the informal economy, in seasonal work, in fixed-term work and in the more empoverished forms of self-employment.

On the contrary, part-time work has been very important[1] in helping to reconcile the working life and family life of adult women. In countries where it is more widespread, it has gradually facilitated full-time work as well and has generally come to be associated with rather generous social policy benefits especially with regard to parental leave, both in terms of length of leave and gradual return to work (with the opportunity, in Sweden and elsewhere of switching to part-time work and back again). Using and modifying Jallinoja's (1989) typology, we can place part-time countries (almost all continental and Scandinavian countries) in intermediate positions between two extremes, the 'forced participation' model of ex-socialist countries where the employment rate is very high but part-time work is almost non-existent, and the 'difficult participation' model where, as almost only in the case of Italy,[2] protective policies exist only for secured jobs, there is an absence of part-time work and the difficulty of access to the labour market helps to form a vicious circle which paradoxically reinforces the recourse to separate labour markets. The fact that female work is more rigidly full-time in countries like Italy is the result of rigorous selection: women only accede to the labour market if their work is more 'highly regarded' than that of men, if they are younger and better educated than the men (Padoa Schioppa, 1994; Schizzerotto *et al.*, 1995), and if they can present these qualities to compensate for the greater degree of reassurance which male workers instil in prospective employers.

---

[1] See Schmidt (1993: 191) where the presence of part-time in the early '70s is one of the factors which correlates highest with increases in the female work force in developed countries from 1960 to 1985; contra with special reference to Italy cf. Bettio and Villa (1996).
[2] In Jalinoja's typology in the 1980s Italy was level with Holland, which, in the meantime, has increased part-time work (see Table 2) and its employment rate for women in central age-groups (see Table 4).

This situation often leads to women having to continue to work under male conditions, to cope with competition, work long hours and sometimes avoid making use of legal maternity provisions, whose costs still terrify many employers since, they are not borne by the general system of taxation. Those who leave the work setting are highly unlikely to be allowed to return. Older women, on the other hand, who are not so well-educated, have no network of contacts or who have left the labour market, probably only have access to the type of work which forms part of the informal economy. This means casual work, not officially registered, which as a result is not reflected in the statistics and is mostly unprotected (Bianco, 1996). Our model in a sense brings 'forced' and 'difficult' participation together for two different groups of women.

This is probably one reason for the visible discrepancy between the ISTAT statistics and the European ones that reflect women's employment rate, especially since the former have been revised to include the many forms of work which have often not been included in official statistics. In times of economic crisis, the discrepancy becomes accentuated and women's work in Italy becomes less visible tending to 'disappear' in part from the European surveys. But this is not compatible with what emerges, as we shall see, from the sociological studies in this field.[3]

Indeed, if we introduce sub-national territorial divisions, the distance from Europe in women's activity rate and its recent growth may be almost entirely accounted for by the situation in the South. In contrast the North has a slow but steady growth like the other EU countries.

Table 3   *Rate of women's employment for the 14-70 age group split on a territorial basis for various years*

	1989	1990	1991	1992	1993	1994	1995	1996
North	43.5	43.6	44.3	44.7	44.1	44.4	45.5	46.4
Centre	41.7	41.7	42.8	42.9	40.2	40.1	41.7	42.3
South	35.1	34.7	34.3	34.6	31.0	30.7	31.3	31.3
Italy	40.1	40.1	40.4	40.8	38.6	38.7	39.7	40.3

Source: elaboration of ISTAT's Labour Surveys, yearly averages, various years.

---

[3] I do not wish to suggest that Italy's lagging behind can be put down to a question of statistical measurement (Bettio and Villa, 1997), but only to suggest that during recessions more women perhaps leave the official labour market. I share the view that a interpretative model should not limit itself to this evidence, but I do not feel that

Clearly, the fall in the national rates reflects a phenomenon that is more marked in the South, still present in the Centre and barely discernible in the more advanced regions of the country. This provides further proof that the fall is more a question of a switch to the grey and illegal economy which is more prevalent in those areas of the country: much of the work is carried out within family firms by 'helpers' or under other informal conditions, but it is clearly inadequate to describe such workers as non-working women. Perhaps the increase in women's education has been regarded too much as a springboard for growth and the cohort effect overcoming the delay (Fadiga Zanatta, 1988). It did seem to be a strategic resource which would bring about change, but there are regions of the country where the younger generation of women with a higher level of education has little advantage, since the labour market has not yet undergone a change to flexible firms, which would justify greater investment in personnel by employers.[4] Neither can the difference in Italy be put down entirely to the shorter working life of women. Even if we consider the employment rate for women in unaffected ages a more comparable group (25-39) separately, we note that the fact that women have shorter working lives does not fully explain things. The difference which seemed bound to diminish in the 1980s has remained and increased in this age group as well.

Table 4   *A comparison of the employment rates for women in the 25 to 39 age group: Italy and Europe.*

	Italy		Europe	Germany	France	Netherl.	UK	Ireland	Spain	Greece
	Istat	Eurost.	12							
1989	62.1	60.9	66.1	64.2	74.2	60.8	70.5	51.1	54.9	57.9
1990	62.2									
1992	63.5									
1993	58.9	57.1	69.8	69.9	77.9	68.4	72.1	60.2	61.9	59.4
1994	59.1	59.4	70.7	74.1	78.2	70.4	71.9	63.5	64.2	60.4
1995	59.8	59.9	--	73.4	78.8	71.2	72.5	65.1	64.7	61.9
1996	60.4									

Source: for Italy our elaboration of the ISTAT Labour Force survey, yearly averages in the first column, and Eurostat data in the second column; for the other European countries, elaboration of Eurostat 1991b, 1995 and 1996a, 1996b.

As regards the 25 - 39 age group who usually have small children, the distance between Italy

---

stressing the 'lack of expansion of the tertiary sector' helps us understand for example the delays which are today more evident in Italy than other Mediterranean countries.

[4] The only important case of an intended change toward 'toyotism', in the South, so far is that of the FIAT factory at Melfi, which does not concern women's work.

and the continental[5] European countries was less marked in the 1980s, and the other southern European countries followed quite closely. This distance has since tended to visibly increase, both compared to more advanced countries and to the other countries in Southern Europe, all of which are catching up on their delayed development. In Italy, however, the recession of the early 1990s affected both the old and the new ways of joning the labour market. It could be asked whether other well-known factors such as the fall in the supply of young workers as a result of discouragement, especially in the south, and the ageing of the population do not combine to magnify a phenomenon for which explanation in terms of women's disenchantment with work outside the home is highly implausible today.

It is well-known that countries which create more jobs in effect discriminate less against women and young people. It might therefore be true that greater opportunity for part-time work or protected forms of flexibility in European countries with a strong tertiary sector and greater tolerance of temporary and less well-protected jobs in other Mediterranean countries have had the same effect of pushing them ahead of Italy. To get work in Italy, women have a clear choice on the one hand, between flexible but unskilled and unprotected jobs in the private sector, and officially recognised jobs under 'male' conditions and with rigid requirements, on the other. Under these conditions, reconciling work and family life rests on what has rightly been called "the ability to perform great feats" (Fagnani, 1992) and is based on women's acceptance of a consistent reduction in their aspirations to produce a family despite continuing to work. Only by restricting fertility and accepting very heavy daily workloads which have been extensively documented in time budget studies is it possible for women to stand up to the tough and difficult conditions of paid work, especially since the division of caring work changes very little when women go out to work (Sabbadini and Palomba, 1994; Bimbi, 1995b). It is hardly surprising therefore that these difficult conditions cannot be borne throughout a working life.

4.   Paid work and the family in surveys of the 1990s

The findings of a series of surveys on the family carried out in the north and centre of Italy would tend to support the argument outlined above. The surveys enable us to compare a relatively uniform and extensive set of data on the family and the everyday life of working women in the late 1980s with some data from the first surveys carried out ten years before in a similar area.

Almost all the surveys show that the percentage of part-time work which effectively takes

---

[5] Denmark has considerably higher percentages but belongs in fact to the Scandinavian type of welfare state.

place is much higher than the official rates considered above. The figures range from 13.9% (Irer, 1991) to 24.5% (Balbo May and Micheli, 1990: 59), 25.8% (Mauri, 1993) and 26.3% (Mauri *et al.*, 1992), but they exceed 30% when women in the 20 or 25 to 50 age group are considered (Barile and Stefanizzi, 1990: 109; Belotti, 1993: 316). At the same time, the percentage of temporary, irregular and seasonal work is always much higher than the official data reflect. If a comparison over time were possible, the difference would probably decrease at the end of the 1980s, especially with regard to working from home (Barile and Stefanizzi, 1990: 107). Likewise, the number of women who have never worked is also falling, but not as dramatically as might be expected; even considering the city effect, it goes from 15.8% in an urban sample from Milan in 1981 (Stefanizzi, 1984) to 15.6% in the 1987 Lombardy survey (Irer, 1991) and 11.5% and 9.6% in recent surveys of women in the central age group in the Veneto and Lombardy areas (Biadene *et al.*, 1994; Barile and Stefanizzi, 1990). Thus, work has tended to become a normal experience for almost all women in the central age groups. We should stress the fact that women in Italy undertake paid work to a far greater extent than would emerge from the official activity ratios, and that they do so in periods of their lives when they also accumulate heavy family burdens. One important item which appears to bring Italy closer to the situation in the rest of Europe is that there is no longer a difference in the rate of employment between married and unmarried women of the same age (Schizzerotto *et al.*, 1995). However the decline in women's employment rates which are related to the number of children, is slowing and this would appear to be typical of Italy at the moment.

Although the categories used by the various research groups do not match perfectly, a certain degree of regularity does emerge. The early studies show a threshold at which the employment rate drops sharply, and which coincides with the birth of the second child. This finding does not emerge from later studies. According to Belotti (1993: 307), for example, it is the number of children in particular that no longer makes a difference to educated mothers.

As a result, all mothers' paid work declines regularly, but without a critical threshold, as a mere function of the number of children; from none to more than two children, the rate falls from 85 to 68 to 53 to 41 with the regularity of a vector. These statistics appear to indicate the number of complications involved in working and managing children rather than a preference to stay at home once the family has been formed. On the basis of this evidence, some studies have found higher activity rates for mothers with one child than for women with no children (Bimbi and Pristinger, 1985: 124).

Table 5   Employment rates for mothers according to the number of children, in surveys
           of north Italy

	Surveys in the late 70s				Surveys early 90s	
	Turin '78*	Lombardy '77	Milan '81	Lombardy '87	The Veneto '91	Piemonte '92
No children	80*	51	54.3	58	65.9	60.5
One child	43*	53	54.1	59	66.3*+	60.7*+
Two children	25*	36**	40.4	54**	51.6++	55.6++
Three children			44.3		28.2+8	

Source: Martinotti, 1982; Barile and Stefanizzi, 1990; Stefanizzi, 1984; Irer, 1991; Mauri et al. 1992, Mauri, 1993. * In the survey on Turin, the categories are respectively "no children and parents under 35", "at least one child under 14", "at least one child over 14 ". **In the Irer study "two or more children". In Mauri's study *+ "children under 6", ++ "children from 6 to 18" +* "children over 18".

This supports the view that motherhood is no longer seen as incompatible with work *in a cultural sense* (and vice versa), although it is still a difficult choice to make since practical problems associated with motherhood interweave and grow (La Mendola, 1992: 66). It seems that women no longer give up work for family; on the contrary, they give up having children in order to have a job (Carmignani and Pruna, 1991: 144).

But this trend requires more explanation. Probably due to the existence of services (especially nursery school for the 3-to-6 year olds, which have a very high attendance), and family support networks which solve the problems associated with very young children better than those associated with children attending school who might in the meantime have gainded a younger brother or sister, it is often the case nowadays that mothers contemplate a return to work immediately after the birth of their child and remain at work, even after the birth of successive children, to simply trying to 'resist' somehow until things become too complicated to manage (Trifiletti, forthcoming). Paradoxically, therefore, the mothers of young, time-demanding children more often remain on the labour market than those with more self-sufficient and, at the same time, 'expensive' offspring. It is for these reasons that, instead of increasing with the age of children as elsewhere, the activity ratio for mothers in Italy actually decreases. The graph for Italy has never consisted of a curve with two peaks and the pattern is still one of 'no return' once women have left the labour market. The way maternity leave is formulated, extremely protective in the first few months and almost non-existent thereafter, has certainly played an important role in this. Even in those areas of Italy where public childcare services have reached European levels (with a crèche coverage of over 25% for children between 0-3 years old) and, therefore, women's employment rate has greatly increased (the province of Reggio Emilia has a women's employment rate which is inferior only to Denmark in Europe) (Reyneri, 1996: 102), these same difficulties in bearing the burden of excessive work loads over time still exist, especially when children reach school age and elderly family members might change from a resource into a care problem. Grandparents, but particularly grandmothers, are an invaluable resource for mothers during the hours not covered by pre-school or for school services on days when children cannot attend. Sometimes children are cared for by their grandparents not only for part of the day but for the whole day (Facchini, 1997: 284). Work outside the home is judged possible by women only to the extent that it is possible to carry it out alongside work for the family, which remains burdensome, cannot be qualitatively reduced and, above all, is not limited to a particular period of time, due to the tendency of grown-up children in Italy to live at home. In all the studies which have examined the transport aspect, for example, the husband's journey to work is always systematically longer than that of his wife. This shows that, as has already been revealed in France (Daune-Richards, 1988), a crucial feature of the desirability of paid work is its proximity to home, which enables woman to have spare-time when the rest of the family is away for at least a minimum of house-work.

In the absence of similar surveys for the south of Italy, we can only gather evidence to indicate that women in this region are much further away from being able to negotiate a change in the division of labour. However, at the same time, there are signs of a desire to move towards modern arrangements at a symbolic level. The huge increase in youth unemployment and its gender differential has been seen as a symptom of "anticipatory modernisation" (Villa, 1992; Bettio and Villa, 1993) and of a wilful refusal to be merely a housewife (Altieri, 1992; Ginatempo, 1994) which is not so very traditional (Mingione, 1993). In a manner of speaking, southern women have already begun to show a *double presence* attitude which very few of them can actually put into practice; sometimes they even go so far as to restrict fertility, a type of behaviour which gives them a sense of belonging to a heteronomous reality (Gullotta, 1993). Time-use studies have amply shown that these aspirations, albeit with great regional differences, remain largely unfulfilled. The national average figures indicates that the birth of a child coincides with an increase in unpaid work by working mothers (one hour extra for each child) at the expense of their leisure time, their sleeping time or time for personal care. However, it only affects unpaid work by the father by a few minutes. He, if anything, tends to increase the hours of paid work outside the home (Palomba, 1997).

5. Is it possible to hypothesise a Mediterranean model for combining family, social policy and paid work for women?

As has been noted on other occasions when studying the relations between the family and 5. women's work, it is impossible to avoid referring to social policy. The state is not merely a distant presence for these relations; its workings intertwine with these aspects in many ways and it might be said that, more generally, its ability to intervene in the shaping of gender relations has increased (Saraceno, 1993). This happens most obviously in the setting up of all services that ease the duties of women not only in looking after children but also for example the elderly, the infirm and the disabled. As regards all these areas in fact, the state has increasingly come to assume that its partial interventions will be supplemented by the adequate functioning of the family, whose burden, falls almost entirely on women of 30 years or older. Secondly, the welfare state obviously safeguards motherhood, working mothers and equality. In Italy, these forms of protection have developed only spasmodically, without reference to a general framework of family policies (which in fact does not exist). These forms of protection are detached from society's shared view of the value of motherhood and similarly disconnected from labour policies (Beccalli, 1985), offering initial protection on an almost categorical basis, which is rather inflexible in its double standards for secured and non-secured work. In sum, it has proved to be dysfunctional and somewhat maximalist. It would have been better to guarantee a more reduced but more flexible form of protection on a universalist basis, involving fewer irreversible choices.

Paradoxically, what little protection there is for working mothers has in this way actually worked against them, making it even more difficult to gain access to a labour market that is modelled on the male breadwinner. The welfare regime, however, as is evidenced in all Mediterranean countries, does not follow this model at all; there is no development of derived benefits or of state support for bringing up children. The family is expected to cope with all its own problems. Social state policies presuppose the success of the family, but do not really support it (Saraceno, 1994; Trifiletti, 1995), unless it is manifestly inadequate.

Perhaps the Italian state has also been backward in its role as principle employer of women. It could have set up more services and created part-time state employment to support these services, with duly qualified positions (Pfau-Effinger, 1993; Meyer, 1994) with a minimum of protection, which is what took place in other countries where there was a high rate of employment for women. The fact that there are fewer gender differences in pay, but only for women with officially recognised jobs, bears witness to this. The state has been even less aware of the subject of work-family arrangements.

If the idea of a Mediterranean model for combining family, work and social policy based on the notion of emancipation *within* the family (Bettio and Villa, 1993) rather than away *from* it, is feasible, this is by no means an invitation to revive old-style cultural interpretations of traditional Italian familism, especially if this is based on purported 'explanations' for it such as Catholicism (Sainsbury, 1996). We must, on the other hand, not lose sight of the difficult task of making paid work compatible with the family, which, for all these reasons, is even more difficult and is, in any case, not felt to be a state responsibility.

6. Employers' flexibility policies

We should therefore be wary of jumping to hasty conclusions about the 'backwardness' of Italy compared to the rest of Europe in adopting new forms of work. Rather, the point is that we are faced with a characteristic combination of backward and modern features which makes it much more difficult both to plan measures and assess their real impact. In all countries which do not hold a central position in the international division of labour, standard Fordist industrial relations have never eliminated atypical forms of work and the current change to flexibility is just as likely to give rise to new types of highly qualified workers as it is to an increase in de-qualified menial or illegal job opportunities (Chiesi, 1995: 60-66).

The convergence of interests between employers trying to respond quickly to the market, improve the effective use of machinery and make the best possible use of human capital on the one hand, and workers wishing to obtain greater freedom in the management of their working hours on the other, is present everywhere and has tended to help the two parties to agree on working hours. This is also true of Italy, but a problem arises from the fact that it takes place under the conditions described earlier, with a twofold labour market divided between well-protected workers and those in the deregulated grey economy. At the same time, the welfare regime is not capable of really protecting the family or of giving autonomy to individuals. In addition, we must not underestimate the important, and sometimes unwieldy presence of the unions, which have always opposed any form of flexibility since they adopted their role of protector of 'secure' workers to stop them from ending up in the informal economy, where there had always been flexibility, albeit of a very different type. Only recently has the Italian Trade Union Congress agreed (in the September 1996 Employment Agreement, signed together with the Government and Employers' association), though not unreservedly, to discuss the subject of flexible working hours with the main aim of tackling the problem of unemployment. It has reserved for itself a close supervisory role to carry on its struggle against overtime as well. Thus, the subject of flexibility has emerged peremptorily in Italy. Recent studies involving a content analysis of the collective union agreements have revealed an increase in the term's usage and additions which have been attributed to its semantic field in the 1990s (Accornero and Di Nicola, 1996). However, most of the changes in working hours which have taken place suit the requirements of the company. Few of the changes introduced are forms of flexibility chosen by employees, and where this is the case, it is not an intention but a consequence. As proof of this we may cite the fact that in most cases the de-standardisation of working hours has had the effect of extending the working week to include Saturday and sometimes Sunday, a return to night-shifts and the introduction of forms of week-end part-time work[6], or the annualization of a multi-week schedule which is often a type of quasi-seasonal work (Cerruti, 1995)[7], found especially in the textile industry. The overall effect has been to effectively increase both competitiveness and the number of hours worked, despite a decrease in the hours contractually agreed upon (Olini, 1994; Gasparini and Olini, 1996). Many flexibility agreements have in fact been accepted to avoid redundancies and to limit the use of overtime which has been made less attractive for employers through the 1996 Budget law, which introduced a 5% compulsory contribution to the National Employment Fund (Law, 1995/549).

Undoubtedly, in Italy as elsewhere, the process, which started within the local branches of large multinational companies is one of the few positive effects of globalization. Because certain schemes have been found to be effective elsewhere (Harker, 1996: 53), they may be put to good effect in terms of maximising and supporting human capital, although they are by no means bound to spread throughout the whole of the private sector. Along these lines, Dupont de Nemours Italiana (Arve-Parès, 1996), for example, operate on a steady basis of telework, flexi-hours and part-time contracts for all career levels. In addition, it has introduced highly sophisticated forms of preventive medicine, counselling and legal advice for its employees; several banks, chains of shopping malls, and some public bodies such as the Province of Milan which offers a choice of many forms of horizontal or vertical 'new part-time'constructions. It is a much more common practice to offset overtime or unsocial working hours against time off, which can sometimes be transformed into leave of absence for family or health reasons. However, workers often complain that they have to work longer hours to earn the same salary they earned with greater ease through overtime (Piazza, 1997).

Another example of good company practice is, that of Sony in Rovereto which has introduced various measures to facilitate parenthood, part-time work, return to work, and job-sharing where two part-time workers can freely agree on their working hours (Comune di Ferrara, 1996). At the moment, it is rarer (and limited to the big banks and the public sector)

---

[6] When the need not to change excessively the working hours of those already employed prevailed.

[7] It has been estimated that 50% of collective agreements since the 1990s contains clauses concerning the change to annualization of working hours (Pero e Treu, 1995).

to find parental leave which is longer or concerns children who are older than that provided for under national law. But leave for the care of other family members or voluntary work is now beginning to be included in legislation (Piazza *et al.*, 1997). This 'fruitful' interpretation of work-family arrangements, however, is unlikely to become generalised in the short term. Although there is a great deal of political and cultural debate (Villa, 1997)[8], these facilities still seem to be isolated avant-garde cases stimulated by the firms' interests and justified by a significant increase of productivity (cf. Marzotto company of Praia a mare). It would be wrong to take these experiences as indicative of real conditions of work, especially for women. The idea of family-friendly work organisation does not seem to be taking off yet, mainly because of a reluctance to discuss the issue of the family we mentioned earlier. This is particularly odd if we consider that it is particularly the mothers with young children who go to work.

And yet, something is changing. For years, term-time contracts were almost forbidden, while part-time contracts were discouraged, and solidarity contracts recommended but not implemented. The only forms of flexibility that were put into practice, under strict union supervision, were the use of overtime for periods of intense activity and the Cassa Integrazione Guadagni (Earnings Integration Fund) for slack periods (with frequent slides into early retirement if the crisis was long-lasting). However, these measures were discriminatory on a gender basis, as indeed are the short-term work-experience contracts (Contratti Formazione-Lavoro) aimed at making young peoples' access to the labour market more flexible (Villa, 1997: 16-18). Now, with the recent introduction of contracts negotiated locally (but still largely defined at a national level), a significant change in course might be taking place. If the present leftist government lasts, it might be able to meet a need by providing a legal and nationally recognized model of flexibility that is backed up by suitable labour policies (De Luca and Bruni, 1993: 99). Along these lines there has been a new move to promote solidarity contracts and recent legalization of work on call (Law, 1996/167) which will be implemented in 1998. But even the sense of entitlement that is felt by workers, and especially by women workers, may undergo rapid change on the basis of showcase-experience and changes in employers' attitudes to women's work which have already been observed (Carmignani and Pruna, 1991: 145).

In Italy, this does not, however, result in expectations for forms of company childcare of which there is hardly a trace in collective agreements. There is a precise historical reason for this: the law which set up a national network of public crèches was intended to replace a

---

[8] It has been said that if there were a tele-work job for every conference on the subject, it would be a good start (Russo, 1996: 5). On the contrary, the number of workers on tele-work have been estimated at less than a thousand in the whole country on the basis of collective agreements (Iannaccone, 1996). Moreover these jobs have generally low technological specialization.

previous law dating from the 1950s which obliged those employing 50 or more women workers to provide a 'camera di allattamento' (baby-feeding room). It was precisely the unhappy memories of workplace crèches with their inferior, charity image from which the new service introduced in 1971 has tended to distance itself. Existing company crèches were usually absorbed into the public system or transformed to give employees priority access to a particular public crèche, or, more rarely, a private one; but this happens less often nowadays. There is greater interest in developing alternative or complementary services which have more flexibility and involve parental participation, such as those promoted by Livia Turco's law on children's rights (Law, 28-8-1997/285).

But other forms of support for parenthood are emerging too. In the private sector, for example, the disadvantages for blue-collar workers with respect to white-collar ones regarding maternity leave are diminishing; in most local contracts the entitlement during maternity leave was 100% of normal pay for blue-collar workers from the 1990s on. This was previously a privilege reserved for white-collar workers only. Items such as paid time off and leave of absence "for serious family reasons"[9] or to attend training courses are also beginning to become more widespread for blue-collar workers. By the same token, in the contracts of the 1990s limited forms of flexibility in the daily hours of work were beginning to be tried out even for blue-collar workers (normally an hour and a half at the most), something already existing for white-collar workers in the private sector. We should also mention that maternity leave has recently been extended to the realms of self-employed, but unfortunately no figures are available.[10] The distance between Italy and the more advanced European countries may be seen from the following example: to ensure the effective enjoyment of parental leave in Sweden, part of it must be at least non-transferrable (Björnberg, 1994), whereas in Italy, parental leave exists only as a form of transfer of optional leave after the compulsory five months' leave, on condition that the woman gives up her entitlement and that both parents are employees in 'secure' jobs; alternatively, the compulsory leave may be transferred only if the mother is dead or disabled. It is therefore significant that today's contracts mention these cases of paternal leave, which should anyway already have been safeguarded by the 1977 law on equal opportunities, but which has, until now, never been applied in this field (Battistoni and Gilardi, 1992: 125-130).

Even the experience of positive action for equality, which should have been the ideal context to establish for convergence between the various needs for flexibility of employers

---

[9] The reasons must be really serious, as is shown by the illustrative examples used: if you or a member of your family have to undergo treatment for drug addiction.

[10] It is known that the overall cost of this item has fallen in the state budget, due to the population decrease. But, for example, leave of absence in the case of adoption which by law is the equivalent of parental leave for childbirth, occurs infrequently.

and employees, turned out not to be so ideal. Initially at least, the training and promotion of women in business prevailed. Studies on organisations, or actions aimed at the valorisation of women as an organisational resource,[11] and above all actions concerning family life were less prevalent. Table 6 shows the division for the first three years of the application of the law for positive action funded by the Ministry of Labour.

Table 6   Types of positive action funded by the Ministry of Labour

	1991	1992	1993
Training and promotion of professional skills	21	37	36
For the elimination of inequality in careers and appreciation			
Of gender difference	10	13	15
Of which in favour of women-run enterprises	3	12	11
Organisational and territorial studies	4	6	8
Training for positive action or union bargaining	5	11	7
Safeguarding motherhood and easing return to work	1	--	4
Total	41	67	66

Source: Ministero del Lavoro e della Previdenza sociale. Comitato nazionale pari opportunità 1993.

Perhaps the most significant aspect is that where forms of flexibility are introduced even with the best of intentions they are only successful when they accompany a lengthy process of cultural consideration which involves working women. The first emblematic attempts at positive action in firms such as SGS (Cazzaniga 1985) or Zanussi (Cazzaniga 1996) were initially resisted by women workers; in fact, this age-old diffidence has only very recently been overcome. Women factory workers, when offered shifts to their advantage, reacted negatively, perceiving their family role as inflexible and non-negotiable and seeing any reduction in working hours as a prelude to future redundancy. If the latter fear is more unrealistic, the former perception is not. It is based on the great burden on working women caused by her family. Far from being an irrational vestige of traditionalism, it is a more general perception of the dangers attached to the 'new' forms of family-friendly flexibility in Italian society, and the suspicion that these new forms might merge into the old forms of women's work which were also flexible, but in a very discriminating way. Along these lines, it is significant that a recent proposal by the ruling centre-left alliance to promote part-time work in public administration has roused very little interest. The intention behind the proposal was to bring to light the illegal position of having two jobs. This is very common in the public

---

[11] This happens only in certain computer firms (Luciano, 1993).

administration sector which, with its effective guarantees such as return to work after a long period of maternity leave, time-off and leaves of absence, has always been family-friendly - almost *de facto* part-time jobs with a 36 hours week - and has therefore been chosen by many women. The private tertiary sector, however, has never been particularly flexible with regard to women's work (Chiesi, 1995).

Further evidence that it is not merely a question of being old-fashioned comes from the fact that when positive action is combined with a cultural preparation which takes account of the role of women in the family, there is much less resistance. This is so not only in well-known cases such as that of Italtel, but also in highly problematic situations such as that of Merloni, located in an area of very high unemployment in the south (Aa.Vv, 1994). The difference lies, in my opinion, in being able to bring to light what women's work really consists of, and in acting on women's sense of entitlement (Lewis, 1996).

7.   Conclusions

The situation in Italy is marked by the scant social visibility of family problems. Also the fact that changes in work and the family have so far left men's working hours virtually untouched has meant that the issue does not cut across the private-public domains but remains, in a sense, more private as it concerns only women. It is for these reasons, among others, that the question has been raised as a public issue to ensure that it ends up on the official agenda. In this light the experiment of planning and innovation in city time management (cf. Balbo, 1991; Tempia, 1993, 1995; Belloni, 1995; Bimbi, 1995a) is of particular significance. The experiment followed a popular proposal of a bill put forward by the women's organisation of the former Communist Party (Women change times, bill 1989; Life-cycle, working hours, city times bill 1990), which was taken up in the reform of the new-style mayors. They were given the task of "coordinating the opening hours of the shops, the public services ... the counters of public administrations, in order to harmonize ...[them] with the needs of service users" (Law 142/1990, art. 36). Various schemes are beginning to be implemented in the large cities, starting with the extension of opening hours for services and shops but also in some cases with 'time banks' or important preparatory studies for opening hours structure plans (Comune of Milan, 1994). All this, however, means that the Italian experience is not chiefly or exclusively centered in the world of work.[12] Whether this is an advantage or disadvantage, it

---

[12] At least 80 local Councils in large ans medium-sized cities have undertaken in various ways to harmonize opening hours, streamline bureaucracy, set up time offices, time banks (approximately 120 until now, considering those already functioning or projected ones) and even structure plans for working hours of the town.

is still too early to tell. The Minister for Social Solidarity, Livia Turco, has had her bill on the reconciliation of working and family times approved by the Cabinet (19/02/98), in compliance with recent recommendations by the EC. The bill supports part-time work, parental leave (within the first 8 years of the child's life) and other types of leaves for care reasons, not only by keeping the post open, but also by anticipating the payment of the end-of service allowance. Incentives are, for the first time, being envisaged for employers who favour the 'harmonising of work and family times'. If Turco's bill becomes law, it will probably foster a cultural change parallel to that of the city time schemes and, as a result, we might be able to look forward to a period of rapid change. However, there is no evidence yet of a more equal division of unpaid work in Italian society.

References

AA.VV. (1994), *Donne frigoriferi e lavatrici. Storia di un'azione positiva alla Merloni elettrodomestici*, Laboratorio delle idee, Studio Mustica.

Abburrà, L. (1989), *L'occupazione femminile dal declino alla crescita*, Torino: Rosenberg e Sellier.

Accornero, A. and P. Di Nicola (1996), *La mobilità nella società italiana*, Roma: Sipi.

Altieri, G. (1992), La disoccupazione femminile italiana: fra specificità e dualismo territoriale. In: *Politiche del lavoro*, 20.

Altieri, G. (1993), *Presenti ed escluse*, Roma: Ediesse.

Altieri, G. (1995), Donne e trasformazioni del mercato del lavoro. In: *Interpretazioni tendenziose*, 1, 2, 46-61.

Arve-Parès B. ed. (1996), *Concilier travail et vie familiale- un enjeu pour l'Europe?*, Stockholm.

Balbo, L. (1974), *Stato di famiglia*, Milano: Etas.

Balbo, L. (1978), La doppia presenza. In *Inchiesta*, 8, 32, 3-6.

Balbo, L. (1982), The Servicing Work of Women and the Capitalist State. In M. Zeitlin (ed.), *Political Power and Social Theory*. Greenwich: JAI Press.

Balbo, L. ed. (1991), *Tempi di vita. Studi e proposte per cambiarli.* Milano: Feltrinelli.

Balbo, L. ed. (1993, 1994), *Friendly. Almanacco della società italiana*, Milano, Anabasi.

Ten Regional administrations have already passed framework laws for such schemes. It is significant, for example, that in one of the studies which inspired these schemes, work is mentioned only in the second updating, as if it were something much harder to change: cf. *Friendly, Almanacco della società italiana*, a project by Laura Balbo, 1993 and 1994.

Balbo, L., M. May and G. Micheli (1990), *Vincoli e strategie nella vita quotidiana*, Milano: Angeli.

Barbagli, M. (1991), *Provando e riprovando*, Bologna: il Mulino.

Barile, G. and S. Stefanizzi (1990), *Donne, lavoro e condizione familiare*, Milano: IRER.

Battistoni, L. and G. Gilardi (1992), *La parità tra consenso e conflitto*, Roma, Ediesse.

Beccalli, B. (1985), Le politiche del lavoro femminile in Italia: donne sindacati e stato tra 1974 e 1984. In: *Stato e mercato*, 15, dic.

Belloni, M.C. (1995), Policies concerning the Organisation of Time in Italian cities, paper presented to the European Forum, Gender and the Use of Time, Florence, European University Institute (forthcoming).

Belotti, V. (1993), La partecipazione al lavoro delle donne coniugate. In: *Polis*, 7, 2, 277-300.

Beneria, L. (1988), Conceptualizing the Labour Force: the Underestimation of Women's Economic Activities. In: R. Pahl (ed.), *On Work*, Oxford: Blackwells.

Bettio, F. and P. Villa (1993), Strutture familiari e mercati del lavoro nei paesi sviluppati. L'emergere di un percorso mediterraneo per l'integrazione delle donne nel mercato del lavoro. In: *Economia e lavoro*, 27, 3-30.

Bettio, F. and P. Villa (1996), Un modello al bivio. In: *DonnaWomanFemme*, 32,4.

Bettio, F. and P. Villa (1997), A Mediterranean Perspective on the Breakdown of the relationship between Participation and Fertility. In: *Cambridge Journal of Economics*, forthcoming.

Biadene, S. *et al.* (1994), *Modelli territoriali e differenze di genere*, Milano: Feltrinelli.

Bianchi, M. (1978), Oltre il doppio lavoro. In: *Inchiesta*, 8, 32, 7-15.

Bianchi, M. (1991), Lavoro di cura, lavoro di servizio, lavoro familiare. In: Balbo (ed.), *cit.*

Bianco (1996), *Classi e reti sociali*, Bologna: Il Mulino.

Bimbi, F. (1995a), Gender Divisions of Labour and Welfare Provisions in Italy. Governmental Policies on Reconciliation of Paid and Unpaid Work for Parents. In T. Williamsen, G. Frinking and R. Vogels (1995), *Work and Family in Europe: the Role of the Policies*, Tilburg: Tilburg University Press.

Bimbi, F. (1995b), Gender Metaphors on Paid and Unpaid Work. Time in Gender Relations, paper presented to the European Forum, Gender and the Use of Time, Florence: European University Institute (forthcoming).

Bimbi, F. and F. Pristinger (1985), *Profili sovrapposti*, Milano: Angeli.

Björnberg, U. (1994), Reconciling Family and employment in Sweden. In: M.T. Létablier and L. Hantrais (eds.) *The Family-Employment Relationship*, Loughborough Cross-National Research Papers. Loughborough: Loughborough University of Technology.

Carmignani, F. and M. Pruna (1991), Le donne nel mercato del lavoro. Vecchi problemi e nuove opportunità. In: G.Bonazzi, C. Saraceno and B. Beccalli (a cura di) *Donne uomini nella divisione del lavoro*, Milano: Angeli.

Cazzaniga, P. (1985), I turni di lavoro in un'azienda elettronica. In: P. Manacorda and P. Piva (eds.), *Terminale donna*, Roma: Edizioni Lavoro.

Cazzaniga, P. (1996), Rosa al lavoro, pro manuscripto.

Cerruti, G. (1995), Produzione snella e banca del tempo, In: *Lettera FIM*, 6, 4/5.

Chiesi, A.M. (1995), Le trasformazioni dei contenuti del lavoro. In: A. Chiesi, I.Regalia and M. Regini (eds.), *Lavoro e relazioni industriali in Europa*, Roma: Nis.

Comune di Ferrara - "European network Work and Family Life"(1996), *Tempi e spazi nell'organizzazione della vita quotidiana/Social Innovation: Time and Space of Everyday Life*, Atti del convegno 26/27-9-96, Ferrara.

Comune di Milano (1994), *Piano regolatore degli orari per la città di Milano*, Milano: Ufficio tempi della città, feb., 3 voll.

Daune-Richards, A.M. (1988), Gender Relations and Female Labour. A Consideration of Sociological Categories. In J. Jenson, E. Hagen and C. Reddy (eds.), *Feminization of the Labor Force: Paradoxes and Promises*. New York: Oxford University Press.

David, P. and G. Vicarelli (1994), *Donne nelle professioni degli uomini*, Milano: Angeli.

De Luca, L. and M. Bruni (1994), *Unemployment and Labour Market flexibility*, Genève: ILO.

Eardley. T, J. Bradshaw, J. Gough and P. Whiteford (eds.)(1996), *Social Assistance in OECD Countries*. London: HMSO.

European Foundation for the Improvement of Living and Working Conditions (1988), *New Forms of Work. Labour Law and Social Security Aspects in the European Community*, Luxembourg.

Eurostat (1991a), *A Social Portrait of Europe*, Luxembourg: Office for Publications of EC .

Eurostat (1991b), *Labour Force Survey. Results 1989*, Luxembourg: Office for Publications of EC.

Eurostat (1995), *Labour Force Survey. Results 1993*, Luxembourg: Office for Publications of EC.

Eurostat (1996a), *Labour Force Survey. Results 1994*, Luxembourg: Office for Publications of EC.

Eurostat (1996b), *Labour Force Survey. Results 1995*, Luxembourg: Office for Publications of EC.

Facchini, C. (1997), Gli anziani e la solidarietà fra generazioni. In: M. Barbagli and C. Saraceno (eds.), *Lo stato delle famiglie in Italia*. Bologna: Il Mulino.

Fadiga Zanatta, A. (1988), Donne e lavoro: istruzione passepartout. In: *Politica ed economia*, 2.

Fagnani, J. (1992), Les Françaises font-elles des prouesses? Fécondité et travail professionnel et politiques familiales en France et Allemagne de l'Ouest, CNAF Recherches et Prévisions, 28, 23-36.

Finch, J. and D. Groves (1983), a c. di *A Labour of Love*. London: Routledge.

Gasparini, G. and G. Olini (1996), *I tempi nelle società complesse*. Roma: edizioni Lavoro.

Gesano, G. (1990), Dieci anni di evoluzione nel mercato del lavoro italiano: 1978-87. Un'analisi per generazioni nel nord-centro e nel mezzogiorno. In: *Economia and lavoro*, 24, 2, 79-112.

Ginatempo, N. (1994), *Donne al confine*, Milano: Angeli.

Guillen, A. (1996), Social Policy in Democratic Spain: the reformulation of the Francoist welfare system, paper presented at the MIRE Conference *Comparing Social Welfare Systems in Southern Europe*, Florence 22/24-2-1996, Iue-Centre R. Schumann.

Gullotta, G. (1993), Un figlio solo e poi basta. In: N. Ginatempo (a cura di), *Donne del sud. Il prisma femminile sulla questione meridionale*, Palermo: Gelka.

Hakim, C. (1993), The Myth of the Rising Female Employment. In: *Work, Employment and Society*, 7, 1, 97-120.

Hakim, C. (1995), Five Feminist Myths about Women's Employment. In: *British Journal of Sociology*, 46, 3, 429-55

Harker, L. (1996), The Family Friendly Employer in Europe. In S. Lewis and J. Lewis (eds.), *The Work-Family Challenge. Rethinking Employment*. London: Sage.

Hochschild, A (1983), *The Managed Hearth*, University of California Press.

Humphries, J. and J. Rubery (1984), The Reconstruction of the Supply Side of the Labour Market: the Relative autonomy of Social Reproduction. In: *Cambridge Journal of Economics*, 8, 331-46.

Iannaccone, M. (1996), Telelavorare in Italia: le novità del 1996, In: *NL. Notiziario del Lavoro*, 81, 14, pp. 56-64.

IRER (1991), *Social Survey in Lombardia*, Milano: Angeli.

Istat (1990, 1993a, 1993b, 1994, 1995a, 1995b), *Rilevazione delle forze di lavoro. Media annuale 1989, 1990, 1991, 1992, 1993, 1994*, Collana di informazione, nn. risp. 20, 12, 26, 23, 17, 18.

Istat. Sistema statistico nazionale (1996, 1997), *Forze di lavoro. Media 1995,1996*, Roma: Istat.

Jallinoja, R. (1989), Women between Family and Employment. In: K. Boh and G. Sgritta (eds.) *Changing Patterns of European Family Life*, London: Routledge.

Jonung, C. and I. Persson (1993), Women and Market Work: the Misleading Tale of Participation Rates in International Comparisons. In: *Work, Employment and Society*, 7, 2, 259-74.

Kickbutsch, I. (1984) Familie als Beruf - Beruf als Familie: der segregierte Arbeitsmarkt und die Familialisierung der weiblichen Arbeit. In I. Kickbutsch and B. Riedmüller (hrsg.), *Die armen Frauen*, Frankfurt: Suhrkampf.

La Mendola, S. (1992), *Gente comune*, Venezia: Fondazione Corazzin.

Lewis, S. (1996), Sense of Entitlement, Family Friendly Policies and Gender. In: H. Helle and I. Thaulow (eds.), *Reconciling Work and Family Life. An Internatinal Perspective on the Role of the Companies*. Copenhagen: Danish Institute of Social Research.

Luciano, A.(1993), *Tornei. Donne e uomini in carriera*, Milano: Etas.

Martinotti, G. (a cura di) (1982), *La città difficile. Progetto Torino 5*. Milano: Angeli.

Mauri, L. *et al.* (1992), *Vita di famiglia. Social survey in Veneto*, Milano: Angeli.

Mauri, L. (1993), *Equilibri. Persistenze e mutamenti nella famiglia in un'area piemontese*, Milano: Angeli.

Meulders, D., O. Plasman and R. Plasman (1994), *Atypical Employment in the EC*, Aldershot: Gower.

Meyer, T. (1994), The German end British Welfare States as Employers: Patriarchal or Emancipatory?. In: D. Sainsbury (ed.), *Gendering the Welfare State*, London: Sage.

Mingione, E. (1993), Le donne del mezzogiorno. disoccupazione, lavoro e mancato sviluppo. In: *Politiche del lavoro*, 20.

Ministero del Lavoro e della Previdenza sociale. Comitato Nazionale Pari Opportunità (1993), *Le opportunità crescono. La legge 125/91 due anni dopo*, Roma.

OECD (1991), *Labour Force Statistics, 1969-1989*, (1994), *Employment Outlook*, Paris.

Olini, G. (1994), I regimi di orario nella contrattazione decentrata: le tendenze dal 1980 al 1992. In: *Lavoro Informazione*, 2, pp. 15-22.

Padoa Schioppa Kostoris, F. (1994), Retribuzione femminile: parità formale, disparità sostanziale nel pubblico e nel privato fra lavoratori e lavoratrici oggi in Italia. In: *Ruolo e prospettive delle donne nell'economia*. Roma: Commissione Nazionale per la parità e pari opportunità tra uomo e donna,9-59.

Palomba, R.(1997), I tempi in famiglia. In: M. Barbagli and C. Saraceno (eds.), *cit.*

Papanek, H. (1973), Men, Women and Work. Reflections on the two Persons Career. In *American Journal of Sociology*, 78, 852-72.

Pero, L. and T. Treu (1995), *Working Time Network*. Milano: Fondazione Pietro Seveso.

Pfau-Effinger, B. (1993), Modernisation, Culture and Part-time Employment: the Example of Finland and West Germany. In: *Work Employment and Society*, 7, 3, 383-410.

Piazza, M., A.M. Ponzellini, E. Provenzano and A. Tempia (1997) *Riprogettiamo il tempo*, vol. 1, Milano: Fondazione Pietro Seveso.

Picchio, A. (1992) *Social Reproduction: the Political Economy of the Labour Market*, Cambridge: Cambridge University Press.

Picchio, A. (1993), Il lavoro di riproduzione, questione centrale nell'analisi del mercato del lavoro. In: *Politiche del lavoro*, 19, 3-35.

Piva, P. (1994), *Il lavoro sessuato. Donne e uomini nelle organizzazioni*, Milano: Anabasi.

Pleck, J. (1977), The Work-Family Role System. In: *Social Problems*, 24, 417-27.

Reyneri, E., (1996), *Sociologia del mercato del lavoro*, Bologna: Il Mulino.

Ronco, W. and L. Peattie (1988), Making Work: a Perspective from Social Science. In: R. Pahl, *cit.*

Russo, P. (1996), *Il telelavoro non è una televisione*. Roma: Stampa Alternativa.

Sabbadini, L.L. and R. Palomba (1994), *Tempi diversi. L'uso del tempo di uomini e donne nell'Italia di oggi*, Roma: Presidenza del Consiglio dei Ministri, Commissione Nazionale pari opportunità.

Sainsbury, D.(1996), *Gender, Equality and Welfare States*, Cambridge: University Press.

Saraceno, C. (1986), Uomini e donne nella vita quotidiana, ovvero per un'analisi delle strutture di sesso della vita quotidiana. In: F. Bimbi and V. Capecchi, *Strutture e strategie della vita quotidiana*, Milano: Angeli.

Saraceno, C. (1992), Donne e lavoro o strutture di genere del lavoro. In: *Polis*, 6, 1, 5-22.

Saraceno, C. (1993), Elementi per un'analisi delle trasformazioni di genere nella società contemporanea e delle loro conseguenze sociali. In: *Rassegna italiana di sociologia*, 1, 19-56.

Saraceno, C. (1994), The Ambivalent familism of the Italian Welfare state, In: *Social Politics*, 1, 1.

Schizzerotto, A., I. Bison and A. Zoppè (1995), Disparità di genere nella partecipazione al mondo del lavoro e nella durata delle carriere. In: *Polis*, 9, 1, 91-112.

Schmidt, M.G. (1993), Gendered Labour Force Participation. In: F.G. Castles, *Families of Nations: Patterns of Public Policy in Western Democracies*. Aldershot: Darthmouth.

Stefanizzi, S. (1984), La produzione femminile, in Comune di Milano - Istituto superiore di Sociologia, *Bilancio sociale di area*, ciclostilato.

Tempia, A. (1993), *Ricomporre i tempi*, Roma: Ediesse.

Tempia, A. (1995), Il rapporto fra tempi vincolati e tempi non vincolati dalla prospettiva degli studi sui tempi delle città, In: *Sociologia del lavoro*, 58, 172-86.

Tobìo, C. (1994), The Family-Employment Relation in Spain. In: M.T. Létablier and L. Hantrais, The Family Employment relationship, *cit.*

Taccani, P. (ed.)(1994), *Dentro la cura*, Milano: Angeli.

Trifiletti, R. (1995), Defining Family Obligations in Italy. In: J.Millar and A. Warman, *Defining Family Obligations in Italy*. Bath: Bath Social Policy papers 23.

Trifiletti, R. (1996), Un modello 'altro' di doppia presenza in Toscana. Lavoro femminile, famiglia e decisione di aver figli. In: *Inchiesta*, 112.

Villa, P. (1992), Donne del Sud: fuori casa dove? In: *Politiche del lavoro*, 20, 5-16.

Villa, P. (1997), *1997 Report: Italy* for the European Commission, Network of Experts "Gender and Employment", Trento, may 1997.

WORK-FAMILY ARRANGEMENTS IN SPAIN: FAMILY ADJUSTMENTS TO LABOUR MARKET IMBALANCES

Anna Escobedo

1.   Introduction

In Spain, the widespread integration of women in the labour market and its impact on family life has been one of the most profound changes in the last two decades. Most Spanish young families can now be considered as dual-earner families, i.e., families in which both parents are active in the labour market, either employed or looking for a job. Fertility rates have sharply decreased in the last few years, resulting in one of the lowest rates in the EU. The low fertility rate is related to young women's strong orientation towards employment, a lack of adequate work-family arrangements, and unstable job conditions for younger generations. Young people are experiencing a delay in their attainment of residential independence and autonomy. Statistics indicate that in 1994, more than half of the 25- to 29-year-olds were living in the parental home.

Most young women are facing a dilemma between work and maternity. Due to long-term, high unemployment, men and women have focused on the continuity of their jobs rather than on the quality of their working conditions. Continuity has been also a main concern for many companies facing changing contexts and economic strains. In the Spanish workplace culture, it is assumed that having a professional career is incompatible with part-time work or with the full take-up of leave arrangements. Although the situation is better in the public sector, family-friendly workplaces are rare in the Spanish context.

This chapter identifies trends and Spanish issues in connection with the work-family debate. The next section presents some features of the economic, social and political context in order to provide a better understanding of why work-family policies and practices are still limited in Spain and only recently have become a social affair and an object of research. The third section presents work-family arrangements available to dual earner families: statutory leaves for working parents and public provision of childcare. The fourth section focuses on the development of work-family arrangements in the workplace. Conclusions are presented in the last section.[1]

---

[1] This article uses information from two studies developed during 1997 at the CIREM Foundation. The first is a report on research developed in Spain between 1987-97 on Reconciliation of work and family life for men and women and the quality of care services (Casas, Balaguer *et al.*, 1997) in the framework of a European overview on the subject (Deven, Inglis, Moss *et al.*, 1997). The second is a qualitative research on equal gender opportunities in 20 Spanish companies (of different activity, size, public and private), including 40 in-depth interviews with different

2. **The framework for work-family arrangements in Spain: labour market features and family trends**

Spanish society is leaving behind a male breadwinner model, established during Franco's authoritarian regime (1939-75). The dual-earner household has become the norm among young adults, as a result of preferences and of necessity, because of job insecurity. Meanwhile, policies that support early parenthood have been inadequately developed. This can be partly explained by the situation on the labour market.

2.1 Labour market features

The Spanish labour market is characterised by a low activity rate, the persistence of high unemployment since the 1980's (over 15% since 1981, 22% in 1996), instability of new employment, and pronounced disparity in working conditions, especially between people with steady jobs and people in temporary employment.

The activity rate has increased in the last decade mainly because of the working patterns of women. The following data from the Spanish Labour Force Survey in 1996 illustrate the situation. In 1996 the female activity rate was 37%, but rates in the 25-29 and 30-34 age groups were 73.9% and 64.4% respectively (88.2% and 94.8% for men), although employment rates were only 47.7% and 45.5% in the same age groups (66.6% and 78.9% for men).

Table 1   Activity, employment and unemployment rate for men and women (1996)

1996 Spanish Labour Force Survey		Total	25-29 year-olds	30-34 year-olds
Activity rate	All	49.6	81.3	79.5
	Women	37.0	73.9	64.4
	Men	63.1	88.2	94.8
Employment rate	All	38.6	57.5	62.0
	Women	26.0	47.7	45.5
	Men	52.0	66.6	78.9
Unemployment rate	All	22.2	29.3	22.0
	Women	29.2	35.5	29.4
	Men	17.6	24.4	16.8

Source: Ministry of Employment and Social Affairs (Http://www.mtas.es)

types of female workers, and 8 personnel managers (Crespo, Artal *et al.*, 1997). The work-family interface was one of the main issues of this research. I want to thank Lluis Flaquer, Teresa Crespo and Laura den Dulk for their helpful comments, and Maria Josep Boix for helping me with the revision of the English text.

Women's strong orientation towards paid work already appears in the student population. Young women have increased their participation at all educational levels and are using education relatively more than men as a strategy to improve their employment opportunities. Nevertheless, female employment opportunities remain unequal at all educational levels, except for the illiterate population (Flaquer, 1995: 299-301). In 1996, nearly one in every four Spaniards in the 18- to 24-year-old group was a university student, 52.6% of whom were women; the employment rate of university graduates was 84.4% (Consejo Económico y Social, 1997: 407-409). The high female unemployment rate also indicates women's orientation to paid work. In 1986, Spain had the lowest female activity rate in the European Union, 27%, which represented 40% of the male rate. In 1996, the female activity rate had reached 37%, which is 58.6% of the male rate, and the employment rate was 26%, which represented 50% of the male rate. It is noticeable that Spanish mothers with children under 3 years have higher activity and employment rates than the female population as a whole (48% and 33% respectively in 1995).

Table 2   Employment status of Spanish women with children under 17 years by age of the youngest child in the 1995 ELFS

Age (years) of youngest child	Employed: Total (%)	Full-time	Part-time	on Leave	Unemployed	Economically Inactive
0 - 2	33	26	5	2	15	52
3 - 9	37	30	7	less than 0.5%	17	46
10 - 16	35	29	7	0	12	52
0 - 16	36	29	6	less than 0.5%	15	50

Source: 'Employment status of women with children under 17 years by age of youngest child, 1995, EU15 + Norway' based on a Eurostat exploitation of the European Labour Force Survey, in *State of the Art review on the reconciliation of work and family life* European Report (Deven, Inglis, Moss *et al.*, 1997)

Although Spain is a heterogeneous country with major differences between regions, and between urban or rural contexts, it happens more and more frequently that when a woman becomes a mother, she does not voluntarily abandon or reduce her work load.[2] Spanish fathers, as in other countries, also have higher rates of activity and employment than the rest of the population. Employment patterns of fathers are very different from those of mothers.

---

[2] A research carried out in Valencia, based on a sample of 619 employed women who gave birth to her first or second child in a large public hospital, found that for half of the mothers the child's birth implied a break with their professional career. Professional factors associated with the break in the job career were low qualification and unstable employment in private sector companies (Escribà *et al.*, 1994).

Table 3   *Employment status of Spanish men with children under 17 years by age of the youngest child in the 1995 ELFS*

Age (years) of youngest child	Employed: Total (%)	Full-time	Part-time	on Leave	Unemployed	Economically Inactive
0 - 2	86	85	1	less than 0.5%	12	2
3 - 9	86	85	1	0	11	3
10 - 16	83	82	1	0	10	8
0 - 16	84	83	1	less than 0.5%	11	5

Source: Deven, Inglis, Moss *et al.*, 1997.

Within the EU, Spain has a low employment rate (33%) and a high unemployment rate (15%) for women with children under 3 years. On the other hand, Spanish working mothers are in the third rank, after Portugese and Greek mothers, in the average number of hours of paid work per week (36.6 average hours per week). Only 5% of working mothers with children under 3 years are working part-time.

Table 4   *Average hours of paid work per week for Spanish women and men with children under 17 years by age of youngest child in the 1995 ELFS*

	Parents with a child under 3 years			Parents with a child under 17 years		
	All employed	Part-time	Full-time	All employed	Part-time	Full-time
Mothers	36.6	18.9	39.9	36.4	18.0	40.5
Fathers	42.7	20.3	43.0	42.6	20.2	43.0
Fathers>mothers	+6.1	+1.4	+3.1	+6.2	+2.2	+2.5

Source: Deven, Inglis, Moss *et al.*, 1997.

In the '90s, part-time employment has grown quickly among the female population. In 1995, 17% of female wage earners and 3% of male wage earners were working part-time. The figures for 1987 were 4.2% and 5.8% respectively.

Below 12 hours per week, social security contributions and social protection are reduced. Under these conditions, the degree of personal choice for part-time work seems to be very low. Part-time work has more to do with low educational levels, the sector of the least qualified services and women returning to employment, than with a family-friendly strategy. There are indications that new trends are emerging and profiles of more qualified part-time workers are appearing in such sectors as health care and education. Part-time work increased again in 1996, 6.8% of all part-time employment contracts signed were permanent contracts (109,991 out of 1,626,233) and 45.1% had a duration of less than 3 months. Whereas part-time work seems to be achieving the objective of promoting greater flexibility in companies, it is only used in a few cases as a means of personal choice to reconcile child bearing and work (Consejo Económico y Social, 1996, 1997; Torns, 1997).

In the last few years, there have been various labour market reforms orientated to reducing labour costs and to introducing flexibility in contracts from the point of view of the employers, with the aim of promoting employment. Various forms of temporary work have been developed. The effects, particularly those of a reform carried out in 1994, have been an excess of precarious working conditions and of different types of 'low quality' contracts, which are mainly affecting the younger generations and all those persons that lose their jobs and try to return to work later on.

In 1987, 18.1% of the employees had a temporary job (from a total number of 8,037,300 wage earners), whereas in 1996, the figure for temporary employment was 33.8% (from a total amount of 9,278,100 wage earners out of an employed population of 12,544,000). In 1996, 8,601,119 new working contracts were registered, 18% more than in the previous year. The annual report of the Spanish Economic and Social Council estimates that about 90% of these contracts had a limited duration, and only about 4% were permanent contracts (*contratos indefinidos*). There has also been a trend towards shorter contracts; 41% had a duration of less than 3 months (Consejo Económico y Social, 1997: 180, 202-207).

In 1997 the main trade unions and employers' associations reached an intersectoral Labour Agreement for Employment that introduced a new type of permanent contract, with lower cost of dismissal, and an agreement to improve the collective bargaining structure, which had become too fragmented. This reform is intended to promote more quality and stability of employment and to reduce the very high rate of temporary employment, which has a negative impact on social conditions and on the growth of the economy.

2.2   Family trends

There are three major family trends connected to the work-family interface: the transition from a family model, based on complementary roles between men and women, to a model based on equal roles; the delay in attaining full autonomy experienced by young people; and the delay in having a first child together with a sharp drop in fertility rates and the increase in life expectancy.

Spain has reached very low fertility rates in the 1990s (from 2.79 in 1975 to 1.18 in 1995). In 1950, there were 363 children under 15 per 100 people older than 65. The ratio was 287 in

1970, and 154 in 1990. In 1995 life expectancy was 81.5 years for women and 74.3 for men. As a consequence, the family situation has changed rapidly and so has the need for family care and social services (Casas *et al.*, 1997).

In Spanish civil and social law, the family is the primary responsible unit for the welfare of individuals. "Someone in need is expected to look first to their family for support" and the definition of the family changes according to the purposes and dates of different laws. Spain has been characterised as belonging to a family of nations (together with Italy, Greece, and Portugal) where family obligations and mutual help are extended beyond the nuclear family (Millar and Warman, 1996: 47-48). Family obligations often include elder parents, grandparents, grandchildren, sometimes siblings or other second-degree relatives. In Spain, care is mostly provided informally by female relatives through the family network (i.e., by mothers, wives, daughters, grandmothers, sisters, or aunts).[3] This assumption is embedded in social regulations and the functioning of important public services, such as health care, that often presume a high availability of homemakers who are willing to provide help.

The system works because there are still age cohorts which include large numbers of housewives (who are getting older and will need help in the future), and because female unemployment is high in all age groups. Leaving the labour market for mothering is still widespread, especially in economically less developed areas, but not as voluntary and acceptable as before, and leaving the labour market is creating greater economic strain in the family. Among women who have completed a longer education, the opposite trend is happening. Flaquer (1995: 303-307) suggests that more educated women have children when they finally find a steady job that ensures their autonomy. They do not want to become housewives after a long and costly education. The problem is that employers are not willingly to offer them steady jobs.

The participation of women in paid work is far from being compensated for by the participation of men in unpaid family work. The study of time budgets and the inequality between women and men is one of the research topics of the last decade (Instituto de la Mujer, 1990, 1995). Within a context of lack of choice in work organisation and shortage of affordable and adequate caring services, the negotiation and reorganisation of housework is one of the possible strategies used by families, and more specifically by women. The effects of these negotiations depend on

---

[3] Data from a research on informal care for the elderly in 1993 indicate that the average age of informal carers was 51 years and 83% were female relatives (45% daughters). About 75% of the informal carers were not active in the labour market (15% retired, 10% unemployed, 50% housewives). Among those with jobs, 57% of men and 83% of women had part-time jobs (Rodriguez *et al.*, 1995; Casas *et al.*, 1997).

the type of partnership, socio-economic status, education and the amount of paid work performed by women.[4]

Opinion surveys show that the family is highly valued in Spain. During the long and unfinished process of economic restructuring, it has provided a safety network for individuals and especially for young people, of whom a large proportion have been able to invest in a long period of education. This constitutes a factor for future change. Coping strategies in Spain, congruent with cultural values, have been intergenerational solidarity through family networks, low fertility and relatively strong traditional family patterns. In this context of lower levels of individualisation (in comparison with other EU countries), more individualistic patterns like cohabitation or divorce imply higher costs. They are in fact more frequent among social groups with higher education and incomes.

Another major family trend is the delay in the process of gaining residential independence and autonomy by young people and in the formation of new families. Sons and daughters stay in the parental home up to an average age of 28. This means a delay in the setting up of new homes, since opinion surveys show that young people consider 23-24 years a good age to do so.[5] In a comparative study based on labour force surveys in six EU countries, Fernández Cordón has estimated that in Spain 58.6% of working males and 77.1% of non-working males aged 25 to 29 were living with their parents in 1994. In 1986, the rate of 25- to 29-year-olds living with their parents was 53.2% for men and 35.3% for women. The corresponding figures in 1994 are 65.3% and 47.6%, which shows that this trend gained ground between 1986 and 1994 (Fernández Cordón, 1997, Tables 1, 2 and 7).[6] Explanatory factors of this situation which are mentioned by different experts are: the instability of the labour market, low wages, insufficient solvency in the face of expensive housing (with the rent housing market working imperfectly and an inclination towards expensive mortgages), a strong family solidarity and permissiveness

---

[4] Parenthood practices have been studied among young couples with children under 3 years old living in a urban and industrial area in Catalonia. Four main family patterns were identified in the organisation of the total amount of work. About 65% were working-class couples who were organised in a traditional way; although women had high egalitarian values, they had big difficulties in the labour market (women did not have paid work or worked part-time). In the other families, both parents were working full time. About 10% were working class couples. While their roles were flexible in relation to the housework, women emphasized their exclusivity in motherhood. About 10% were high-middle class with higher education. They both participated in child rearing and were flexible on parenthood roles, hardest chores being done by paid home-helpers. Finally about 10% were couples with medium education and higher incomes, as a result of working long hours in the family business. They delegated child rearing more easily to relatives or childcare services, while women usually decided on and organised the household daily life (Brullet, 1998 pp. 461).

[5] EL PAÍS, 28/4/1997, Díaz, M.J., 'Seis de cada diez trabajadores de 25 a 30 años viven todavía en la casa de sus padres' article based on the following mentionned research of Fernandez Cordón.

[6] This trend is also common in Italy and Greece and sharply contrasts with the other countries studied (France, Germany and the UK).

along with the maintenance of traditional family ideals. The main related effects of the postponement of residential independence are the important drop in marriage and in fertility rates, and a more difficult transition to adulthood: "The non-controversial fact is that having a job does not guarantee full independence anymore. The role of the family becomes essential to making socially acceptable the new type of precarious underpaid jobs, which are said to be necessary for economic competitiveness" (Fernández Cordón, 1997: 604). Furthermore, in Spain new families are mainly constituted through marriage, involving a long and costly process of emancipation. Family obligations and co-operation are shaped during these long periods when parents and adult children live together (Flaquer, 1995).

Values and behaviours are changing, but the consequences for the broad group of under 30s (or under 35s) who have not yet decided on their family pattern developments are still unknown. Social expectations and the very unequal distribution both of paid and unpaid work are at the core of social dilemmas that affect these younger generations.

Family policy is very weak in the Spanish welfare state. In 1994, Spanish expenditure on social protection benefits was distributed as follows: old-age pensions (32.6%); sickness (26.0%); invalidity (8.1%); survivors (10%); family (0.8%); unemployment (17.4%) and others (5.1%). Spain had the second lowest rate in the EU on family protection benefits, with 6.8% in 1994 (2.9% in 1980). The EU average of family benefits was 7.7% of total expenditure on social protection benefits in 1994 (9.2% in 1980).[7]

Valiente (1995) explains this low attention to family policy "in terms of the rejection of the family policies formulated during Francisco Franco (1936-1975) authoritarian regime by post-authoritarian policy-makers. Francoist Family policies were both pronatalist and antifeminist. (...) The salience of family programs in Francoist official discourses and propaganda was such that they were remembered by political elites and the population in general long after 1975 (...) most political and social actors have associated all family policies with the symbols displayed and the measures enacted during Franco's regime. They have thus tried to avoid policy-making in the area of the family." (Valiente, 1995: 33). As a result, women's groups that have supported egalitarian family policies in other countries (women's movements, state feminists, women's sections in trade unions), have had different orientations and political priorities in Spain (Valiente, 1996).

---

[7] Data from Internet statistical pages of the Spanish Ministry of Employment and Social Affairs: 'Tabla SEI-16. Gastos en prestaciones de protección social, según función, en términos SEEPROS, en los países de la Unión Europea'.

Recently, the demands on family and care services have been growing. Care services are developing in Spain with difficulties and as a mixture of public and private services. They are thougt to be a major source of employment in the next few years if adequate public measures and support are provided (Jiménez et al, 1998). [8] Social care services are an important source of female employment in the EU countries with higher female activity rates, especially in Northern Europe (Anttonen and Sippilä, 1996). As employment policies are higher on the political agenda than family policies, this may be a way of building a social consensus to devote more resources to care services that are necessary to the reconciliation of family and employment and to gender equality.

3. Work-family arrangements provided by the state: statutory leaves for working parents and public provision of childcare

This section contains a description of the work-family arrangements in principle available to working parents in Spain, i.e., provided by the state either through public funding or through legislation. Statutory provisions are limited and have not been prioritised in the social policy budget distribution until now. Tobío (1994, 1995) suggests that dominant social institutions are scarcely aware of the new problems which are arising and that working women are developing individual strategies which cannot be considered a model for the future, rather they must be seen as temporary solutions. For example, a large number of informal arrangements are now possible because of the availability of a high unemployment rate among women, a high percentage of non-active grandmothers, and because of strategies based on residential proximity.

3.1 Statutory leave arrangements for working parents

Leave arrangements can be defined as regulated forms of absence from normal work to facilitate parenthood and the care of children. They are intended to protect simultaneously, in different proportions, the interests of employees, employers, and society in general. Leave arrangements for working parents consist of maternity leave, paternity leave, parental leave, reduction of working hours, and leave to care for a sick child.

---

[8] A study on proximity services and employment in a medium-sized city in the Metropolitan Area of Barcelona has estimated that domiciliary services (domestic service, childcare or care for the elderly) constitute over 80% of employment creation opportunities. The services with greater development possibilities in relative terms are those related to caring for specific groups -children and elderly people- because of scarce supply and growing demand (Jiménez, 1996).

The regulation of leave arrangements in Spain has been modified several times since 1989 and new changes have been announced. Coverage, duration and related benefits have been improved. There is a trend from an incomplete and subjective protection of maternity towards a more complete and objective protection of family responsibilities (for both women and men). This means that "legislators begin to think more in terms of parental leave and not only of maternal leave" (López, 1996: 313). Regulation is spread between labour and social security legislation, with different laws regulating absences and related benefits.[9] In some cases statutory entitlements are developed in collective and company agreements, mainly in the public sector, but information in this sense is scarce and changeable. Thus, the description below is restricted to statutory provisions.

Usually leave arrangements start with the birth of the child, although maternity leave can be taken in the final period of pregnancy and some labour health regulations protect pregnant women. Women are entitled to change working conditions which may be considered dangerous, and to use related pregnancy' health services during working hours without loss of earnings.

Maternity leave is a 16-week paid leave for working mothers, plus two extra weeks for multiple births. At least six weeks must be taken after the child's birth, while the remaining 10 weeks can be taken before or after the birth. The mother can maximally transfer the last four weeks to the father if this does not endanger her health. The mother receives an earnings-related cash benefit directly from social security at a high level of replacement.[10] To qualify for this benefit, she needs to have contributed to social security at least 180 days in the last previous 5 years and be contributing at the beginning of the leave. During this period the employer has to pay the employer's contribution to social security, which is an amount equivalent more or less to 30% of the maternity benefit.[11] Since 1997, adopted children under

---

[9] Main legal references are: *Texto refundido de la Ley del Estatuto de los Trabajadores, Texto refundido aprobado por Real Decreto Legislativo 1/1995 de 24 de marzo, BOE 29/3/95; Ley General de la Seguridad Social, Texto refundido aprobado por Real Decreto Legislativo1/1994 de 20 de junio, BOE del 29/6/94; Ley 4/1995 de 23 de marzo de regulación del permiso parental y por maternidad.*

[10] This earnings-related benefit is equivalent to 100% of a regulating basis used to calculate different types of benefits from social security. As reference, the sickness benefit provided by the Social Security fund is 75% of this regulating basis, although it is often supplemented by the employer through collective bargaining. In 1998, this regulating basis can vary between 79,280pts (480 ecu) and 322,700pts (1956 ecu) which is the top ceiling. In 1994, maternity was detached from sickness contingency (*incapacidad laboral transitoria*) and the benefit was then improved to 100% of this regulating basis.

[11] The employer's contribution per employee to the social security fund was equivalent to 31.79% of the before mentioned regulating basis in 1997, and will amount to 30.8% of it in 1998. This may vary depending on different types of contracts, some kind of contracts that promote employment requiring a lower contribution from employers.

nine months give the same rights as biological children in respect of maternity leave (Fernández Cordón, 1998: 86).[12]

During the first 9 months after the child's birth, employed mothers are entitled to one hour of absence during the working day without loss of earnings. This period can be divided into two half-hours or be replaced by a half-hour shortening of the normal working day. If both parents are working, the mother can transfer this right to the father. This absence is paid for by the employer.[13]

At the birth of the child, the father is entitled to 2 days of absence, which are paid for by the employer. The father can take the last four weeks (or less) of the maternity leave if the mother transfers this right to him. He can take the first six weeks after the birth to care for the child if the mother dies.

Working parents can take unpaid parental leave to care for a child, from birth up to the third year. When both parents are working, only one of them can make use of this benefit, but they can divide the leave between them. During the first year, the right to keep the working position is guaranteed and it is taken into account as a period of effective contribution to social security. During further periods of leave, this right applies only to a workplace of the same category (and in the same town only for civil servants); hence, the employee has to wait until a vacancy is available. The whole leave period is taken into account for seniority purposes, and the employee on leave is entitled to attend continuing training. If the employer hires as a substitute an unemployed person who has been receiving unemployment benefits at least for a year, the social contribution to be paid for this substitution will be reduced.

Furthermore, there is the possibility of working-time reduction with proportional reduction of earnings. A working parent can reduce his/her working day to between a third and half of its normal duration to care for a child until the 6th year or to look after a disabled child. It is defined as an individual right, so both working parents can use it.

Parents can also take two days' leave to care for a sick child or for other family reasons (serious illness or death of a relative to a second degree of consanguinity or affinity). It is an individual right, paid for by the employer. The employee has to inform the employer

---

[12] Until 1997, working mothers and fathers that adopted a child were entitled to 8 weeks of absence starting from court judgement (of adoption or previous fostering) if the child was under 9 months, and to 6 weeks if the child was over 9 months and under 5 years old. The leave is paid under the same conditions as the maternity leave. When both parents are working, only one of them can make use of this benefit.

[13] This measure is called 'Breast-feeding leave' although it is not useful to that purpose. In Spain there is a very low rate and duration of breastfeeding, in contrast with other European countries. Medical culture and practices are mentioned as the first explanatory reason, working conditions seem to be the second reason.

previously and justify his absence from work. The entitlement is extended to four days if travelling is required.

Improvements in Spanish legislation are counteracted by the precarious character of employment. The legislation was conceived within a context of stable employment contracts for an unlimited period of time, but nowadays a growing proportion of young people are in temporary and unstable employment. In addition to this, the fact that parental leave and the childcare working-time reduction are not paid for is another factor which hinders their use, even among those who have a steady job. Experts suggest that the use of parental leave is quite infrequent. There are no studies which evaluate the impacts of legal improvements, the numbers and characteristics of the users, or the factors associated with take-up rates or with cost and benefits.

The cost of leaves is shared by families (which support those who suffer loss of earnings in non-paid leaves and especially women who face problems in their job career); employers (who pay for short-term leaves, the social contributions of the maternity leave, and replacement cost); and the state which covers the employee's earnings during the maternity leave and benefits related to social security contributions in the case of parental leave.

Maternity leave, although mostly paid for by social security, is perceived by employers as an important cost for the company, and results in dismissals. However, there is no quantitative data about the number of dismissals available. It is significant that in April 1997 the Spanish Equal Opportunities Commission proposed an act to prevent employers from dismissing pregnant women under any circumstance. A pregnant woman can be made redundant if 'objective reasons' are claimed that are not related to her pregnancy, but to developments in the activity of the company. It is easy to take advantage of such a clause, and during 1997 various cases were reported in the press. In the Spanish labour legislation, the protection of motherhood is not guaranteed to the necessary extent in the case of dismissal, the renewal of temporary contracts or an adverse employment selection (Pérez del Río *et al*, 1998).

3.2   Public childcare provision

In Spain, public childcare is developed from an educational perspective rather than as a social care service for families with working parents. Consequently, public services for children over 3 years old are widely developed in connection to educational goals, while public provision (and supervision of private care services) for children under 3 years old is scarce and incomplete.

Paid arrangements for childcare in private homes do exist but are not regulated as a childcare provision.[14]

The Spanish education system was reformed in 1990 through a general education act (*Ley Orgánica General del Sistema Educativo - LOGSE*). School is mandatory for children between 6 and 16 years old. It is free of charge in public centres and subsidised in many private centres. This act also concerns the right to education for children under 6 years old, and regulates early childhood education before compulsory school in two different stages: a first pre-school stage for the under 3s and a second pre-school stage for children from 3 to 6. As education is a decentralised responsibility for 7 regional governments (out of 17), there are regional differences at this pre-school stage.

The second pre-school stage is largely publicly funded and there is a policy commitment to provide schooling for all children in this age group. Parents pay no fees in publicly-managed schools. Schooling rate for children between 3 and 5 years old is about 89.2% in 1996-97.[15] Nearly all 4- and 5-year-olds attend nursery schooling. An increasing number of centres provide meals and care outside of school hours (school hours are approximately between 9.00 to 12.00 and 15.00 to 17.00).

The first pre-school stage (for the under 3-year-olds) is characterised by a low public funding in centres: about 5% in 1993-94 (increasing from 0.8% for children under 12 months to 11% for 2-year-olds). For children under 3 years, the statistics may be less complete and may not include some publicly-funded services provided by local authorities. The LOGSE can be implemented until the year 2002[16] and there is no political commitment to guarantee childcare services at this stage. Services are generally available on a full-day and all-year basis. Public funding is provided by local authorities; regional governments and some services can get support from the Ministry of Social Affairs. Parents pay half or more of the costs in privately managed centres but less than 20% (according to their incomes) in services managed by public authorities (European Commission Network on Childcare, 1996: 53-58).

In the last few years, new types of public services have been set up (at local and regional level) which provide more flexible models of caring for early childhood, in an attempt to meet the specific demands of different families. A few municipalities offer a good service (either

---

[14] "The laws which affect these carers are those of the domestic service, which regulate the status of these people as workers (...) Nevertheless, as in other countries, the domestic service is in Spain de facto an informal sector of the economy where legal measures are hardly applied." (Valiente, 1995, p. 332).

[15] Data from Internet statistical pages of the Spanish Ministry of Education and Culture.

[16] The complete implementation of this part of the LOGSE was stated for the year 2000, but has been postponed until 2002 (RD 173/1998 de 16 de febrero). Private centres are not obliged to register until this date. Thus, data for the under-3 childcare services will be uncomplete until then.

from the point of view of quality or coverage of needs). Publicly managed services are associated with high standards of quality and shortage of services.

Most of centre-based provision is in private centres that are not publicly funded. Families where both parents are employed with a net income below a specified level can benefit from a tax relief (a maximum of 15% of the cost in 1997). Three types of privately managed nursery schools can be described. First, expensive nursery schools with good resources and an educational project, targeted at a minority of families that can afford them. Second, nursery schools attached to co-operatives of professionals with a definite educational project and of good quality. And third, the traditional nurseries (*guarderías*), the most numerous, with no educational project, which may not comply with or operate outside established regulations (Casas, Balaguer *et al.*, 1997). According to the LOGSE, all private centres have to be registered and adapted to the regulated quality standards before the year 2002.

Family day-care (childminding), which constitutes an important part of the public supply of childcare for the under 3s in other EU countries, is thought to be very uncommon and is not regulated in Spain (Karlsson, 1995). Paid care at the child's own home is a bit more common for families who can afford it, either through the regular or the informal economy. There is no public supervision nor data available.

A research exploring needs of families with children under 4 years old (Delgado, 1994: 102-111), based on a national sample of 1200 families, gives some indications as to how children are cared for while parents are at work, and the scope of informal childcare arrangements. In the group of children whose mother had paid work (33% of the whole sample), 30.9% were attending a private childcare centre; 20.5% a public one; 4.1% other centres; and 44.8% did not attend any childcare centre. Among these children, 60.1% spent more than 5 hours per day in the childcare centre; 36.2% between 3 and 5 hours; and 3.7% less than 3 hours per day. Finally, the main carer of the child during the working day was: the working mother (32.9%); the childcare centre (32.2%); a grandmother (18.7%); a paid caregiver (8.6%); another relative (3.0%); the father (2.8%); a grandfather (1.5%); a neighbour (0.3%).

These results indicate that an important proportion of working women still manage to be the main carer of their child during the day, with the help of childcare services. Informal and unpaid care provided by relatives, especially by grandparents, is the third most-used resource (23.2%) besides childcare services (either in centres or at home), and parental care. It has to be noted that 61.5% of these families (57.3% in the whole sample) had grandparents living near the home (ibid.: 66-67).

4.   The development of work-family arrangements at the workplace

Family-friendly policies and practices have not been introduced in Spain under this heading. Some positive action measures for women have been introduced in a few companies, although these measures are mainly related to selection, promotion and continuing training. The social debate in Spain has been focused on the economic crisis and unemployment, labour market flexibility for employers, the professional qualification and competitive strength of companies. Thus the quality of work and working conditions, flexibility in a wider sense that takes into account the employees' needs, are far less developed issues. From the gender equality perspective, the main focus of attention has been placed on the integration into the labour market, women's employment and unemployment, hardly questioning the present organisation of work.

The Instituto de la Mujer, a governmental service responsible for equal opportunity policies between women and men, has promoted a series of studies about women's employment and industrial relations in different sectors and occupations. Many studies have focused on the adaptation of women to company structures and cultures long conceived according to the professional career of men without family caring responsibilities. Caring responsibilities are frequently perceived as an obstacle to women's performance at the workplace and their career opportunities. The relegation of women to the domestic context and to their family duties is a central argument in the discourse on the discrimination of women in the labour market (Instituto de la Mujer, 1990, 1995).

For example, dysfunctional behaviour patterns at work associated with maternity have been observed, like temporary absenteeism related to the upbringing of children in more rigid and difficult working situations. It is a common prejudice, to construct and attribute hypothetical absenteeism, out of all proportion, to the whole cycle of female activity (Martinez Quintana, 1991). Female absenteeism is a topic of discussion, and different researches study this subject trying to identify cultural stereotypes and to quantify realities.

On the other hand, results of research on collective bargaining (Pérez del Río *et al.*, 1993, 1996) highlight the lack of attention given to women's working conditions, protection during pregnancy, maternity leave or leave to care for sick children, in contrast with the importance given to matters related to business and trade union representation, or to other social security issues. One explanation for this is the rare presence of women at the negotiating table. In trade unions, there is a problem with the representation of interests of workers who are under greater work-family strain, as they do not usually devote time to this kind of activity.

4.1   The 'latitude for adjustment' in companies in Spain

The family-friendliness of companies can be understood in different ways and varies according to national contexts. Holt and Thaulow define as a family-friendly workplace "one which in practice grants its employees plenty of scope for adjusting their work according to their various family needs" and "latitude for adjustment between working life and family life as the sum of the formal and informal flexibility" available at the workplace. To satisfy family needs means not only providing practical and emotional care, which is traditionally a more female-oriented responsibility, but also providing economic support. This second form of family friendliness is traditionally more male-oriented. It means adequate pay, security in employment or the possibility of additional income, a practice which in Spain is quite frequently used by men working paid overtime (Holt and Thaulow, 1996).[17]

The informal dimension is important in Spain, thus the use of the concept "latitude for adjustment" is fruitful. Another useful tool is the concept of a sense of entitlement defined "as a set of beliefs and feelings that enable individuals to voice and make visible their needs to modify traditional structures in order to reconcile work and family demands" (Lewis, 1996). The subjective sense of entitlement affects the use, widening or narrowing, of the available latitude to adjust work to family needs. Thus the economic context in Spain and a male-oriented work culture tend to limit the use of formal flexibility; on the other hand, there is a great number of informal work-family arrangements that are not quantified.

In Spain, as in other countries, while the public sector tends to develop formal opportunities that are offered through law and public provision, most private companies tend to limit them. So, working in the public or the private sector is a relevant variable. In the public sector most workers are civil servants or permanent employees, trade unions are strong, the sense of entitlement is high and bureaucracy proceedings and labour rights are respected. Some public institutions have developed social benefits that are useful as work-family arrangements. However, in institutions and companies in the public sector new trends have also appeared, such as the use of temporary employees and self-employed workers, and management oriented towards improving economic results, which may reduce this family friendliness.

In private companies, there is a difference depending on the size and nationality of the firm. Large and multinational companies are expected to have better developed personnel

---

[17] Holt and Thaulow suggest that companies in countries where welfare state services are less well developed and where women are still seeking full integration into the labour market are more likely to offer economic support and provision of services that enable parents to concentrate on work. In countries where women have achieved a central position either in the labour market or in the political system, where childcare is publicly guaranteed, the present trend is to grant employees flexibility and autonomy to fulfil family responsibilities. Flexibility can be offered to employees at no direct cost but affects the organisation of work and the workplace culture (*ibidem*).

policies and social benefits. But the company's economic development and the sector of activity in which it operates are also very important variables. There is a general trend to restrict or reduce personnel in order to increase productivity. In some cases, the effects of this are work strain and consequently more constraints upon work-family arrangements, as it is more difficult to have one's work covered by someone else. For example, it is quite a common practice for a worker on maternity leave not to be replaced, even if her wage is paid during this period by social security. These kinds of solutions create strain in the work team and the perception that professional duties are not being fulfilled.

The replacement of the person on leave is an important issue, strains at the workplace and overburdened colleagues are to be avoided. The public sector and large companies seem to reorganise their work and hire substitutes more easily. In the smaller companies, informal agreements and reorganisations are helpful. The possibility of anticipating and discussing these situations in confidence contributes to finding the best solutions. Nevertheless, results from a qualitative research with in-depth interviews of female employees and personnel managers in 20 Spanish companies (Crespo *et al.*, 1997)[18] have shown quite a lot of fear and distrust of women working in private sector companies who went on maternity leave or used the breastfeeding leave in contrast to women with a steady job in the public sector. The following translated fragments from these qualitative interviews illustrate this.

'With the first child, they asked me not to take the breastfeeding leave. However, this half an hour leave was sacred to me. It makes a difference to either reach the nursery at 6 or at nearly 7 in the evening. Of course I took my leave. As result, first I lost my position and finally I lost my job (...) Now I have a temporary job and I would like to have another child. But I can't. I can't. If I get pregnant they would sack me (...) Of course they would tell me that I am very good in my work and that I will be up in the list, and thus in a year I could come back... but meanwhile you are completely defenceless.' (Qualified technician in a private company, woman, 36 years, 2 small children, main provider of her family income)

'An employee informed me that she was pregnant after she had been promoted through a formal, open competition. Her boss reacted to the news very badly, very violently. He told her that she should have warned him before taking part in the competition. Of course she would not have won the post then.'
(Personnel manager in a public sector company, man, 38, 2 small children)

---

[18] See foot-note 1.

'Problems? I don't know. For example when I came back from maternity leave, I was relegated to a lower position. Why? I don't know. I am still waiting for somebody to explain it to me.'
(Qualified technician in a private company, woman, 32, 2 small children)

'When I gave birth, I made a terrible mistake which I will never repeat. After two weeks I went back to work. It was awful, after a month I was so depressed and anxious that the same person who previously had asked me if I would be able to continue with my job told me to go home and rest.' (Economist in a private company, woman, 37, one small child)

'When I told my new boss that I was pregnant he congratulated me. I felt very comfortable all the time (...) Now after the maternity leave I have an hour less per day because of breastfeeding, I have to be at work from 9 till 2, the remaining hours I have for myself, so I can arrange things better for my work' (Clerical worker, civil servant in a large public institution, 32, one small child)

The qualitative research shows various conditions that influence the use of leave arrangements. First, the mother's qualification and expectations for her professional career. Mothers in the qualitative research that had not taken the full maternity leave were among the better qualified women in leading positions. A second condition is the mother's employment contract. Under a temporary contract, job protection provided by the law is frail, which makes women decide to shorten their maternity leave or to delay maternity until they have a steady position. Thirdly, the characteristics of the company (branch, economic situation, workplace culture) determine replacement policies and this in turn influences take-up rates. Finally, the paid or unpaid character of the leave is of importance. As parental leave and the reduction of working hours is unpaid, several respondents said that it was difficult for them to afford these solutions.

Childcare facilities provided by the employers are unusual. It is easier to find examples of employer's involvement in subsidising places than of employer's childcare provision at the workplace. In the public sector, there are examples of financial help for working parents with children established as social benefits in special collective agreements. There are very few examples of nurseries at the workplace. In the past, there were some, for example, in hospitals for nurses, but they have disappeared because of their cost for employers. Families usually prefer services near the child's home. A personnel manager in a large public institution suggested that including this kind of social benefit could be an interesting strategy in the collective bargaining, as it is relatively cheap and easier to agree on than direct wage increases, which are more restricted in the public sector nowadays. Nevertheless, this kind of agreement also requires the support of the trade unions.

'We have developed a social action plan that includes monetary help towards people with children under 3 years (...)But this subject was not a priority for the trade unions and then it was postponed (...) They know that money invested in this will not be available for other purposes they ask for (...) Maybe next year.' (Personnel manager in a large public institution, man, 47, 2 children)

Examples of banking hours or flexible working hours were found in the qualitative interviews. Often the flexibility is informal, or it is based upon individual agreements. On the other hand, flexibility appears to be related to overtime, either paid or unpaid. In Spain overtime is an important issue, which is regulated by law and collective agreements. Unpaid overtime appears in the qualitative interviews with women, as something really difficult to avoid as it is associated with a positive commitment.

In general, work-family arrangements are perceived as a women's affair and as social benefits, rather than as social rights for both parents. Due to the economic trend and labour market conditions, there is a low sense of entitlement, so that people do not ask for this kind of arrangement. Women feel that they have to demonstrate their value, show that they are as efficient as men at all times, and are not guilty of absenteeism. In most private companies, personnel policies are not planned in the long term. The public sector has a different perspective in that respect but is now under budgetary restrictions. There is a common assumption that reducing working hours, or taking parenthood leaves, is a cost for the company, and hinders efficiency and thus the development of the professional career, if it is not a first stop towards dismissal. 'You have to be there'; absence can be understood as evidence of low commitment (Crespo, Artal, *et al.*, 1997).

4.2   Positive action programmes in companies in Spain

In recent years, some positive action programmes to support equal opportunities between women and men have been developed in companies and in trade unions, and promoted by governmental Equal Opportunities services. The programmes Optima and Luna-Now are two of the most significant examples. As an indicator of the Spanish situation, it is interesting to know what happens with these pilot programmes, what measures are more likely to be implemented at the company level, and to what extent the issue of work-family arrangements is introduced in positive action programmes in private companies.

Optima was launched in 1995 by different governmental Equal Opportunities services (Instituto de la Mujer at the national level, Emakunde of the Basque Government and the Instituto Andaluz de la Mujer). The aim was to introduce equal opportunities between men and women in human resources management as a way of improving efficiency and results. In 1997, after a diagnostic study and the approval of a positive action plan at the company level, nine companies obtained the public recognition that they contributed to equal opportunities. Seven of them are large private companies in different industrial sectors (food, chemistry, technology and health services), one is a medium-sized consultancy company, and the last one is a large public company that produces tobacco (Instituto de la Mujer et al, 1996 and 1997).

The public tobacco company is the one that has most clearly developed measures including work-family arrangements, in the framework of a continuing training programme directed at low qualified women with family care responsibilities, for whom it was difficult to participate in company training schemes. As continuing training was offered outside of working hours, and this could not be changed, childcare facilities at home were offered to a group of 158 women in order to allow them to attend the training activities (Tubert and García, 1996).

Luna-Now was launched in 1996 by a major Spanish trade union, Comisiones Obreras (CC.OO.). Five private and five public firms took part in the first stage of this programme (most of them large companies, with at least 30% female personnel). The agreement between the companies and the trade union included a diagnostic analysis and the implementation of an action plan, while the trade union provided training in equal opportunities to the employees' representatives.

After the diagnosis made in these companies, some results were highlighted. The lack of awareness about the indirect discrimination of working women, and that no demands are made to overcome it, is a major problem for the implementation of positive action.[19] Equality is often understood as women doing the same as men. More professional human resources management and formal procedures contribute to overcoming discrimination. Lower and middle management are identified as an obstacle when traditional backgrounds determine their attitude towards women; thus, maternity and family responsibilities are used as a reason for not promoting them. Situations of discrimination affect the motivation, expectations, and

---

[19] Some examples of indirect discrimination are: traditions and values that affect the choices of managers when hiring and promoting people; the absence of training for the jobs women do, the obsolescence of job descriptions and task evaluations that affect wages.

commitment of women working in production and clerical work. They are sceptical about their possibilities, and the lack of trust and motivation reinforces the stereotypes. In contrast, young highly qualified women who are entering staff tasks in most companies show high expectations and commitment. 'They were ready to make any kind of effort necessary to make a good career, including sacrifices in their personal and family life such as not taking maternity leave. Time was the major issue for these women' (Méndez-Vigo, 1997).

Both programmes include the issue of reconciliation in the catalogue of objectives and positive actions proposed. Information already available indicates that the measures actually developed in the companies are focused on the selection, promotion and continuing training of women. The kinds of proposals that spontaneously appear to reconcile working hours and family care are developed with a view to facilitating women's attendance at the workplace and training activities (some childcare facilities, flexibility in working hours to adjust family needs at more qualified levels) rather than to spending more time at home (through working time reductions, leave arrangements, facilities to work at home).

In some European countries with a more consolidated position of women in the labour market, positive action for women has evolved towards family-friendly programmes oriented towards providing a better balance between working time and family time for women and men. Time appears to be an important restriction in special periods of family life, such as young parenthood or long-term illness. This is not the case in Spain, where the focus is still on promoting the entry of women in the labour market, and the main deficiencies are in paid work and income maintenance.

Finally, Spanish data reveal a great diversity between different regions, rural or urban contexts, as for example the Madrid and Barcelona metropolitan areas. This means that the needs of young families also vary. Mothers and some fathers in urban contexts, with a more consolidated position in the labour market, and under more time pressure, are facing new priorities and moving towards new demands for flexibility to adjust family and other personal requirements.

'It is not easy to say as a working father 'I'm leaving earlier because the baby-sitter has to go'. Sometimes when I do the answer is 'Oh, you are the baby-sitter of your daughters!' instead of 'you are the father of your daughters'. I have heard this so many times. Nobody would say it to a mother (...) Yes I take some flexibility to care for my daughters, to attend meetings at school, to pick them up if they get sick.' (Personnel manager in a public company, man, 38, 2 small children)

There are diversified needs, and policies are just starting to provide more diversified work-family arrangements. If economic strains decrease, this movement will be become more visible.

5.   Conclusions

The changes that have taken place in other countries over a long period of time have taken less than twenty years in Spain, in a context of economic crisis, restructuring and globalisation. Spanish women are still moving out of the home and the private sphere. Women are evincing a strong orientation towards education and labour market participation, but they still need to gain economic independence and they need more public consideration, both in the labour market and the political sphere.

Social care services are not extended enough. This affects women's professional opportunities in two ways: personal constraints and fewer jobs available in the public sector, which in other countries has provided good family-friendly opportunities. Innovative social legislation has been developed with scarce economic resources. The lack of support schemes, especially acute in early parenthood, upsets the balance between work and family life. Childcare services vary quite a lot depending on regional and local contexts, but in general terms, childcare for children under 3 remains an unsolved problem.

The combination of family caring responsibilities and paid work is mainly perceived as a woman's affair. Men, particularly fathers, are perceived as the main providers of the family's income, even if this is not always the case because of unemployment or the diversification of family situations. The ways in which young mothers manage to combine paid work and family care depend very much on their employment and family situation, and on the availability of informal help through the family network.

Women are competing for equal opportunities in the labour market, without questioning the dominant patterns. As arrangements to meet family needs are felt to be private matters, employees lack a sense of entitlement to develop strategies to reconcile working time and family time, even to make use of the opportunities provided by current laws. As in other countries, whereas the public sector tends to develop formal opportunities, most private companies tend to restrict them. In precarious working conditions, such as temporary employment, such basic rights as job continuity are not guaranteed in the event of pregnancy.

Young women face a dilemma between work and motherhood. Maternity leave is perceived as a problem, while the use of unpaid parental leave or working time reduction to care for a child is rare. Maternity leave is something that a working mother bargains about if she has a temporary job or if she wants to maintain her career expectations. Companies are demanding more and more flexibility and availability, but until now it has not been easy to use this flexibility to the benefit of employees.

High and long-term unemployment has exerted an enormous pressure both on working conditions and on family life. In order to provide for family needs, families have focused on maintaining employment and family incomes, which often requires more than one income. A large proportion of the current jobs for young people do not provide economic autonomy and a safe start for a new family. Thus, a major strategy in Spain has been the family adjustment to these labour market imbalances. Young adult people stay longer in the parental home while prolonging education and women postpone having children and have fewer children. All this is combined with a higher appreciation of and expectations for the family, which acts as the main welfare network.

This situation may be changing as the economic situation is improving and the need for more quality and security in work is gaining more consensus. A shift towards more stable jobs and more reliable labour commitments would provide more security and confidence to make long-term family decisions, and also more room to focus on the quality of work.

WORK-FAMILY ARRANGEMENTS IN SPAIN

I. Flexible working patterns	II. Parental leave arrangements
- Increasing part-time work (in 1995 17% of women and 3% of men) mainly through employer demand in low qualified service jobs. Recently new trends point to more opportunities of part-time work in qualified jobs. - Traditional patterns of work in the home and the informal economy that provide flexible opportunities in a framework of precariousness (low payment, lack of social protection and public control) - In qualitative research flexibility appears associated with long working hours and unpaid extra hours in order to meet production requirements.	- During pregnancy (possible changes in working conditions, right to attend health services during working hours) - Maternity leave (16 weeks paid by social security, a minimum of 6 weeks after the birth, the last 4 weeks can be taken by the father) - Paternity leave (2 days paid by the employer) - Breast-feeding leave (1 hour per day until the child is 9 months old, paid by the employer) - Unpaid parental leave until the 3rd year of the child. During the first 12 months the position is guaranteed. - Unpaid childcare working-time reduction (between half and a third of full-time) until the child is 6 years old or for a disabled child. Proportional reduction of earnings. Individual entitlement. - Leave to care for a sick child (2 days paid by the employer, 4 in the case of need of travelling). Individual entitlement.
III. Childcare provisions	**IV. Supportive measures**
- Low publicly-funded provision in the first pre-school stage (under 3): about 5% in 1993-94 (0.8% for children under 12 months to 11% for 2-year-olds). Most of centre-based provision is in private centres that are not publicly funded. - High publicly-funded provision in the second pre-school stage (3-6 years): about 84% in 1993-94, nearly all 4- and 5-year-old children. An increasing number of centres provide meals and care outside school hours. - Family day care is uncommon and not regulated in Spain. Individual care at the child's home is more common for families who can afford it, either through the regular or the informal economy. There is no public supervision. - Important role of grand-parents in the care of grand-children when both parents work.	In the last years some positive action programmes to support equal opportunities between women and men have been developed in companies and in trade unions, and promoted by governmental Equal Opportunities services. The issue of reconciliation between work and family needs appears in the catalogue of objectives and positive actions measures proposed through these programmes. Measures developed, however, are mainly connected to selection, continuing training and promotion of women.

Types of work-family arrangements in Spain, see Chapter 1, Figure 1.

References

Anttonen, A. and J. Sipilä (1996), European Social Care Services: is it possible to identify models?, *Journal of European Social Policy, 6(2),* 87-100.

Brullet, Cristina (1998), Relacions de gènere i dinàmiques familiars a Catalunya. In: Giner *et al.* (ed.). Barcelona: *La Societat Catalana.*

Casas, Ferran (dir.), Irene Balaguer, Teresa Crespo, Anna Escobedo and Maria Gómez (1997), *Spanish report on recent research literature on reconciliation of work and family life and the quality of care services*, (unpublished report). Barcelona: CIREM Foundation.

Consejo Económico y Social (1996), El trabajo a tiempo parcial, *Colección Informes* Número 4/1996. Madrid: Departamento de Publicaciones del Consejo Económico y Social.

Consejo Económico y Social (1997), Memoria sobre la situación socioeconómica y laboral de España en 1996, *Colección Memorias* Número 4. Madrid: Departamento de Publicaciones del Consejo Económico y Social.

Crespo, Teresa (dir.), Carmen Artal, Anna Escobedo and Gemma Tubert (1997) *La voz de la mujer trabajadora en España,* (unpublished report). Barcelona: CIREM Foundation.

Delgado, Ana M., Teresa Gutiérrez del Alamo and Francesca Majó (1994), *Los servicios de atención a la primera infancia: Necesidades del grupo familiar.* Madrid: Ministerio de Asuntos Sociales.

Deven, Fred, Sheila Inglis, Peter Moss and Pat Petrie (1998), *State of the Art Review on the Reconciliation of Work and Family Life for Men and Women and the Quality of Care Services.* Final Report for the European Commission Equal Opportunities Unit (DGV). London: British Department of Education and Employment.

Escribà, Vicenta, Conxita Colomer, R. Mas and R. Grifol (1994), Working conditions and the decision to breastfeed in Spain. In: *Health Promotion International*, 9, pp. 251-258.

European Commission Network on Childcare and other Measures to Reconcile Employment and Family Responsibilities (1996), *A Review of Services for Young Children in the European Union*, European Commission. Brussels: DGV-Equal Opportunities Unit for Women and Men.

Fernández Cordón, Juan Antonio (1997), Youth residencial independence and autonomy: A comparative study. In: *Journal of Family Issues,* Vol. 18 No.6, pp.576-607 .

Fernández Cordón, Juan Antonio (1998), 'Spain' in European Observatory on National Family Policies (1998) In: *Developments in National Family Policies in 1996,* Employment and Social Affairs. Brussels: Commission of the European Communities.

Flaquer, Lluís (1995), El modelo de familia española en el contexto europeo, pp. 289-312. In: Moreno, Luis y Sarasa, Sebastián (comp), *El Estado del Bienestar en la Europa del Sur*. Madrid: CSIC-IESA.

García, Cristina and Gemma Tubert (1996), Equal opportunity in the workplace. The Optima programme', in CIREMINFORMA, *Newsletter of the Centre for European Initiatives and Research in the Mediterranean*, num. 11, April 1996, Barcelona: CIREM Foundation

Holt, Helle and Ivan Thaulow (1996), Formal and Informal Flexibility in the Workplace. In: Suzan Lewis and Jeremy Lewis (Eds.) (1996), *The Work-Family Challenge. Rethinking Employment*. London: SAGE Publications.

Instituto de la Mujer (1990), *Síntesis de Estudios y Encuestas del Instituto de la Mujer 1984-1990*. Madrid: Ministerio de Asuntos Sociales.

Instituto de la Mujer (1995), *Síntesis de Estudios y Encuestas del Instituto de la Mujer 1990-1994*, Madrid: Ministerio de Asuntos Sociales.

Instituto de la Mujer, Emakunde, Instituto Andaluz de la Mujer and Fundació CIREM (1995), *Catálogo de acciones positivas. Programa OPTIMA*, Ministerio de Asuntos Sociales.

Instituto de la Mujer, Emakunde, Instituto Andaluz de la Mujer, *Boletín Informativo del Programa Optima*, num. 1, 2 (1996) and 3 (1997).

Jiménez, Eduard (1996), Job creation, local labour market segmentation and proximity services. A practical case: Sant Feliu de Llobregat (Catalonia), paper presented at the *European Symposium of Labour Markets Developments, Warwick 16-18 May 1996*, Barcelona: CIREM Foundation.

Jiménez, Eduard, Fernando Barreiro and Joan Eugeni Sánchez (1998), *Los nuevos yacimientos de empleo. Los retos de la creación de empleo desde el territorio*. Barcelona: CIREM Foundation.

Karlsson, Malene (1995), *Family Day Care in Europe*. Brussels: European Commission, DGV- Equal Opportunities Unit for Women and Men (V/5187/95-EN).

Lewis, Suzan (1996), Sense of Entitlement, Family-friendly Policies and Gender. In: Holt, Helle and Thaulow, Ivan (eds.) *Reconciling Work and Family Life. An International Perspective on the Role of Companies*. Copenhagen: The Danish Institute of Social Research.

López, Isabel (1996), Evolución en España de la normativa sobre los permisos parentales. *Infancia y Sociedad. Revista de Estudios*, 34-35, pp. 313-320.

Martínez Quintana and Maria Violante (1992), *Mujer, trabajo y maternidad. Problemas y alternativas de las mujeres que trabajan*. Serie Estudios n°30. Madrid: Instituto de la Mujer, Ministerio de Asuntos Sociales.

Méndez-Vigo, Marisa (1997), Positive actions in European companies: Spain. Paper presented at a *European meeting 'Integration of equality in Enterprises' Athens, June 1997.* Barcelona: ACTIVA.

Millar, Jane and Andrea Warman (Eds.) (1995), Defining Family Obligations in Europe, *Bath Social Policy Papers,* No. 23. Bath: University of Bath, Centre for the Analysis of Social Policy.

Pérez del Río, Teresa, Fernanda Fernández and Salvador Del Rey (1993), *Discriminación e igualdad en la negociación colectiva*, Serie Estudios n°36. Madrid: Instituto de la Mujer.

Pérez del Río, Teresa, Maria Amparo Ballester and Maria Pons *et al.* (1998) *La discriminación por razón de sexo en la negociación colectiva (1996-97).* Serie Estudios. Madrid: Instituto de la Mujer.

Rodriguez, P., T. Sancho, M. Alvaro, and M. Justel (1996) *Las personas mayores en España. Perfiles. Reciprocidad familiar.* IMSERSO. Madrid: Ministerio de Trabajo y Asuntos Sociales.

Tobío Soler, Constanza (1994), The family-employment relationship in Spain, pp. 41-47 in Hantrais, L. and M. T. Letablier (Eds.) *The Family-Employment Relationship*, Cross-National Research Papers. Loughborough: Loughborough University.

Tobío Soler, Constanza (1995), Changing gender roles and family-employment strategies in Spain, pp. 79-85. In L. Hantrais and M.T. Letablier (Eds.) *The Family in Social Policy and Family Policy*, Cross-National Research Papers. Loughborough: Loughborough University.

Torns, Teresa (1997), Part-time employment, a new feature on the Spanish labour market. In: European Industrial Relations Observatory On-line, European Foundation for the Improvement of Living and Working Conditions. Http://eiro.eurofound.ie.

Valiente, Celia (1995), Family Obligations in Spain. In: Jane Millar and Andrea Warman (eds.) *Defining Family Obligations in Europe*, Bath Social Policy Papers No. 23, Centre for the Analysis of Social Policy. Bath: University of Bath.

Valiente, Celia (1996), The Rejection of Authoritarian Policy Legacies: Family Policy in Spain (1975-1995). *South European Society & Politics,* Vol.1, No. 1, pp. 95-114. London: Frank Cass.

WORK-FAMILY ARRANGEMENTS IN SWEDEN: FAMILY STRATEGIES

Elisabet Näsman

1.   Introduction

For some considerable time now, Sweden has attracted attention due to the unique combination that there is a very high degree of labour force participation amongst women, high fertility rates, extensive public childcare and a growing proportion of fathers taking parental leave in order to care for their new-born babies. The problems of reconciling work and family in Sweden are, to a large extent, treated as public rather than private issues (Moen, 1989). Swedish public policies have the explicit aim of enabling women to combine work and motherhood, to increase equality between men and women in everyday life, and to support children's development. Public policy measures and workplace options have become part of a family's strategies for negotiating and organising the household and its interfaces with public services and the labour market.

   Today, Sweden, like many other European countries, struggles with unemployment and financial problems. The problems in the labour market and cuts in public spending have, however, left the ways in which Swedish families manage their everyday life fundamentally unchanged. After a short historical introduction, this chapter will analyse how dual-income families reconcile work and family life. How do men and women use existing work-family policies? Do higher unemployment rates affect take-up rates? And what is the role of workplace conditions in family strategies used to reconcile work and caring responsibilities?

   The next section provides a historical overview of public work-family policies in Sweden. Section 3 addresses the question as to how fathers and mothers use existing facilities. There are major differences in the male and female patterns of parental leave. One of the factors which explains the different patterns are conditions and practices in the workplace. Section 4 discusses workplace conditions and work-family arrangements.

2.   From the nuclear family to the dual-earner family

At the beginning of this century, the legislation on working hours often discriminated by gender with the official purpose of protecting women. An example of this kind of legislation is the law of 1909 prohibiting women from working at night. During the first decades of the century, these laws were gradually replaced by gender-neutral protective legislation. The first work-family policies also emerged in this period. For instance, at the beginning of the century, a law was passed which gave mothers the right to take a break during the working day to breastfeed their child. The first act on Working Hours was realised in 1919 after pressure from the labour movement and regulated a 48-hour working week. One of the main reasons for the demand for an 8-hour working day and a 48-hour working week was to make more time available for family life. In 1937, employers were not allowed to dismiss female employees because of marriage or pregnancy. The law was replaced by a gender-neutral law in 1945, and by the Employment Security Act in 1974.

Paid leave was realised in 1937 and additional options for mothers were contained in a law passed in 1955. This law was further developed in 1974 whose most important change was the introduction of a common right to leave of absence for both parents, rather than maternity leave for the mother only, as well as gender-specific options; i.e. parental leave. Parental insurance was also introduced in 1974 and has been changed several times since then, which mainly involved increases in the number of benefit days, and changes up and down the scale of benefit levels. In 1979, a law was passed giving parents with pre-school age children the right to reduce their working day to three-quarters of a full-time job and the right to full-time leave until the child is 18 months old. This legislation was further developed several times during the 1980s and 1990s.

In 1971, a separate taxation for husband and spouse was introduced. In 1979, a law was introduced prohibiting discrimination by gender in the labour market, the Equal Opportunities Act. In its preparatory stage, the law stated that for men equality would lead to the right to take responsibility for their children under the same conditions as women, and that men would have the same responsibility for the home and an equal right to children and to an emotional life (The government bill on the Equal Opportunities Act 78/79).

Sweden is also known for its substantial system of public childcare. A resolution from the Swedish Parliament in 1985 specified that all children over the age of 18 months should be entitled to attend public day-care. Publicly subsidised childcare services have been greatly extended since the 1960s. Nowadays, a majority of Swedish children aged 1-6 is enrolled in public day-care.

These are the main legislative changes that form the background to the present situation and the developments mirror the changes in public policy and ideals. One of the objectives of Swedish family policy since the 1930s has been to create equality between men and women. However, up to the 1960s political action was dominated by a family ideal based on complementary gender roles of equal value, rather than equal roles. A woman's rights in marriage were based on her responsibility for looking after the home and children, whereas the man's rights stemmed from his responsibility for supporting the family. In the 1960s, the debate on sex roles gathered impetus, and new ideals emerged. Marriage as an institution was increasingly equated with other forms of cohabitation. In a process of individualisation, men and women were increasingly placed on an equal footing as citizens, employees, partners and parents. This has had a tremendous impact not only on the family but also on the labour force.

In addition, changes took place in the labour market in the 1960s and the 1970s. Demand for labour rose sharply, especially in the public sector, and the labour reserve consisting of unemployed or immigrant labour did not sufficiently meet the demand. This labour shortage was exacerbated by the fact that general working hours were shortened during this period. Women were in demand on the labour market and being gainfully employed was increasingly worth their while. Part-time jobs were favoured since working 20 hours per week or longer, proportionately entitled women to the same social benefits as did full-time work. Furthermore, marginal tax went down for part-time employees in the 1970s, while it rose for full-time employees.

Accordingly, the proportion of women in the labour force has been growing throughout the post-war era, thereby increasing the number of gainfully employed people and altering the composition of the labour force. Through part-time work, women's gainful employment rate increased. Today, women constitute almost half the labour force (48% in 1996) compared to one-third in 1960. The participation of Swedish women in the labour force is very high, even among those with pre-school age children. The fact that women have entered the labour market by means of part-time work meant that their share of total working hours did not increase as fast. However, since the beginning of the 1980s the increase in part-time work has stagnated and the number of 'short' part-time jobs has decreased. In addition, women started to take part in the labour force without interruptions for childbearing and childcare. Parental leave followed by part-time work meant that there was a considerable drop in the proportion of women who left the labour market after childbirth. In 1984 the proportion was less than 6%.

From the end of the 1980s, the fact that men used the parental leave system became a major issue. Unions as well as government organisations have campaigned in various ways to stimulate fathers to use parental leave. Development programs have targeted companies in order to stimulate an increase in the proportion of fathers that take parental leave and research has uncovered hindrances in the workplaces. Nowadays, women, in terms of gainful employment and working hours, have approached the male employment pattern and men, in terms of absenteeism in connection with the care of young children, have approached the pattern of women, although the change in the male employment pattern is much smaller than in the female pattern (see section 3).

In Sweden, three-generation families are rare. When elderly people are in need of daily care, this is mostly given in the form of some public service at home or in some kind of institution. Relatives are often involved to some extent, but mostly in terms of social and emotional support rather than practical care. Accordingly, Swedish middle-aged women are not under the pressure of the so called sandwich-situation to the same extent as in other countries, where demands are put on her simultaneously by children and elderly parents. There is, however, as part of the social insurance scheme, a legislation that gives an employee the right to leave of absence with a compensation for loss of income, if he/she is needed as a carer by someone who is seriously ill. The person who has fallen ill may give someone of his/her own choice, not necessarily a relative, this right for 60 days per year, and 80 per cent of the loss of income is compensated for. All employees have this right irrespective of the duration of the employment.

Nowadays, young people start their own household earlier than they used to in the 1960s. Young couples start cohabiting without marrying and without having children. To finish their education and find employment is prioritized before childbearing for both men and women (Hörnqvist, 1994). To a large extent, Swedish women and men control their childbearing, by using easily available techniques of contraception. The total fertility rate declined in Sweden during the late 1970s, rose again during the mid 1980s, reaching replacement level in 1990 (2.1), and has since dropped to 1.5 in 1997 (Sundgren Grinups, 1998). This pattern is mainly the result of postponement of the first child until a later age. There is no sign in Sweden of an increase in the number of people who opt for childlessness. Furthermore, most women who have one child also have a second and many of them, especially the highly educated women, have a third (Martinell, 1992). Families who have only one child are not becoming more common. Births are closely spaced in time and there has been a tendency to speed up childbearing. This, according to Hoem (1993), is closely linked to the development of a "speed premium" in the parental insurance scheme. A parent may retain the level of income compensation, paid after one birth, during parental leave, for the next birth, if the interval between the two births does not exceed thirty months, even if the parent has a drop in wages in between the births, due to part-time work for instance. Close spacing of births may also mean that the woman stays away from her workplace for several years, but still keeps her employment, as she is protected by job security legislation. The parental leave system is a crucial part of family strategies in balancing work and caring responsibilities. The next section will present the system in more detail.

3.   Fathers and mothers taking parental leave

3.1   Parental leave

The parental leave legislation in Sweden includes a number of different options for mothers and fathers. It is, however, a support system to parents that is closely related to employment, in terms of entitlements and benefit levels, and thus produces incentives[1] for employment, long working hours and career-making before childbearing. The parental leave scheme consists of pregnancy leave, paternity leave and parental leave allowance. Presently, the situation is as follows.

During her pregnancy, a woman is entitled to be transferred to other duties if she has a physically heavy job that she cannot do because of her pregnancy, or has been suspended from work under the Work Environment Act. If the employer cannot transfer her, she can draw pregnancy allowance in two cases: firstly, when her capacity for work is reduced by at least one quarter on account of the pregnancy and she has a physically heavy job. Or secondly, when she has a job that she cannot do because of risks in the work environment. Pregnancy allowance may be drawn for a maximum of 50 days but no earlier than 60 days before the expected date of birth. Pregnancy allowance cannot be drawn during the last 10 days before the expected date of birth. Pregnancy allowance can be drawn on a full-time or part-time basis. Loss of income is compensated for 80 percent.

Fathers are entitled to 10 days leave on a temporary parental allowance following a child's birth or adoption. These "daddy days" are the greatest success in the parental leave system, and currently 80% of lost income is compensated for. These benefit days may be drawn at the same time as the mother is on parental leave, but have to be drawn within the first 60 days of the child's life. This is the option most often used among fathers. The peak was in 1989. Since then, the proportion of fathers who draw this kind of cash benefit has dropped steadily, but it is still at a high level. In 1995, 81% of fathers made use of this option. On average the number of "daddy days" drawn has also decreased somewhat since the beginning of the

---

[1] Parents are biological parents, parents who plan to adopt or have adopted the child, foster parents, other legal guardians or someone who cohabits with the parent and with whom the parent is or has been married or has or has had a child of their own. A parent has to take care of the child during parental leave. A person who is the sole legal guardian is entitled to all the days and so is one of the parents if the other is not entitled to any parental allowance or, due to sickness or handicap, is unable to take care of the child during the period under which parental allowance may be drawn. In order to get an allowance, however, they have to be registered for an income for 6 months. In all the allowances mentioned here there is a ceiling level for the compensation allowed which presently is 273000SEK.

1990s, when the number of days drawn was close to 10, but it is still more than 9 on average (RFV, 1996; 1998). If those decreases are related to the increased unemployment rates, the effect is not very strong.

Diagram 1   Daddy days. Fathers who have drawn cash benefit for daddy days, annually relative to number of children born 1986-1995.

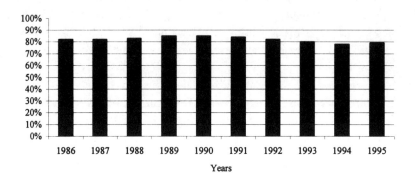

Source: RFV 1996

When a child is born or adopted, parents may draw a parental allowance in order to care for the child for 450 days.[2] The days of parental allowance are divided equally between the parents. A total of 420 days can be transferred to the other parent. The mother can start drawing the parental allowance 60 days before the expected date of birth. A parent may draw full, three-quarters, half or quarter of their parental allowance.

The allowance covers 80% of wages during the first 360 days and the minimum benefit 60 Swedish crowns for a further 90 days.[3] The 450 benefit days may be drawn at any time until the child is 8 years old or has completed the first class of school. The parents cannot be on leave together except when multiple births are involved.[4] The following table shows the proportion of fathers amongst those who drew this kind of benefit days and the proportion of days on leave during the years 1986-1995. Parts of days on leave are summarised into full days.

---

[2] A parent is entitles to parental leave from work if she/he has been employed during the last six months or a total of at least 12 months during the last two years.
[3] In order to get 80% of the wage during the first 180 days of allowance the parent has to be registered for an income above the level of the minimum benefit for at least 240 days before confinement.
[4] In case of multiple births, the parents are entitled to another 180 benefit days per each child above the first.

Table 1.　　*Proportion of fathers among those who drew cash benefit days when a child was born and the proportion of benefit days drawn by fathers, yearly 1986-1997, percent.*

Year	'86	'87	'88	'89	'90	'91	'92	'93	'94	'95	'96	'97
Fathers, %	23.0	24.5	23.1	24.6	26.1	26.5	26.9	27.0	28.1	27.9	31.1	30.9
Days taken by fathers, %	5.9	7.3	6.3	6.6	7.1	7.7	8.6	10.1	11.4	9.6	10.6	9.9

Source: RFV1996, 1998

The proportion of fathers and the proportion of benefit days drawn by fathers has not changed during the years of relatively high unemployment rates evidenced in Sweden since 1991. The conclusion we may draw is that the tendency for couples to increasingly share the experience of parental leave has not changed as a result of an increased risk of unemployment. The few indications we find of young men risking their job in favour of parental leave (Näsman, 1992) and the fact that they are sometimes discriminated against at recruitment level, because they may still have children and take parental leave (Kugelberg, 1993), does not change the overall tendencies. But the effect of unemployment is visible in public statistics as an increase in late childbearing among young parents.

The proportion of fathers who share parental leave becomes clear only if we look at a period longer than one year, since fathers tend to take leave later in the child's life and the 450 leave days may be drawn over a period of many years (RFV, 1996). This kind of longitudinal analysis is only available for parents of children born in 1991. Most of these parents had drawn all their days during the child's first 30 months. In that period leave was shared by 50% of couples. The mother drew all the days in 49% of cases and the father all his days in 1% of the cases (RFV, 1994). In the latter cases, the fathers drew 198 days of leave on average. Cases where this happens may be, for instance, situations where the father is the only one entitled to leave days with a benefit level above the minimum level, when he is employed while the mother is a student, for example (Näsman, 1992). For couples who shared the benefit days during the child's first 30 months, the fathers drew two months of cash benefit days on average (RFV, 1994). The fathers who take leave days early in the child's life tend to take more days off. In general, fathers more often take the first leave days before the child is six months old; in 1990, almost one quarter of the fathers and as many as 13.8% did so before the child was three months old (RFV, 1994). Fathers more often draw benefit days during the summer and in December (RFV, 1994; 1998). Since these are periods which, by tradition, are used for joint family activities, the parental leave pattern can be interpreted as a way for some parents to be on leave together by combining the mother's vacation days with the father drawing benefit days. Another pattern that may be related the fact that fathers more often than mothers draw cash benefit days part-time (Röcklinger, 1987). Part-time leave may be used to attend a child's celebration of the end of the semester in daycare and school at Christmas and at the beginning of the summer.

The proportion of fathers taking leave also increased after the introduction of a mother and a father month, while the proportion of benefit days drawn by fathers was reduced. If this becomes a tendency in the future, it may mean that the introduction of a father month has set a norm for the period a father is expected to be on leave. An alternative explanation is that the reduction of the benefit level for the remaining days during a time period made it hard for many couples to afford the father taking off more than "his" month. In 1998, the difference in allowance level disappeared. The household economy has frequently been given as an explanation by parents for the father's small share of parental leave, even when the benefit level was 90%. In many cases, however, the real reduction in income is due to the reduction in benefit levels, much less so than to the percentage reduction, due to the combination of marginal taxes and the ceiling for compensation of loss of income.

The parental insurance is, however, not the only reason for parents´ absenteeism when a child is born. The Childcare Leave Act entitles parents to take leave of absence during the first one and a half years of their child's life, and the separate right to cash benefit days. A parent may thus be on unpaid leave at first, and draw the cash benefit days afterwards, ending up with a total of 990 days of leave of absence at most. The unpaid leave is not registered at a national level, so we do not know to which extent the unpaid leave option is used.

Once the parents are back at work, an important option in the parental leave scheme is the right to temporary leave when a child is sick or contagious or when the child has to go to the doctor or to the child health centre. Parents are entitled to temporary parental allowance 60 days per year per child. This also applies for 60 of these days if the person who normally minds the child falls ill or is contagious. A temporary parental allowance may be obtained if the child has not reached the age of 12 or, if a doctor certifies that the child has special needs for care and supervision, until the child has reached the age of 16.[5] Benefit days can be transferred to someone else who takes leave from work in order to care for the child when the child is sick or the person who normally minds the child is sick. Benefit can be paid for a

---

[5] This right also applies when a parent has to take one of the children to the doctor and leaves another child in need of care by the other parent. Furthermore it applies when a parent is visiting a child that is treated at an institution, when a parent is educated in how to take care of the child or is needed as part of the treatment. There is a special regulation for children who are covered by the Disabled Persons Act. The entitlement to temporary leave is not limited to those with an employment of a certain duration.

whole, three-quarters, half or a quarter of a day, depending on how much time the parent has to take off work.

3.2   Two parents - two working lives

Most women as well as men participate in the labour force before they have their first child, and they continue to do so as parents of young children, fathers more frequently even than childless men. Public policies such as the fiscal policy of separate taxation for husband and spouse, parental leave options and publicly subsidised daycare for children, all contribute to the financial incentives for women to take on paid labour (Sundström, 1987). Many women, however, give other than economic reasons for working (Nordenstam, 1984).

When both parents have returned to work after parental leave, family strategies have to reconcile the demands of family and work. For most working parents, access to publicly subsidised day-care outside the home, is a crucial option, while at the same time many parents schedule their working hours in order to reduce the hours the child spends in this type of care (Jacoby & Näsman, 1989). The local regulation of public daycare may form an obstacle for parents using these strategies. Cuts in public spending have resulted in larger child groups in public daycare, increased fees and reduced possibilities for part-time care. This combination of changes makes it hard for parents to find a good solution. Larger groups of children call for a reduction of hours in daycare. Reduction in part-time options, i.e. with reduced fees, is an incentive for longer working hours. Combined with other changes in public policies, which have reduced the level of income in families with children, the incentive to work longer hours has become strong. Single parents, of course, find it even harder to manage this jigsaw puzzle of hours and money. Single mothers work longer hours on average than women in two-income families, and as the households of single mothers have a lower level of living standard than the two-income households, they can thus less afford costly solutions to the puzzle. Transport and travelling hours to and from work are other parts of the puzzle for which single parents have a harder time making ends meet. In sum, single parents are dependant on public services, public transport and public financial support to a much larger extent.

In the two-income family, the parents combined working hours is a crucial issue. Most men, including fathers, work full-time, while many mothers work part-time. This is the most common combination of working hours. Next, in terms of frequency, come situations in which both work full-time. The expressed ideal amongst a majority of men as well as women is for both parents to work part-time in order to reconcile work and parenting. Scheduling the hours in a day or week turn the family work pattern into a type of family shift work system.

This is done in order to be able to combine shorter hours for the children in day-care outside the home with longer hours of work for both parents. In terms of gender equality, this type of family shift means that fathers take sole responsibility for the care of their children on a regular basis (Jacoby & Näsman ,1989; Näsman, 1992).

Most mothers work part-time by making use of the option in the parental leave system to take part-time leave of absence from a full-time position. They may reduce their working hours to 75% of normal hours until the child is 8 years old, or at any later date, before the end of the child's second year at school. The parent has the right to return to full-time work on two months' notice. The income loss due to reduction in working hours is not compensated for. Compared to part-time in other countries, part-time to most Swedish women does not mean a marginalized position in the labour market. Short part-time contracts are rare (less than 20 hours per week) which means that most part-timers have job security and get social benefits (Sundström, 1987; Statistics Sweden, 1995). There is, however, some discrimination towards part-timers. Some of them are replaced at work and are subjected to worse conditions in terms of job content, pay and career development. In one study, 20% of the parents who had reduced their working hours had experienced these kinds of drawbacks (Jacoby & Näsman, 1989).

While part-time is a strategy for mothers for a long period of time, it is rarely a strategy for fathers. If men are on part-time leave following the birth of a child, it is more often for short periods of time, during which they draw cash benefit days part-time. In a 1989 survey of parents with children born in 1986, only 8 per cent of fathers had made any use at all of this option during their child's first three years, and all of those who had, had also been on full-time parental leave (Näsman, 1992).

Within the family, the fact that a woman works part-time means that there is an unequal division of domestic duties. If we take into account paid and unpaid work, we can see that men and women have the same work load, in terms of hours at work, but that the women do the unpaid work to a larger extent than men and that men do more of the paid work, which is a crucial difference (Rydenstam, 1992).

This pattern thus makes women lose economic independence and also an aspect of the quality of life, since their spare time is split up into bits and pieces to a larger extent than that of men. In many households, however, there is a heavy workload on both parents and shortage of time is an often mentioned problem in dual-income families with children (Rydenstam, 1992; Jacoby & Näsman, 1989).

Once the children grow up and do not demand so much care, parents work more hours in the labour market. The total workload is thus also heavy in families with schoolchildren. Fathers do, however, increase the hours spent on domestic work, when the workload of the mothers becomes heavier (Nermo, 1994). Some parents, mothers as well as fathers, who lose their job, describe the first period of unemployment as a positive experience due to the increase in the hours they can spend freely with their children (Näsman, 1996).

Table 2   *Fathers among the parents who drew cash benefit days to care for a sick or infectious child and days drawn by men 1986-1997, relative numbers, %.*

Year	'86	'87	'88	'89	'90	'91	'92	'93	'94	'95	'96	'97
Men	40.6	41.1	41.3	40.9	41.2	41.0	40.9	40.7	40.4	39.5	38.7	38.3
Benefit days	34.4	35.2	34.8	34.5	34.5	34.1	34.3	32.9	33.5	31.2	31.0	31.0

Source: (RFV, 1996, 1998)

For a family with working parents a reduction in working hours will not be enough for them to cope, if acute problems should arise in the family. Temporary parental leave is that part of the parental leave system that is most evenly divided between mothers and fathers. Table 2 shows the proportion of fathers among parents who drew this kind of cash benefit and the proportion of days drawn by men 1986-1995.

The regulations have been changed slightly every two years since 1986, but the proportion of fathers who use this option and the proportion of days that men draw, have not changed to any great extent over the years (RFV, 1996). There has, however, been a small decrease in the proportion of fathers and the proportion of days they have claimed since 1990, which may be a result of the increase in unemployment rates and consequently, in the increase of insecurity in the labour market.

Less than half of the parents entitled to this option, draw this kind of cash benefit and the number of average days drawn per child, per year, is 7 out of a total possible number of 60 days. This stable pattern is seen to extend in the period 1986-1995 (RFV, 1996). The new option, introduced in 1996, to transfer cash benefit days to someone other than the parent was mainly used by women who transferred their days off to another woman.

Before July 1995, parents were also entitled to cash benefit days for parent education. In addition, they could draw benefit days to visit the child at the day-care centre, two days per child, per year, while the child was four to twelve years old. Now this is an option for parents with a handicapped child only. These cash benefit days may be drawn on a part-time basis. This has also been an option for fathers. Of those who, for a year, drew this kind of cash benefit, more than a third were fathers in the years when it was an option open to all parents. In 1997, the proportion of fathers was somewhat higher (38.4%), and they used 41% of days taken up (RFV, 1998).

3.3   Parental leave as a parenting strategy for mothers and fathers?

I will conclude that, since the option for fathers to take parental leave was introduced in 1974, fathers have consistently used some options in the system. If we consider the long leave when a child is born, there has been a steady increase in the proportion of days taken up by fathers, and in the proportion of fathers that take up at least some of these benefit days. The recession in Sweden at the beginning of the 1990s and the increase in unemployment that followed and seems to have steadily increased since, may have had an impact, but has so far not produced any fundamental change in pattern. Fathers opt for some of these leaves even during economically hard times and in periods of insecurity on the labour market. The fathers used to take the daddy days, and quite a large proportion of fathers share the long parental leave when the child is born, which constitutes a large proportion of days, on average. They also, make use, to a large extent of the option of taking temporary leave to care for a sick child, and they use the opportunity to take leave to be with their child in the day-care centre or at school.

In spite of this, the male and female patterns for parental leave are very different. Most women opt for full-time parental leave over a long period, followed by unpaid part-time leave and, occasionally, temporary leave if the child is sick. Men prefer to take a short period of leave when the child is very young, and then return to work full-time. Half of all fathers share the long full-time leave for short periods and many draw these cash benefit days on a part-time basis. A minority of fathers shares the responsibility of staying at home when the child falls ill, or visits the child at the daycare centre or at school. Thus, long parental leave for women has become a feature of everyday life, fathers leave, to many children, is exceptional, and is related to peak periods in life and to temporary needs.

The complex motives of parents underlying these patterns have been debated at length, so I will not elaborate here. I will simply address one critical question. Do fathers really take care of their children when they draw cash benefit days or are they doing something else? This is a question never asked when women are concerned. The question is, of course, based on the assumption that men would not want to take care of their infants. The fact that almost half of fathers do not share a long parental leave may support this idea. The distribution of parental leave over the year is another argument in favour of this critical stance. Anecdotal evidence is often put forward showing that fathers take leave during their holiday, thus doubling their income, or that they go hunting, or paint the house, etc., during their leave. Instead, however, there are arguments that indicate that fathers actually father during their leave. A change in legislation prohibiting parental leave during holidays did not decrease the number of cash benefit days drawn by fathers. The variation in fathers' parental leave during the year does not necessarily indicate an abuse of the law. The question instead may be what kind of fathering activities the policy aims to support through parental leave. Studies on leave-taking fathers, generally quote fathers who describe their parental leave as a positive experience of childcare. The fact that many fathers do not draw cash benefit days except for daddy days may be explained by a number of other factors besides the fathers' unwillingness. Some of the most obvious reasons are that the mother lacks interest in sharing, the risk of monetary loss, and obstacles in the workplace (Näsman, 1990; Näsman, 1992). Loss of income is compensated for only up to a ceiling level that is not very high. This means that quite a number of well-paid parents, fathers more often than mothers, get a lower level of compensation than generally stated. Case studies demonstrate the intricate calculation parents make, counting income, taxes, paid and unpaid leave days, holidays, etc., in order to find the best combination of available options (Näsman, 1997). In this decision-making process, various arguments related to the mother as well as the father may be used in the negotiation, including time to spend with the child, the child's hours spent in the day-care centre, time for travel, household income, job security, career opportunities, workplace family policy, workplace demands and other work environment conditions. The next section discusses the role of workplace conditions.

4.   Workplace conditions and work-family policies

Workplaces are traditionally organised according to a male breadwinner model. This implies that low family duties of the male employee fit the demands of the workplace. The working father is typically looked upon as a reliable member of the workforce, with a high attendance rate and a readiness to take on further duties and to accept increases in working hours in order to promote his job security, career opportunities and to increase his pay. Working mothers are typically labelled as the opposite, ready to leave their job, to take leave and to refuse overtime and more responsibility. The caring father and the bread-winning mother face problems in a workplace culture based on these traditional stereotypes and values. Parental leave legislation does not only offer the right to be on leave of absence but also protects individuals against negative effects. Parents who try to make use of their legal right to opt for parental leave may be discriminated against. In a study of the impact of parental leave on working conditions, some men and women described problems they had faced when they asked for parental leave. Furthermore, most men and women who had been on parental leave full-time were discriminated against upon returning to work. Some were replaced or else discriminated against when returning to work part-time. But this was not a common pattern. A majority of men and women did not report any negative impact on salary increase, opportunities for on-the-job education or for career development. About a quarter of the women who had been on leave full-time and/or part-time reported a negative impact on some of these conditions and the same was the case for about 20 % of the fathers who had been on parental leave (both full-time and part-time). The unions did not, according to these parents, supervise the implementation of this legislation by the employer. No examples of decreased job security was found when those with a permanent post were taken into account, which is exactly what the legislation applies to. The employers respected the legal protection of this fundamental right (Näsman, 1992).

Discriminatory practices related to parental leave are, however, not the only ways in which a workplace may form an obstacle to parenting. Factors such as the work organisation, staff size and workload in the workplace may leave some employees free to take leave and adapt their work to parenting, while others are expected not to make any adaptations of this kind. So-called key persons, experts, supervisors, managers and those who are part of a small staff find it difficult to get parental leave. The fact that most of the fathers who described these kinds of problems and all of the women who did so, were on parental leave nevertheless, makes it probable that their descriptions reflect real problems at their workplaces and not only the need for fathers to find an excuse for not answering to the public image of an ideal father. According to employers there are obvious drawbacks for companies to parental leave rights. Commonly mentioned drawbacks are planning difficulties when parents take temporary leave on short notice, the difficulties and costs in finding competent substitutes and, generally, disturbances in the production process and administrative costs incurred when staff come and go irregularly. In some professions there is also a risk that parents, during a long leave, cannot maintain their competence level. (Näsman, 1992; Ljung &Nettmark, 1998)

Workplace culture is another important factor in this respect. The workplace culture may consist of views concerning the typical worker and normal behaviour at the workplace that are taken for granted. Such views may make parenthood and the care demands of children into non-issues. This is a form of invisible and informal regulation, which is an obstacle to the caring parent and may even make it hard to claim formal parental rights. Such views and norms are often gender-based (Näsman, 1997).

In order to create a new scope for parenting activities in such cases a parent has to initiate a negotiation concerning the boundaries of normal behaviour, thus widening the scope for action allowed by the ideal, or at least, the accepted employee. The first male policeman at a police station to ask for a reduction in working hours, which was his legal right, was told by a superior officer that it was self-evident that this law did not apply to police work. The father's insistence prevailed, however, when he appealed to a higher level in the hierarchy.

This opened perspectives for other police officers at the station, male as well as female, to make a similar appeal (Näsman, 1997).

Important aspects include whether the caring activities of parents are seen as optional. In other words, a worker cannot normally be expected to adapt in these ways, especially if he is male. If this is how management sees the situation, the adaptations that are made may be deemed as exceptions and consequently penalised. In this respect, the fact that most fathers make their parenthood felt at the workplace by staying at home in order to care for their new-born baby, may be an important breakthrough. The fact that men also share the long leave and take a relatively large proportion of days off when a child is ill, means that a large proportion of Swedish employers experience men taking short-term parental leaves. Since it is the short and unpredictable leaves employers see as the major problem, discriminating women in the recruitment phase and with respect to promotion is not any longer a way to avoid these problems. Workplaces with a predominantly male staff more often experience the men taking parental leave than the women and vice versa (Jacoby & Näsman, 1989). The Swedish labour market which is highly gender segregated, and where women mostly work in the public sector and men in the private sector, thus entails that a large proportion of private employers experience parental leave among their male staff more often than among their female staff.

In a recent local survey to employers, the proportion who had experienced men taking parental leave, staying at home with a sick child, or making use of the opportunity to work flexible working hours or to work at home, was almost equal to the proportion who had experienced women making use of these options. There was, however, a large gender difference in part-time employment. The proportion of employers who had experienced women working part-time was as twice as high as the proportion who experienced men working part-time (Ljung & Nettmark, 1998).

Workplace cultures vary. Statistics demonstrate vast differences between professional groups and between local regions in the proportion of fathers that make use of their parental leave rights (RFV, 1998). Furthermore, surveys show that men take leave more often if they work in the public sector and if their partner works in the private sector (Näsman, 1992). There is also a difference between workplaces dominated by male staff and workplaces dominated by female staff, in that the latter seem to offer more options that are specifically oriented towards childcare needs (Näsman, 1997). Some management cultures actively oppose parenting demands, others take up a neutral position but accept and adapt to the formal rights, and others still promote parenting through family-workplace policies. The first and last type of management culture mentioned seem to be in the minority, while the second type is the dominant type (Näsman, 1992; 1997). Sometimes there is also tension within a workplace. In some workplaces, the culture at the shop floor level is more accepting than at management level. This produces a hidden and informal scope for parenting activities. In other cases, top management tries to implement new family policies, but has to struggle with the traditional negative norms and values at lower levels in the organisation (Näsman, 1997).

The extent to which formal rights are offered without negative sanctions and the extent to which options are offered over and above formal rights, is a matter of discretion and can sometimes be described in terms of an implicit contract of mutual understanding and adaptation between an employer and an employee. Since reallocation of tasks is often chosen as a solution by management, solidarity among colleagues may also be part of such implicit contracts (Petersen, 1989; Näsman, 1990).

Parenting options in the workplace sometimes supplement legislation. In a recent local study of small and middle-sized companies the majority of employers (77%) answered yes to the question: Do you think that employers ought to take responsibility for the family situation of employees over and above the legal rights? Close to half of the employers offered additional options, the most frequent ones being flexible working hours, greater options to work part-time, opportunities to work at home and prolonged parental leave. Increased compensation for loss of income during parental leave and help with childcare were other options that were offered (Ljung & Nettmark, 1998).

Some options in the workplace form general parts of the work organisation as such. Scheduling family life also means varying it when parents work day and night. Irregular hours and shift work is the traditional way for parents to combine family and work, a pattern documented from the 1960s onwards. Later on, flexitime became a common phenomenon, starting among white collar workers, but it is now also found in work organisations that were regarded as unsuitable before, among men working shifts in factories and among hospital staff in intensive care units. The next step in this development is an individualisation of working hours with the help of computerised scheduling run by local workgroups themselves. At very short notice, workers can find out if they can change or otherwise rearrange their work schedule (Näsman, 1997). Temporary leaves, and being late or leaving for childcare reasons are important options here. This type of working time organisation offers a wide scope for parenting activities in the workplace.

Other options are to make reconciliation possible, not by dividing hours between work and family but by integrating these two spheres, for instance by making an employee available as a parent while at the workplace. This entails running errands during working hours and communicating by telephone with the children, the daycare staff or the other parent at home. A majority of Swedish men in the Nordic study were able to communicate with their family during their working day and about one third of fathers were regularly in contact with their children during working hours. The fact that children were allowed to visit them and even stay at the parent's workplace was another strategy that was mentioned. These options were mostly not stated formally, but were informally accepted by supervisors and work mates. The management demonstrated their acceptance when they installed a telephone in the factory for the workers to use for private phone calls (Näsman, 1997).

A general pattern found in the Swedish population included in the Nordic study was that men had more opportunities for general flexibility in attendance and working hours. These options were not targeted especially to child-care needs, but were available for whatever reason the employees had to make use of them. Women, on the other hand, had better access to options targeted specifically to childcare needs (Näsman, 1997). In the case study, however, the male-dominated workplaces were found to offer a wide scope for parenting of both kinds. In a Swedish metal plant, fathers made extensive use of the right to daddy days, shared the long parental leave with their wives, used their flexitime options for care purposes and were on some type of temporary leave when the child was ill. Some of the fathers were more frequently on temporary leave for this reason than their partners, because this type of leave was easier to get and was accepted to a larger extent at the metal plant than in the workplace of their partners. This was a strategy openly applied by fathers and accepted by their supervisors and even at higher levels in the organisation. Company policy stated that men as well as women have a right to take parental leave, and further stressed that there ought to be no negative consequences for parents who made use of these rights. This policy was accepted at lower levels in the organisation as well, both among supervisors and work mates. The policy also got support from the labour union (Magnusson Granqvist, 1993). The management's policy was to promote fathers' usage of these options. Parenthood and fatherhood were positively valued in the workplace, as taking care of a young child was expected to foster flexibility and make the father more mature. These characteristics were seen as positive for production, since they fitted into the new demands on staff in cases where a new work schedule was introduced. The staff manager at the plant thought that paternal leave was profitable for the company (Magnusson Granqvist, 1993).

Similar ideas concerning a positive impact were also found in a recent Swedish study of small and middle-sized companies. Employers mentioned gains the company could make when employees use their legal right to parental leave: the staff achieved a better balance between family and working life, and created the necessary distance to their work. Parental leaves also made people more mature, increased their social competence, sense of responsibility and increased their productivity when they came back. There was a positive spill-over from security in family life to the company. The leaves also gave the employer the opportunity to try out new staff members as substitutes. Furthermore, parental leaves were an important way to recruit and keep competent staff members (Ljung &Nettmark, 1998).

5. Conclusion

My conclusion is that the tendency to develop a positive view of work-family arrangements in the workplace may be the best option in the future, even if times are hard, economically. On the other hand, I see a risk in the tendency for the labour market to move towards increased individual responsibility. The demands for a very efficient and profitable organisation caused by the need for increased productivity places heavy demands on workers. Workplace demands for flexibility also means demands on children and on the public day-care system. For single parents, these demands may be hard to manage. At the same time, Swedish public debate stresses high demands on parents to be successful, as such. Parents are thus caught in a pressure situation. If we look at the issue from a children's perspective we can only hope that they will not suffer when working life as well as family life become parts of a larger family project, focussing on a dual career for both men and women. The fact that some children today see unemployment as a good thing, since that makes the parents available to them, calls for a discussion concerning the extent to which it is morally justified for parents to turn unemployment into a meaningful experience by reorienting themselves towards parenting, and, on the other hand, how working life may be organised in such a way that makes parenting activities an accepted part of a woman's as well as man's working life as good lifetime employees.

References

Hoem, J. (1993), Public Policy as the Fuel of Fertility: Effects of a Policy Reform on the Pace of Childbearing in Sweden in the 1980s. In: *Acta Sociologica* 36:19-31.

Hörnqvist, M. (1994), Att bli vuxen i olika generationer. In: Fritzell, J. & Lundberg, O. (eds) *Vardagens villkor. Levnadsförhållanden i Sverige under tre decennier*. Stockholm: Brombergs.

Jacoby, A. & E. Näsman (1989), *Mamma Pappa Jobb. Föräldrar och barn om arbetets villkor*. Stockholm: Arbetslivscentrum/Brevskolan.

Kugelberg, C. (1993), Föräldraskap och arbetsliv. In: A. Agell *et al* (eds) *Om moderns familjeliv* och familjeseparationer. Stockholm: SFR.

Ljung, P. & S. Nettmark (1998), *Samarbete, Kommunikation, Ansvar*, Department of Thematic Studies, Linköping university, 1998:1.

Magnusson Granqvist, M. (1993), *Arbetsplats Verkstäderna.*arbetsrapport, Socialhögskolan, Lunds universitet.

Martinell, S. (1992), Fruktsamheten nu och i framtiden. In: *Välfärdsbulletinen* 2:5-7.

Moen, P. (1989), *Working parents. Transformations in Gender Roles and Public Policies in Sweden.* Madison: Univ. of Wisconsin Press.

Nermo, M. (1994), Den ofullbordade jämställdheten. In: J. Fritzell & O. Lundberg (eds) *Vardagens villkor. Levnadsförhållanden i Sverige under tre decennier.* Stockholm: Brombergs.

Nordenstam, U. (1984), *Ha barn, men hur många?* Information i prognofrågor 1984:4. Stockholm: Statistics Sweden.

Näsman, E. (1990), *The importance of Family Policy for Fathers' Care of their Children.* Brussels: European Commission, report DGV/B/4.

Näsman, E. (1992), *Parental Leave a Workplace Issue?* ISRRD - Unit of Demography, Stockholm university.

Näsman, E. & C. von Gerber (1996), *Mamma Pappa Utan Jobb.* Stockholm: Rädda Barnens Förlag.

Näsman, E. (1997), Föräldraskaperts synlighet i arbetsplatskulturer. In: Jens Bonke (ed) *Dilemmaet arbejdsliv – familjeliv i Norden,* Nordiska Ministerrådet Tema Nord 1997:534, Copenhagen.

Petersen, H. (1989), Perspectives of Women on Work and Law. In: *International Journal of the Sociology of Law,* 17, pp 327-346.

Rydenstam, K. (1992), *I tid och otid. En undersökning om kvinnors och mäns tidanvändning, 1990/91.* Levnadsförhållanden, rapport no 79, Statistics Sweden, Stockholm.

Röcklinger, A. S. (1987) *Hur används föräldraförsäkringen?* In: Barnfamiljerna och arbetslivet, Socialdepartementet, Stockholm.

Sundgren Grinups, B. (1998), *Försörjning och omsorg i förändring,* Göteborgs universitet, Institutionen för socialt arbete 1998:4, diss.

Sundström, M. (1987), *A Study in the Growth of Part-time Work in Sweden,* Almqvist & Wiksell, Stockholm, diss.

Sources:
Riksförsäkringsverket (RFV) 1990, 1994, 1995, 1996, 1998.
Statistics Sweden 1995.

EUROPEAN REGULATION AND INITIATIVES ON WORK-FAMILY POLICIES

Jacqie van Stigt, Anneke van Doorne-Huiskes and Joop Schippers

1. Introduction

During its forty-year existence, the European Community (later: European Union) has increased its involvement with 'women's issues'. Even though the Community has been based on principles of efficiency from its establishment, on several occasions measures that have been taken have also contributed to the principles of equity. In 1957, the principle of equal pay for men and women was already set out in the Treaty of Rome. Since the 1970s, this principle has been expanded with a number of Directives aimed at ending all other forms of discrimination in the area of employment. Later still, the principle of equal treatment was also introduced in the domain of social security, and legal and vocational rules. The recognition of this principle led to the promotion of equal opportunities in the 1980s.[1] While early regulation and measures taken were directly inspired by ideas on competition and efficiency, equal treatment and social policy have become independent goals that exist alongside those already in existence.

While the promotion of equal opportunities was still focussed very much on employment as a world apart, the causes of unequal treatment more often than not can be traced to the interaction between the public sphere of labour and the private sphere of family and care. As a result, the European Union (EU) has become more and more active in the last decade in promoting reconciliation of work and family life. Over the past ten years, Directives setting minimum standards for maternity leave and parental leave have been adopted, and a Council Recommendation on Childcare has been introduced, which is supplemented by a Commission Guide of good practice.[2] A Framework Directive on how to combine work and family is still under consideration. The Structural Funds, especially the NOW (New Opportunities for Women) Initiatives now play a more active role in the development of services. There is

---

[1] The EU distingues a number of measures:

* Directives, which oblige Member States to adapt their national legislation within a certain time, in accordance to the content and intent of the directive;

* Recommendations, which request Member States to pursue a certain policy (so-called soft law), and

* Action Programmes, which intend to stimulate the realization of policy in each Member State (Goedhard *et al.*, 1992).

[2] European Commission, DG V, Social Europe. Work and childcare: implementing the Council Recommendation on childcare. A guide to good practice. Supplement 5/96. Luxembourg, 1996

support for networks, conferences, seminars and other ways to promote co-operation and exchange.[34]

While measures taken in the 1970s and 1980s arose from ideas of justice, i.e. equal opportunities for men and women, a substantial shift in thinking took place in the 1990s. Economic arguments have been foregrounded concerning the importance of labour participation and employment of women, but also, for example, childcare as a new growth industry and a source of employment. Nowadays, work-family policies have become an integral part of the social and economic policy of the EU, and it could even be argued that the discussion of women's employment as it relates to family responsibilities has contributed much to the integration of social and economic policy at the EU-level.

This chapter explores the historical development and context of work-family policies in the EU. The role of the Union and plans concerning work-family policies in the future are also considered. The question as to what extent the European Union has actually contributed to an improvement of the possibilities for reconciling work with family life is answered in the last section.

2.   From equal pay to equal treatment: the 1970s

Initially, the only action undertaken to promote equal opportunities for women was the inclusion of article 119 in the Treaty of Rome (1957), concerning equal pay for men and women. The article was adopted to alleviate the French government's fears that lower pay for women would prove to be a competitive advantage for the other Member States (Roelofs, 1995).

In the early 1970s, more scope was created for joint social policy, of which equal opportunities was (not yet an integrated) part. There was more money available and there was political support. One consequence was the founding of the Equal Opportunities Unit, under

---

[3] The EC Childcare Network and other Measures to reconcile Employment and Family Responsibilities, 1986-1996, A Decade of Achievements. DG-V, Brussel, 1996.

[4] Beside these instruments the European Commission also stimulates research, exchange and action projects to accelerate developments. For that, a network of experts have been set up to advise the Commission. The first network in this area was founded in 1983: Women and Employment. Other networks are for example the Network on Childcare (see section 3) and the European Network of Women (ENOW). The European Trade Union Confederation (ETUC) has founded a women's committee as did the agricultural organization COPA. And there are networks on affirmative action in companies, on diversifications of occupational choices, on equal opportunities in education, on equal opportunities in radio and television, and so on. In 1993 the Black Women in Europe Network was founded.

the Directorate-General of Employment, Industrial Relations and Social Affairs (DG-V). The Equal Opportunity Unit is responsible for the so-called Equal Opportunities Action Programmes (see section 3). Another measure was the establishment of an ad hoc advisory Committee on Equal Opportunities for Women and Men for the European Commission (Commission Decision 82/53/EEC).[5]

In 1974, the Social Action Programme of the EC focussed attention on the disadvantaged position of women. The lack of adequate facilities for working mothers was considered one of the major causes of the unequal position of women. And so the proposal in the Social Action Programme was formulated as follows: "to give immediate priority to the problems of providing facilities to enable women to reconcile family responsibilities with job aspirations" (Pot, 1992:60).

In the 1970s, a number of Directives concerning the equal treatment of men and women came into effect. Firstly, the EU adopted the Directive on equal pay for men and women in 1975 (Directive 75/117 of 10/2/1975, Pb 1975, nr. L45). The second Directive relating to equal treatment between men and women in the labour market was introduced in 1976 (Directive 76/207 of 9/21976, Pb 1976, L39). The principle of equal treatment is related to the accessibility of the labour market, to career opportunities, to the accessibility of vocational training and to terms of employment. The third EU-Directive is about equal treatment between men and women in the domain of social security (Directive 79/7 of 19/12/1979, PB 1979, L6). This Directive prescribes gradual implementation of the principle of equal treatment between men and women in that domain.

3.   The first two Action Programmes: policy in the 1980s

After the initiatives in the 1970s focusing on equal opportunities policy, which resulted in a number of directives, a different approach was chosen in the 1980s. The emphasis shifted from regulatory policy to process and action policy (Roelofs, 1995). The First four-year Action Programme for equal opportunities 1982-1985 focussed on the one hand on implementing and endorsing existing equal opportunities legislation, and on achieving greater equality in actual practice through Positive Action Programmes and other instruments on the other hand. The programmes and instruments did not include child-care facilities. Although the European Commission did recognize the link between care for children and equal opportunities, policy measures were kept limited. Yet a Recommendation on positive action

---

[5] Since the 1st of January 1996 social partners also take part in this commission as full members instead of

was adopted on the 13th of December 1984. This Recommendation called on Member States to take away the existing inequalities in the professional lives of women and to promote mixed (i.e. men and women) employment through a policy of affirmative action. One of the activities mentioned is the redistribution of paid and unpaid work between men and women.

A Directive on parental leave and leave for family reasons, formulated in 1984, was vetoed by the United Kingdom. A second aim was to build up the network of public (child-care) facilities and services. This resulted in a report on services for children under the age of three.

The Second Action Programme (1986-1990) outlined that more concrete measures have to be taken. In this programme, the European Commission proposes recommendations for action in the field of daycare facilities. A network of European experts was installed in 1986 to advise the Commission. The first task of the Network on Childcare was to conduct a study of the different types of childcare available in the various Member States. This kind of information had not been available until then. The publication of the Network's report 'Childcare and Equality of Opportunity' (Moss, 1988) to a large extent provided the information needed.
The most important recommendations were that:
1. a global directive on childcare provisions should be drawn up (see section 4);
2. changes should be encouraged in organizations to make it easier to combine paid work and care for children, to be achieved via a system of leave provisions, for example maternity leave, parental leave and special leave to care for sick children.

Other tasks of the Network were to monitor developments, evaluate policy choices, to collect and circulate information and to draw up criteria for defining quality for childcare services. The Network was mainly focussed on childcare for children up to ten years. In 1991 the network was renamed the Network on Childcare and other Measures to reconcile Employment and Family Responsibilities, to demonstrate the broader context of the reconciliation of work and family. The Network was dissolved in 1996.

Under the Second Programme, most Member States intensified their efforts in the field of childcare. Especially in the Netherlands, which always lacks behind in this field, the EU dimension functioned as an eye opener, and resulted in Stimulating Measures on Childcare.

In the 1980s, two Directives came into force: the fourth Directive on equal treatment in a company and sectorial measures with regard to social security (Directive 86/378 of 24 July 1986, Pb 1986, L225). The latter concerns social security measures for employees and self-

observers.

employed persons, who work in companies or branches of industry. The fifth Directive prescribes equal treatment for self-employed men and women (Directive 86/613 of 11 December 1986, Pb 1986, L359). The protective measures on pregnancy and motherhood of self-employed women are especially important for women who work in the agricultural sector.

4.   Shift from specific to general policy: the Third Action Programme 1991 - 1995

The Third Action Programme 1991-1995 differs from the first two in that it is an attempt to create an interface with the Union's general structural and socio-economic policy. The ageing of the labour force will lead to a shortage of skilled workers. Therefore the European Union came to realise that it cannot afford to exclude women from the labour market. Women have to become better integrated into the labour process, quantitatively as well as qualitatively. This programme also focuses on the threats a unified European market poses to women.

Efforts to improve the position of women on the labour market are no longer seen as a specific and limited kind of policy. Equal opportunities policies started to become an integrated part of the social-economic and structural policy of the European Union. Key concepts are the co-ordination, complementation and integration of policy, at the European, national and regional levels (Roelofs, 1995). For the first time the concept of mainstreaming is mentioned in reference to the World Women Conference in Beijing.

Explicit attention is focussed on measures to reconcile work and family life. One of the most important pillars of this Action Programme is New Opportunities for Women (18 December 1990). This structural fund targets training and employment projects for women.

The Third Action Programme has three main aims:
- to implement and develop legislation;
- to integrate women in the labour market, and to undertake activities whose purpose it is to make it possible for women to reconcile their domestic and professional obligations;
- to improve the social position of women.

Partnership (more responsibilities for social partners: see, for example, the Directive on Parental Leave to be discussed below) and regular evaluations of the implementation of the programmes and the actions taken are first becoming the basic principles of implementation.

Under this Action Programme, the Recommendation on Childcare was approved of by the Council of Ministers (in 1992) and a code of conduct was drafted as part of the Action

Programme set up to implement the Community Charter of the Fundamental Social Rights of Workers, and point 16 in particular: "measures should also be developed to enable men and women to reconcile their occupational and family obligations."

The principles and objectives of the Recommendations on Childcare are: affordability; access to services in all areas, both urban and rural; access to services for children with special needs; combining reliable care with a pedagogical approach; close and responsive relations between services and parents and local communities; diversity and flexibility of services; increased choice for parents; coherence between services; basic and continuous training appropriate to the educational and social value of work.

Reconciliation of work and family life is recognised as a shared responsibility between men and women, but also as a responsibility of national and local government, of social partners, and of individual services. Reconciliation has to be approached in a broad sense; measures have to be taken with regard to services, leave arrangements, the workplace, and greater involvement of men.

In the same period, the Directive on Maternity Leave and the Directive on Parental Leave were also adopted.

The ETUC (European Trade Union Committee) Women's Committee started the lobby for the Directive on Maternity Leave. It proposed a paid leave of sixteen weeks. The European Commission announced a draft directive on this subject in 1990, which was presented as part of the Social Action Programme and as an elaboration on the Framework Directive on Health and Safety, in accordance with the ETUC's recommendations. But after consulting the social partners, the Commission opted for a directive that, in fact, only established minimal norms, which the member states were free to supplement if they so desired. The minimum provision was to be fourteen weeks of paid leave. In the end, the political decision-making process resulted in a fourteen-week leave, but not in full payment of wages. Instead employees received the same benefit they would receive on sick leave. The Directive was finally adopted on 19 October 1992.

In June 1996, a Directive on Parental Leave (OJ L145 of 19.6.1996, p.4) was adopted by the Council of Ministers. This Directive rounds off a discussion ongoing since 1983 (see section 3), when the Commission put forward proposals for a legal instrument relating to parental leave. In December 1995, negotiations between trade unions and employers led to a Framework Agreement on Parental Leave which involved ETUC, UNICE and CEEP (the united European employers organizations). Pursuant to Article 4 of the Agreement on Social

Policy[6], the signatory parties requested the Commission to put forward a proposal for a Council act implementing the agreement (COM (96) 26 final of 31.1.1996). This was the first collective labour agreement at the European Union level. The social partners also decided to open negotiations on flexibility in working time and security for workers, which led to the framework agreement on part-time work (see section 6).

In the Directive on Parental Leave, the minimum requirements for parental leave provisions for the European Union (excluding the United Kingdom and Northern Ireland) are outlined. According to Clause 2, the parental leave provision entitles women and men to an individual right to parental leave on the grounds of birth or adoption of a child to enable them to take care of that child for at least three months, until a given age of up to eight years to be defined by Member States and/or social partners. This right should be granted on a non-transferable basis.

In addition to parental leave, workers should be entitled to time off from work, on the grounds of force majeure for urgent family reasons such as sickness making the immediate presence of the worker at home indispensable (Clause 3). The Member States will have two years to implement the Directive which states that all matters relating to social security are for the consideration and determination of individual Member States and lets all contentious areas such as payment to workers on leave pass.

5.   Mainstreaming work-family policies in the social and economic policy of the EU

During the first half of the 1990s, the concept of mainstreaming was actually realized. The Treaty of Maastricht (1992), the Social Action Programme 1995-1997 with its supplemental guide to good practice concerning work and childcare, and the Green and White Papers on European Social Policy all reflect this mainstreaming principle. But it was not only equal opportunities policies that became an integrated part of social policy. Social policy also came to be recognized an essential part of good economic performance; social policy contributes to economic productivity instead of generating a loss of income. Thus, equal opportunities policies and social policy became an integrated part of the economic policy of the European Union.

The contribution that social policies make to economic performance and to achieving the

---

[6] This Agreement on Social Policy states that, when a draft Directive is obstructed by lack of unanimity between the Member States, the Commission can ask the social partners to 'take over' the subject. When they come to an agreement, the Council of Ministers can be requested to turn this agreement into a stringent Directive.

economic and social objectives of the Union, is set out in Article 2 of the Treaty of Maastricht; "The Community shall have the task (....) to promote throughout the Community a harmonious and balanced development of economic activities, sustainable and non inflatory growth respecting the environment, a high degree of convergence of economic performance, a high level of employment and of social protection, the raising of the standard of living and the quality of life, and economic and social cohesion and solidarity among Member States" (SDU, 1993).

In the protocol on social policy of the Maastricht Treaty, which is mainly based on agreements between the social partners made the previous year, Article 6 relates to the position of women on the labour market. This Article incorporates the text of Article 119 of the Treaty of Rome, and supplements it with a statement that each Member State can take measures to facilitate women to practise a profession or to prevent or compensate for disadvantages in their career (Article 6, p. 3). This statement has a broader meaning than the Recommendation on Positive Action of 13/12/1984 as it includes not only actual employment, but also refers to the past and future labour market situation (see also Devroe and Wouters, 1996).

The Social Action Programme 1995 - 1997 states that equal opportunities should be promoted in all relevant policies affecting employment, with particular emphasis on de-segregation of the labour market and reconciliation between family life and paid work. The labour market participation of women is seen as an important factor in international competition. The Action Programme is supplemented by 'Work and childcare: a guide to good practice'. This guide is meant to stimulate initiatives on childcare in all Member States and gives detailed suggestions towards implementing the Recommendation on Childcare. Not only childcare but also leave arrangements, the environment, the structure and organisation of work and the workplace and the role of fathers are taken into account.

The globalization of trade and production, the huge impact of new technologies on work, society and individuals, the ageing of the population and the persistent high level of unemployment were all challenges addressed in the Green Paper on Social Policy (1993).
The Green Paper also gives explicit attention to the reconciliation of work and family life: "there is now a broad consensus that, given the aspirations of women themselves, an ageing workforce and expansion of the service sector, women will constitute an increasingly crucial component of the workforce at all levels. The question of their rights and opportunities is thus vital for the future of the economy" (p. 24). And: "it is primarily women who are faced with conflicting employment and family responsibilities. This can result in women failing to

realize their full potential. Social and labour market structures continue to operate on the assumption that women are primarily responsible for home and childcare while men are responsible for the family's economic and financial wellbeing. This conflicts with the new reality. Dual income and lone parent families are increasingly common, while the number of sole breadwinner families has declined dramatically. The gender-based division of family and employment responsibilities not only constrain women's lives but also deprives men of the emotional rewards resulting from the care and development of children" (p. 25).

The Green Paper points out the necessity of a combined labour market and social policy to develop the rights and opportunities of women. Promoting equal opportunities for women and men in a changing European society implies "that the highest priority should be given to measures which will enable individuals, men and women, to achieve a better balance in their private and their working lives" (p. 57). Measures to be taken are:

- encouraging more flexibility in careers and working hours;
- promoting innovative ways to combine household and working responsibilities;
- promoting the provision of childcare facilities;
- eliminating direct and indirect discrimination in the labour market, including that concerning lay-offs and part-time work;
- giving increased attention to women's labour market difficulties in the context of the social dialogue.

The mainstreaming of policies to develop and promote the rights and opportunities of women in all relevant policy areas is also mentioned in the White Paper on European Social Policy. For the first time, attention is given here to the diversity between women. Regarding work-family policies, the White Paper says (p. 42): "the growing participation of women in the economy has been one of the most striking features of recent decades, suggesting that there is now an urgent need, in the interest of society as a whole, for working life and family life to be more mutually reinforcing. (....) Changing demographic trends makes that the responsibility for elderly dependants is moving up the social agenda, although childcare is still the major problem for working parents in many Member States. New social infrastructures are needed to support the household and the family, and the question of how families can be helped to carry the costs remains to be addressed. Progress towards new ways of perceiving family responsibilities may slowly relieve the burden on women and allow men to play a more fulfilling role in society. However, greater solidarity between men and women is needed if men are to take on greater responsibility for the caring role in our societies."

The White Paper issues a warning that flexibility in employment should not lead to new pressures on women to return to the ranks of the non-salaried population or to be obliged to accept paid work at home away from the community.

Drawing on the experiences of Member States, and with a view to fostering greater co-operation, the European Commission will:

- follow up the Childcare Recommendation by assessing the implementation of the Recommendation, establishing baseline data on childcare infrastructure and services in the Member States, and looking at ways of addressing the issues of stereotypes roles of the sexes in society;
- undertake an economic assessment both of the job-creation and reflationary potential of child and dependent-care infrastructures and services. In the light of this assessment, the Commission will make appropriate proposals.

The White Paper also relates to atypical forms of work, such as part-time work. This type of work is coming to be seen more and more as a way of combining work and family life, although it does not provide the same rights and protection as standard full-time work. A draft Directive on part-time work was vetoed by the United Kingdom. The developments in the field of atypical work led to the conclusion that new measures were needed and had to take account of the principles of the ILO Convention on part-time work adopted in June 1994. If no progress was made in the Council, the Commission would initiate consultations with the social partners under the Agreement on Social Policy (see also section 4). This is exactly what happened (Social Europe, social dialogue - the situation in the community in 1995, 1995).

A framework agreement on part-time work was established on the 14th of May 1997 after months of difficult negotiations between the ETUC on the one hand and the UNICE/CEEP on the other. In this agreement, part-time work is seen as a contribution to the overall European strategy on employment.

The agreement sets out the general principles and minimum requirements relating to part-time work, and voices the intention to do the same for other types of atypical work in the future. Outlines are:

- to ban discrimination of part-time workers;
- equal treatment between part-time and full-time workers;
- to improve the quality of part-time jobs;
- to assist the development of opportunities for part-time work on a basis acceptable to employers and workers;

- if an employee refuses to switch from part-time work to full-time work or vice versa, this can never be a reason for dismissal;
- if possible employers will take into consideration a request by an employee to reduce or to increase working time;
- the social security system has to be adapted to suit part-time work, in order to protect workers engaged in such work.

The consulting process of the social partners in each of the Member States has started.

6.   The Fourth Action Programme 1996 - 2000

The Fourth Action Programme emphasizes the exchange of information and experiences regarding good practice in the field of equal opportunities for men and women. Together with the struggle against unemployment, the promotion of equal opportunities is mentioned as a priority of the Union and its Member States. Again it is stated that equal opportunities policies must be a part of all relevant policies, and mainstreaming is the key word. The results from the other three Action Programmes have to be consolidated and developed even further, because inequalities between men and women still exist in the European Union, especially in the area of employment and wages. The role of the social partners is emphasized more and more. But other partners such as local governments, NGOs, and public and private institutions are also mentioned. Partnership is another key word in this Fourth Action Programme.

One of the main aims of this programme is to reconcile work and family life for women and men. Action fields are the organization and the flexibility of professional life, and the combination of responsibilities. Measures aiming at setting higher standards for the care of children and other dependents will be proposed by the Commission, possibly within a framework directive.

The supporting text relates to other, linked areas as well. For example, there are references to the influence that "fiscal incentives and obstacles for dual earner households" might have on women's care strategies. Other issues mentioned are: career breaks policies, policies on working time, and the social infrastructure and care provision. The Fourth Action Programme also suggests a basis for the use of Structural Funds to finance "efforts aimed at reducing constraints on women (care services)".

The discussion on the Fourth Action Programme has resulted in the inclusion of articles related to work-family policies in the Treaty of Amsterdam (16/17 June, 1997). In the chapter on social politics, Article 118 states that the Member States will be supported in realizing equal opportunities for and equal treatment of women and men on the labour market. More specifically, Article 119 states that each Member State can take measures to facilitate the underrepresented sex to encourage them to practise a profession or to prevent or compensate for disadvantages in their career (see also Article 6, p. 3 of the Treaty of Maastricht). Member States have to strive first of all to improve the situation of women in professional life (Article 119: 4).

7.   Future plans

The EU continues to evolve its reconciliation policy, both as an integral part of its economic strategy, and as a key component of family and equal opportunities policy (Large, 1997).

Work-family policies is an area in which the European Union has built up a lot of creative thinking and experience. The EU can provide a framework as well as the means to explore new and radical approaches to reconciliation which could be used (more) by Member States (Moss, 1997).

The monitoring and reviewing of the implementation of policies are placed high on the agenda. Nowadays partnership is a key feature of the method the Commission uses to bring forward proposals in the social field. Especially the role of the social partners, i.e. the social dialogue, is being emphasized more and more. Networks and cross-national components in the NOW programme are also widely used. Apart from the benefits to knowledge, increased cross-national exchange, collaboration and comparison may have a cumulative powerful effect by raising expectations (for example, see section 3: the developments in childcare in the Netherlands) and in speeding up the dissemination of new ideas, policies and practices (Moss, 1996: 28).

The reconciliation of work and family is placed in a broader perspective. Good childcare is not the only important issue. Other care needs, like the care for elderly dependents, are also recognized. In addition, the role of fathers is getting more attention.

Other new items could be: the costs and benefits of different public and workplace policies; action research on initiatives to encourage more equal sharing of family responsibilities between men and women; and the exploration of implications for reconciliation employment and family life of the economic, technological, demographic and social changes that are sweeping through all European countries (Moss, 1996: 33).

The White Paper, the Fourth Action Programme and the Network on Childcare more specifically mention measures to be taken in the field of childcare:

- to improve and increase co-ordination between two Directorate-Generals: DG V and DG XXII (education);
- to develop standards for childcare services and infrastructure in the Member States;
- to introduce a second NOW initiative to provide more funding for childcare services;
- to evaluate the qualitative and quantitative aims for the improvement of childcare services;
- to use this evaluation as a contribution to the development of the labour market policy.

However, a more integrated and co-ordinated approach is needed, not only in relation to childcare, but also in relation to all issues concerning work-family policies. The White Paper suggests a framework directive covering the issues of reconciling professional and family life, and proposes setting higher standards for the care of children and other dependents. This directive should combine the current directives and recommendations with new initiatives, in order to cover the whole field of work and family life. Employment policy, social policy, reconciliation policy and care policy should all be linked. This is one of the biggest challenges facing the European Union in the future.

8. Conclusions

The European Union is characterized by a long-standing interest and increasing involvement in the relationship between paid and unpaid work: the reconciliation of employment and family responsibilities (Moss, 1996). In 1957 the principle of equal pay for men and women was already set out in Article 119 of the Treaty of Rome. Since the 1970s, this principle has been expanded with a number of Directives about the accessibility of the labour market, about education and vocational training, about terms of employment, social security, etc. The promotion of equal opportunities was realized through Action Programmes, Directives, Recommendations and Funds.

In the last decade, the European Community has become more and more active in promoting the reconciliation of work and family. While anti-discrimination measures in the 1970s arose from ideas of justice, i.e. equal opportunities for men and women, a substantial shift in thinking took place in the 1990s. Economic reasons were foregrounded concerning the importance of the labour participation and employment of women, but also, for example, childcare as a new growth industry. Efforts to improve the position of women on the labour market were no longer seen as a specific and limited type of policy. Equal opportunities policies started to become an integrated and full part of the social-economic and structural policy of the European Union. The Fourth Action Programme 1996 - 2000 continues in this line towards mainstreaming.

It is only recently that more attention is being given to the link between different fields of policy. New proposals cover a wide range of measures and conditions that enable and support reconciliation, and include terms and conditions for employment, working hours, tax and social security, leave arrangement and childcare services. The need for family responsibilities to be shared more equally between men and women is also recognized (Moss, 1996).

The increased labour participation of women has led to a change in the structure of the labour force. This has required social transformation on an enormous scale. Family life has been altered. A change in women's working status has demanded a change in the role that men perceive themselves as having within the family. It demands a whole new social contract (Large, 1997, p. 5; cf. OESO, 1991).

The question is to what extent the European Union is contributing to this social transformation. When it comes to an obvious structural improvement in the position of women at the macro-level, the results achieved in the majority of member states by the Union's equal opportunities policy are meagre. The wage gap between men and women in the EU has changed slightly. The same can be said about segregation on the labour market. Women still do the more unpaid work, in spite of the enormous increase in their labour market participation.

EU law has given women more legal instruments, but the equal opportunities policy has a restricted scope. This is largely a result of the decisive role which the Member States themselves play in the Union's decision-making process. As long as decisions have to be taken unanimously, it is highly unlikely that the EU will ever be able to achieve more than the least progressive Member States have. The networks play a vital role, but they are not very effective, mainly because of the very limited financial resources available.

Nevertheless, some measures have functioned as an eye opener, particularly in the Netherlands. The Recommendation on Childcare in particular laid the foundation for the two Stimulation Measures on Childcare taken by the Dutch government. Also, the Netherlands have integrated the activities of the NOW Initiatives into their domestic employment and training programs.

In the southern Member States, where until recently nothing had been arranged in the field of work-family policies, the European Union has provided a framework within which they can operate.

One of the most important points to emerge from this discussion is the notion that equal opportunities policy, social policy and economic policy are intertwined. This notion is also reflected in the current emancipation policy of the Dutch government. It opens new ways that provide room for reconciliation of work and family policies and, because the economic necessity of this process has come to be recognized, the social basis for reconciliation measures is growing.

References

Devroe, W. and J. Wouters (1996), *De Europese Unie. Het verdrag van Maastricht en zijn uitvoering: analyse en perspectieven.* Leuven: Peeters.

European Commission (1994), Green Paper on European Social Policy: options for the Union. Brussels, 17 November 1993, COM(193) 551. Luxembourg: Office for Official Publications of the European Community.

European Commission, DG V (1985), *Ontwerpresoluttie van de Raad betreffende de goedkeuring van een nieuw programma op middellange termijn - Gelijke Kansen voor vrouwen (1986 - 1990).* COM (85) 80 def. - 85/C356/06

European Commission, DG V (1991), *Gelijke kansen voor vrouwen en mannen: derde communitaire actieprogramma op middellange termijn 1991-1995.* Vrouwen in Europa, nr. 34. Brussels: European Commission.

European Commission, DG V (1994), White Paper on European Social Policy, *European social policy; a way forward for the union.* Luxembourg: European Commission.

European Commission, DG V (1995), *Voorstel voor een besluit van de Raad betreffende het Vierde communitaire actieprogramma inzake gelijke kansen voor vrouwen en mannen (1996 - 2000).* COM (95) 381 def. - 95/0206(CNS)

European Commission, DG V (1995), Social Europe, social dialogue - the situation in the community in 1995. Luxembourg: European Commission.

European Commission, DG V (1996), *The EC Childcare Network and other Measure to reconcile Employment and Family Responsibilities, 1986-1996, A Decade of Achievements.* Brussels: European Commission.

European Commission, DG V, Social Europe (1996) *Work and childcare: implementing the Council Recommendation on childcare.* A guide to good practice. Supplement 5/96. Luxembourg: European Commission.

European Commission, Social Europe (1997), *Progress report on the implementation of the medium-term social action programme 1995-7,* Supplement 4/96. Suppl. 5/96 is: Work and childcare: a guide to good practice. Luxembourg: European Commission.

ETUC, UNICE/CEEP (1997), Framework agreement on part-time work. Brussels: European Commission.

Goedhard, E.A. *et al.* (ed.)(1992) *Vrouwen en arbeidsmarktpositie binnen de EG.* Deel 1,2 en 3. Heerlen: Open Universiteit.

Large, J. (1997), Childcare and the female labour supply - the EU perspective. In: J. Gierveld, J.J. Schippers and J.J. Siegers (eds.), *Childcare and female labour supply.* Amsterdam: Thesis Publishers.

Moss, P. (ed.)(1988), *Childcare and Equality of Opportunity. Network on Childcare*, Brussel.

Moss, P. (1996). In: S. Lewis and J. Lewis (eds.)(1996), *Employment and Family Responsibilities.* London: Sage

Pot, L. (1992), In: E.A. Goedhard *et al.* (ed.) *Vrouwen en arbeidsmarktpositie binnen de EG.*, deel 3, p. 60. Heerlen: Open Universiteit.

Richtlijn 96/34/EG van de Raad van 3 juni 1996 betreffende de door de UNICE, het CEEP en het EVV gesloten raamovereenkomst inzake ouderschapsverlof

Roelofs, E. (1995), In: A. Van Doorne-Huiskes, J. Van Hoof and E. Roelofs (1995), *Women and the European Labour Markets.* Heerlen: Open Universiteit.

SDU (1993), *Dossier Maastricht: verdrag betreffende de Europese Unie.* Den Haag: SDU.

EPILOGUE: TOWARDS NEW PATTERNS OF RESPONSIBILITY FOR WORK-FAMILY POLICIES?

Anneke van Doorne-Huiskes, Laura den Dulk and Joop Schippers

1.   Differences in work-family arrangements

Are there differences between the work-family arrangements within firms in the various Western European countries and, if so, are these differences related to the way welfare states in Europe are institutionalised? This is the central theme of this book, worked out in chapters on the Netherlands, the United Kingdom, Germany, Italy, Spain, and Sweden. The choice of these countries was based on welfare state typologies, as developed by Titmuss in the seventies and by Esping-Andersen later on. This typology was presented in Chapter 1.

To summarise briefly what has been said before, it is clear that work-family arrangements do differ. Probably, and that seems to be the first important conclusion, one could better speak of "packages" of work-family arrangements. Work-family arrangements consist of several measures, regulations, and facilities: minimal or substantial systems of public childcare; minimal or substantial possibilities for part-time work; minimal or substantial opportunities for leaves and career interruptions; minimal or substantial possibilities for flexibility in working times and tailor-made arrangements. Of course, at the national scale, firms do differ. Companies with many female workers are generally under greater pressure to develop facilities which meet the need for work-family reconciliation than firms which are dominated by men. In most countries, public organisations are more concerned about equal opportunity policies and work-family facilities than private firms are. But besides these different patterns within countries, countries themselves could be characterised by the way work-family arrangements are organised, made available and institutionalised. These institutionalised patterns reflect the basic assumptions and taken-for-granted ideas about gender roles and divisions of tasks between women and men on which welfare state regimes are based. During the last decade, many feminist scholars have challenged the gender-neutral approach in mainstream welfare state theories. By focussing on the gendered character of welfare states, they have improved and enriched the body of knowledge about welfare states.

What sort of packages of work-family arrangements have we met in the preceding chapters? The Netherlands is primarily characterised by a pattern of part-time work, in combination with minimal public childcare and few statutory leaves. The main strategy couples use to cope with conflicting demands on time seems to be the "one-and-a-half-earner" model: men being primarily responsible for the family income and working full-time and women working part-time and primarily responsible for care at home. This model is becoming increasingly common and certainly more representative of the Dutch way of life than two full-time working partners in one family.

Germany could be characterised by long parental leaves in combination with few public childcare facilities. The Netherlands and Germany share the political view that responsibility for the upbringing of children is primarily a task for parents and not for the state. The institutions or lack of institutions in the work-family field, in both welfare states still reflect this basic assumption. Times are changing, however. The number of dual earner couples is rising rapidly in both countries. Work-family regulations and institutions are hardly able to keep pace with changes in the behaviour of (young) women and men.

Although historically there has been more economic pressure on families in Britain to earn two salaries than has been the case in the Netherlands or in Germany, government involvement in work-family arrangements is low. Family responsibilities are primarily seen as private, and state involvement is only provided when families appear not to be able to fulfil their tasks.

Entirely different is the picture in Sweden in this respect. Owing to a relatively long tradition of working women and dual-earner couples, the Swedish welfare state offers a broad range of statutory leaves and a substantial system of public childcare.

The pattern is the reverse in the Southern European countries Italy and Spain. It is only recently that the (official) number of working women in these countries began increasing. Work-family arrangements have not adapted to these new developments. The number of part-time workers is low, also among women, and childcare facilities for children under 3 are rare. Informal help, from families and grandmothers in particular, still fill these gaps, but this situation will undoubtedly change. We will return to this point later.

Opportunities of flexible work arrangements
An important development on the labour markets in Europe is flexibility. Flexibility has an ambivalent connotation in relation to the reconciliation of work and family life. On the one hand, increased workplace flexibility has the potential of giving employees more freedom regarding their work schedule, which can be used as a means to make paid work compatible with caring tasks. On the other hand, employers can use flexibility as a means to extend opening hours, to respond to changing market demands, and to employ people according to peaks in the workload.

There are different types of flexible work arrangements. Flexitime or flexible work hours consist of flexible starting and finishing times. In most cases, employees have to be on the job during certain core hours but can vary the time they start or finish work. Core hours may be one period or divided into two periods, one in the morning and one in the afternoon, with a flexible lunch period in between. The degree of variability differs between or within organisations. Some employers may prefer their employees to have a flexitime schedule that is permanent or at least fixed for a period of time. Others let their employees schedule their work hours on a daily basis. This may depend, among other things, on the type of work involved (Gottlieb et al, 1998).

Job sharing, as a type of part-time employment, means that two persons share the responsibility, salary, and benefits of one full-time position. It makes it possible to reduce work hours where there is a need for a full-time position.

Telework or flexiplace is an arrangement in which employees work at home for all or part of the workweek. Whether or not telework makes it easier to reconcile work and family life is not clear. It does help reduce commuting time, and employees are often free to schedule their work hours. But telework does not diminish the need for childcare (Gottlieb et al, 1998).

A compressed workweek is another example of flexible work arrangements. In the Netherlands, in those sectors that have implemented a 36-hour workweek (banking and the public sector), a four-day, nine-hour, workweek becomes a possibility. Although the extra day off can be used for caring tasks, long workdays can create difficulties in bringing and picking up children from childcare (depending on general opening hours).

Besides these flexible work arrangements, flexibility is also associated with fixed-term contracts and precarious employment. The increasing number of people with fixed-term or temporary employment are often not eligible for, for instance, parental leave or leave for family reasons. Furthermore, irregular work schedules, schedules that change on short notice, or work at odd hours are difficult to combine with childcare facilities. Childcare facilities that are open 24 hours are rare and often children can only be placed there during regular weekly hours. The effect of flexibility in the workplace on the combination of paid and unpaid work depends in large part on the degree of employee control over their work schedules and compatibility with other work-family arrangements, such as childcare.

2. The relation between government policies and activities regarding work-family arrangements within firms

There is little research on the role of employers and organizational provisions in Europe. What data there is suggests that when the development of work-family arrangements are left to market forces, differences between industries and organisations emerge. Organisational characteristics, such as size, proportion of female personnel, public/private sector, and economic position, influence the decision whether an organisation will develop facilities. According to Suzan Lewis (Chapter 3), within the context of low government involvement and an ideology which considers family responsibilities as private, work-family arrangements will be constructed as a business case dominated by calculations concerning cost and benefits. Without public provisions and regulations, employers are able to choose those arrangements which fit best the needs of their particular organisation. However, organisational needs and the needs of employees do not always coincide. Furthermore, differences between industries and organisations raise the question of equality of access to work-family arrangements. Some workers will have access to facilities, while others do not. From an equal opportunities perspective, this is not desirable. In addition, a wide range of public facilities, such as those in Sweden, could create a cultural climate in which organisations are willing to supplement legislation and take it for granted that employers have family responsibilities. Such a positive relation between public policy and employers provisions can be seen as a win-win situation.

Even in a situation of high public provision, implementation of work-family policies still takes place within organisations. As has been shown in various chapters, workplace conditions play a major role regarding the use of facilities. Precarious employment or the workplace culture may block the use of public provisions. Thus, even though minimum public provision is desirable from an equal opportunity point of view, employers still have a major role to play in the matter of arrangements and regarding adjustments to specific workplace conditions.

Southern European model?
One question that can be raised when analyzing the provision of work-family arrangements is whether there is a distinctive Southern European model. According to Trifiletti (Chapter 5), the family is the unit with primary responsible for the welfare of individuals in the Southern European Welfare state. In first instance, people have to look for family support when they are in need. This assumption is embedded in social policy and regulations. Both in Italy and in Spain, family obligations and mutual help extends beyond the nuclear family. Family obligations include grandparents, grandchildren, and sometimes siblings or other relatives (Millar and Warman, 1996). Hence, informal care through the family network is very important in both countries. And women are the main providers of informal care. Anna Escobedo argued in Chapter 6 that this system works because there are still age cohorts which include large number of housewives and because of the high unemployment among

Spanish women. But the increasing number of women participating on the labour market will put pressure on this system of informal care within the family.

Furthermore, both Spain and Italy are characterised by a strong division between well-protected workers and those in the deregulated grey economy. Employees in the regular institutionalised labour market, such as civil servants, white-collar workers, and private wage-earners of medium and large enterprises working on a full contract with job security, receive generous protection. But there are large numbers of under-protected workers who are not entitled to benefits for, for example, sickness, maternity, unemployment and high earnings related pensions when they retire (Ferrera, 1996). According to Ferrera (1996), it is precisely this trait of dualism which separates Southern European countries from the other continental conservative-corporatistic welfare states. As a consequence, statutory work-family arrangements are not equally accessible. People need a stable job in the formal labour market in order to be able to use existing policies. Irregular workers in weak sectors without job security rely on employers' provisions. However, the idea of family-friendly organisations has, until now, not received much attention. Anna Escobedo showed that, in the Spanish context, companies have been focussing on continuity rather than on the quality of working conditions. In the Spanish workplace culture, it is assumed that having a professional career is incompatible with part-time work or the full use of statutory maternity and parental leave. As in Italy, work-family workplace arrangements are still very rare in organisations.

Other countries
Within the Netherlands and Germany public-private partnerships deserve attention. In the Netherlands, childcare facilities for working parents are largely based on employers' contributions. Wolfgang Erler shows that in Germany, public-private partnerships develop new initiatives, for instance, in creating additional childcare facilities in big cities. These new public-private childcare schemes break with old concepts and traditions: experiments are being carried out on extended opening times, mixed age groups, and the integration of handicapped children in "normal" childcare institutions. These new forms of public-private partnerships could probably arise in welfare states, which historically belong to the conservative-corporatistic tradition. This is different in Sweden, where public provisions are still the most important part of work-family arrangements. Parental leaves could be considered as key elements in Swedish attempts to reconcile working life with family life. However well integrated family life may be in public debates and in the organisation of work, in comparison with other European countries, even in Sweden, male and female patterns regarding parental leaves are different. Long parental leaves for women have become a feature of everyday life, as Näsman (Chapter 7) puts it, while a leave for the father is

exceptional and related to peak periods in life and to temporary needs. This is in part due to still existing traditional stereotypes and values in the culture of the workplace. Ideas about what is "normal behaviour" at the workplace sometimes deny the claims of parenthood and turn care demands of children into non-issues within the workplace. Besides old cultural images, there are practical obstacles as well. Such factors as workload and responsibilities sometimes make it difficult to use the right to parental leaves. This specifically holds for managers, supervisors, so-called key persons, and experts, most of whom are male.

3. Concluding remarks

Comparative research among the member states of the European Union reveals that more statutory work-family arrangements are accompanied by less gender inequality in labour markets. In countries with a more extensive government policy regarding work-family arrangements, women have higher labour participation rates and the gender gap in wages is smaller (Den Dulk *et al.*, 1996). This evidence gives weight to the question whether future developments of work-family arrangements as a public policy can be expected in the near future within Europe. This will depend in part on the state of the economy and the employment situation. Countries with more economic growth and less unemployment, could in general afford better public facilities. This also holds for employers. In a growing economy with reliable prospects, employers will be more willing to create labour conditions that fit the needs of their workforce than in a declining economy. An economy of growth, moreover, is favourable to a more diverse workforce because many workers are needed. The more diverse a workforce is, the greater the pressure on employers will be to provide facilities which support the reconciliation of work and family life.

But this is not the whole story. It is not just the state of the economy which counts. Other developments are relevant as well, social developments which could lead to shrinking welfare state institutions, to the introduction of more market forces in social organisation, and to more personal responsibility for the citizens of the European Union to organise their private lives, their working lives, and their social security. Such developments are supported by a process of increasing individualisation and by a still increasing level of education for most European citizens. It could well be possible that governments in Europe become more inclined to turn public facilities which until now have been financed by public funds over to the marketplace. This process is already taking place, albeit - in line with different national traditions - more in some countries than in others. Regarding work-family arrangements, this could lead to more variety and liberty in options and to more tailor-made facilities that fit the particular needs of people, depending on their stage in the life cycle. It could also imply, however, the danger of more social inequality among citizens. Increasing inequality between citizens will take its toll on the equality between women and men and among women as a group.

Whatever the direction of future work-family arrangements will be, the fact that more and more women have paid jobs seems to be irreversible in Europe. This fact in itself is creating a strong pressure to redefine the way in which work is organised. New forms of work organisation have to take into account that workers do have more responsibilities than their paid work alone.

References

Dulk, L. den, J. van Doorne-Huiskes and J. Schippers (1996), Work-Family Arrangements and Gender Inequality in Europe. *Women in Management Review*. Vol. 11, No. 5, p. 25-35.

Ferrera, M. (1996), The 'Southern model' of Welfare in Social Europe. *Journal of European Social Policy*, No. 6 (1), p. 17-37.

Gottlieb, B.H., E.K. Kelloway and E.J. Barham (1998*). Flexible Work Arrangements. Managing the Work-Family Boundary*. Chichester: John Wiley & Sons.

Millar J. and A. Warman (1996). *Family Obligations in Europe*. Family Policy Studies Centre.

ABOUT THE AUTHORS

Anneke van Doorne-Huiskes studied sociology at the Utrecht University, where she also wrote her thesis concerning labour market participation of higher educated women, which she defended in 1979. Since 1991 she is a professor in Emancipation research/Women's studies at the Erasmus University Rotterdam. From 1988-1993 she worked as a professor at the Agricultural University of Wageningen, to lecture on 'Women in labour organizations'. In addition, she has worked since 1987 as an independent consultant for her own consultancy-agency. Her publications concern a wide range of themes with respect to women and the labour market. She is a senior member of the staff of the research school AWSB and co-operates with the research school ISC. Presently, she is also chair of Tecena, a board of experts that is to advance the mainstreaming of emancipation and gender issues among public advisory councils in the Netherlands.

Laura den Dulk studied sociology at the Erasmus University Rotterdam. She is presently a Ph.D. student at the Netherlands School for Social and Economic Policy Research (AWSB). Her current research is an international comparison of workplace work-family arrangements in different welfare state contexts. The project is partly funded by the Netherlands Organization of Scientific Research (N.W.O.).

Wolfgang Erler, is a sociologist at the German Youth Institute (DJI) in Munich. His main fields of research have been the position of women at the labour market, work-family issues, and rural and regional development. Presently he is studying social movements dealing with childcare and family support in Germany.

Anna Escobedo, studied economics at the University of Barcelona. She is a researcher at CIREM Foundation in Barcelona. She is participating in a Training and Mobility Research Programme on 'Family and Welfare State in Europe' co-ordinated by the Mannheim Centre for European Social Research. During the programme she stayed at the universities of Roskilde (Denmark) and Tampere (Finland) for several months.

Suzan Lewis is currently Reader in Psychology at the Manchester Metropolitan University and co-director of a multi-site Work Life Research Centre located at MMU, UMIST and the Institute of Education, London. She is the author of numerous books and articles on work and family. In addition her edited books include The Work Family Challenge, Rethinking

Employment (co-edited with Jeremy Lewis) and Dual Earner Families, International Perspectives. She is also the founding co-editor of Community, Work and Family, a new international journal for academics and professionals in the field. She has recently co-ordinated a transnational study of young workers' present and future orientations to work and family in five European countries. Current projects with the Work Life Research Centre include the development of a benchmark of good practice for workplace initiatives to support work life balance, and a study of the impact of organisational change and the family.

Elisabet Näsman took her doctoral exam in sociology and became assistant professor at the Department of Sociology at Uppsala University. She has been researcher and research leader at the Swedish Centre for Working Life and senior lecturer at the Demography Unit, Stockholm University and at the University of Örebro. Presently she is acting professor in Child studies and head of the Department of Thematic Studies at Linköping University.

Joop Schippers is an associate professor of economics at the Economic Institute/Centre for Interdisciplinary Research on Labour Market and Distribution issues (CIAV), Utrecht University. His main field of research is labour economics, especially issues concerning labour market inequality between men and women. The latter theme was also the subject of his doctoral thesis (1987), a study on wage-rate differentials between men and women. From 1993 to 1997 he was a member of the Netherlands National Council on Equal Opportunities (Emancipatieraad). At present he is a member of Tecena, a board of experts that is to advance the mainstreaming of emancipation issues among public advisory councils in the Netherlands.

Jacqie van Stigt got her degree in Work and Organisation psychology at Utrecht University in 1988.Up until 1995 she worked as a freelance researcher specialising in labour and emancipation policy. Thereafter she worked as a policy adviser for various organisations including the *Directie Coördinatie Emancipatiebeleid* (a governmental organisation concerned with the co-ordination of emancipation policy), the *Instituut Vrouw & Arbeid* (The Institute 'Women and Work'), and the *Emancipatieraad* (the National Council on Equal Opportunities). In 1997 she worked as a research assistent at Utrecht University for the Law Faculty's Institute of Economics. She is currently employed by FNV Bondgenoten as a labour relations policy adviser.

Rossana Trifiletti is researcher at the Department of Political Science and Sociology of Florence (Dispo) and assistant professor in Sociology of the Family and in Social Policy at the faculty of Political Science, University of Florence, Italy. Her main fields of interest are Sociology of the Family, Social Policies, Gender and Welfare States, Comparative Welfare

State Analysis, Women's Work, and History of Sociological Thought. She took part in several European networks about social and family policies and is presently working in a CNR research project on poverty and the reform of Italian welfare system and in a research for the Ministry of Social Affairs on local welfare systems of big Italian towns.